The Life of
HORACE WALPOLE

From a picture by E. Edwards

ENTRANCE OF STRAWBERRY HILL

THE LIFE OF
HORACE WALPOLE

By

STEPHEN GWYNN

HASKELL HOUSE PUBLISHERS LTD.
Publishers of Scarce Scholarly Books
NEW YORK, N. Y. 10012
1971

First Published 1932

HASKELL HOUSE PUBLISHERS Ltd.
Publishers of Scarce Scholarly Books
280 LAFAYETTE STREET
NEW YORK, N. Y. 10012

Library of Congress Catalog Card Number: 76-160467

Standard Book Number 8383-1302-7

Printed in the United States of America

CONTENTS

LIST OF ILLUSTRATIONS

INTRODUCTORY

SO much has been written about Horace Walpole that I make no pretence of having exhausted the study of it. But a biographer, sitting down simply to tell the story of a life, to make a personality and a career familiar and if possible interesting to others, must be thankful for the work of earlier hands. Miss Dorothy Stuart's recent volume in the " English Men of Letters " series makes it unnecessary for me to attempt any detailed study of Horace Walpole's books, while Austin Dobson long ago put together all the details that a student of bibliography can require.

But of course the main authority for Walpole is himself, and the labours of Mrs. Paget Toynbee, completed after her death, have endowed us with eighteen volumes of his letters to which are added three of Madame du Deffand's letters to him. This definitive edition is a monument of scholarship ; but I sometimes ask myself whether I should have ever read Walpole's letters through for pleasure—as I did more than once—had I not owned Cunningham's less intimidating publication. Even that has nine volumes, and stout ones.

This book is compiled for readers not even so moderately courageous as myself.

I express my special indebtedness to Mr. H. Avray Tipping for the two admirable articles on Strawberry Hill published in *Country Life* of July 5 and 12, 1925, and to my friend Mr. Edward Hudson for leave to reproduce from them the photograph of that fatal vase in which pensive Selima, gold-fishing, came by death and immortality.

S. G.

July, 1931.

9

CHAPTER I

PARENTAGE AND BOYHOOD

WHEN Horace Walpole caused his portrait by Sir Joshua to be engraved, his direction was that it should be inscribed simply "Horace Walpole, youngest son of Sir Robert Walpole, Earl of Orford." That was how he desired to be noted and known, although by the year 1759, when this instruction was given to McArdell the engraver, he had acquired a very considerable reputation in his own right. There was perhaps a touch of affectation in this modesty; yet, oddly enough, the description by which he chose to be recognized was liable to challenge. To begin with, his baptismal name was Horatio, and, though in settling that Horace was the better form for an English gentleman, good taste guided him, there was probably another motive for stereotyping this alteration. He was determined to separate himself from all appearance of association with his godfather, Horatio Walpole, Sir Robert's brother, whom he cordially detested. He had indeed no affection for any Walpole, except Sir Robert; and was even that affection natural as between parent and child?

For the great statesman whose name he bore, and to whom he behaved as a dutiful and affectionate son, he came to have a kind of hero-worship. Yet we have good reason to believe that the tie between these two was not a tie of blood; and though there is no indication that Horace Walpole doubted of his parentage, contemporary opinion doubted, or rather, did not doubt. Since this book is an attempt to study the life of a very odd character about whom we know a very great deal, it would be absurd to ignore the positive statement that he was the child of Lady Walpole, not by Sir Robert but by Carr, Lord Hervey—all the more because this offers an explanation for much in the man that challenges inquiry, as if a mastiff sire were supposed to have produced an elegant Italian greyhound.

Moreover, the statement comes from an honourable and candid recorder of tradition. Lady Louisa Stuart was the last survivor of that society in which Horace Walpole passed his whole existence and of which his letters are the completest reflex. She was forty years his junior; he had been the contemporary—younger, but still a contemporary—of her famous grandmother, Lady Mary Wortley Montagu. But when he was, to borrow Lady Louisa's phrase, a " humoursome old bachelor " in his fifties, he was intimate at the house of her mother, Lady Bute, and he and the clever girl laughed much together at the same people. It is clear that she liked him with limitations, but it is clear that he had her liking, and some of her respect. We know enough of Lady Louisa, Walter Scott's close friend and confidant, to be certain that she would never have retailed mere scandalous gossip about a person whom she had liked and respected. But she had the temper of a social historian, and when she sat down, well on in the nineteenth century, to recall happenings then already more than a hundred years old, she retained the eighteenth century's freedom and did not let her pen be constrained by any false delicacy.

The purpose for which she wrote in 1830 was to put together some introductory anecdotes of Lady Mary Wortley Montagu for an edition of Lady Mary's *Letters*. These anecdotes, she explains, were based on certain journals kept by Lady Mary and left by her to her daughter Lady Bute, who carefully guarded and finally destroyed them. But passages were sometimes read aloud to a small circle, and, late in her life, Lady Bute permitted her daughter to read some portion on condition that nothing was transcribed.

Lady Bute died in 1794; so we are depending on what Lady Louisa remembered when she was eighty-two of what she had read before she was fifty. On the other hand, what she read then had been written by Lady Mary when the events were fresh and vivid.

The story of the Walpoles is told as it concerns Lady Mary's friend, "the beautiful Dolly Walpole," Robert Walpole's sister, who (unlike her brother) was "endowed with only a moderate portion of sense." Mr. Walpole, not yet Sir Robert, had brought her to town "in hopes that her beauty, the pride of his county, might captivate something superior to a Norfolk squire." But, according to Lady Mary Wortley's transmitted account, "being immersed in politics, and careless of what passed at home, he left his sister to the guidance of his wife, an empty coquettish affected woman, anything rather than correct in her own conduct or spotless in her fame; greedy of admiration and extremely dissatisfied at having to share it with the younger, fairer inmate." Accordingly, if we are to believe Lady Mary, Mrs. Walpole allowed and even encouraged the girl to compromise herself, while Lady Mary, though still unmarried, acted as "her simple friend's protecting genius." But in an evil hour, while the good genius was away from London, Dolly Walpole was led into an acquaintance with Lady Wharton and told all her secrets to a "woman equally unfeeling and unprincipled, flattering, canting, affecting prudery and even sanctity, yet in reality as abandoned and unscrupulous as her husband himself. So," Lady Louisa adds (with perhaps a touch of deprecation), "said the journal." The result was that in one of these confidential conversations, when Mrs. Walpole had done something particularly spiteful, and Mr. Walpole happened to be out of town, Lady Wharton pressed the girl to leave her brother's house for a few days and be her guest.

"Now, Lord Wharton's character was so infamous, and

his lady's complacent subserviency so notorious, that no young woman could be four-and-twenty hours under their roof with safety to her reputation. Upon Mr. Walpole's return home, enraged at finding whither his sister had betaken herself, he flew to Lord Wharton and thundering for admittance, demanded her aloud, regardless who might hear him. My lord, not at all inclined to face him in this temper, thought it safest to abscond, so crept privately out of his own house by a back door, leaving my lady to abide the pelting of the storm. Sir Robert, it is well known, was at no time apt to be over delicate or ceremonious ; he accosted her ladyship in the plainest of English, bestowed upon her some significant epithets, and without listening to a word of explanation, forced away his weeping sister, with whom he set out for Norfolk the next morning."

This startling tableau of manners in Queen Anne's reign had a comfortable sequel. "After doing penance for two or three years in a very dull retirement " at Houghton, her brother's house in Norfolk, Dolly Walpole " had the good luck to light on a more capital prize in the country than she had ever aimed at in London, the person being Lord Townshend, one of the most unblemished statesmen and respectable gentlemen of that age." He was not young, " he had been a long and sincere mourner for his first wife, the sister of Lord Pelham " ; but being a great Norfolk landlord (indeed illustrious for his introduction of the turnip to that county), he naturally met the exiled beauty, immediately fell in love with her, and they were married. It was on receiving the news of this alliance, contracted in 1713, that Lady Mary, who herself had been married in the previous year, sat down and wrote the history of Dolly's adventures.

Lady Louisa Stuart, having recounted all this, remarks very justly that it accounts for that excessive dislike of Lady Mary Wortley which appears again and again in Horace Walpole's letters. " His mother and she had been antagonists and enemies before he was born; and if they continued to keep up the outward forms of acquaintance-ship, which of course brought them often into contact, they would naturally hate each other all the more."

Lady Louisa, though a staunch partisan of her grand-mother, does not carry on the vendetta; she admits that Horace Walpole's affection for his mother " was so much the most amiable point in his character, and his expressions whenever he names or alludes to her are so touching, come so directly and evidently from the heart, that one would fain think of her as he did." But, she goes on to say, the opinion of Lady Walpole's character which Lady Mary transmits does not rest " solely nor yet principally " on Lady Mary's authority. It was so current that, when Captain Gulliver gravely vindicated the reputation of Lord Treasurer Flimnap's wife from a scandalous charge of intrigue with the " Man Mountain," everyone understood an ironic application. The " Lord Treasurer " of Great Britain showed no Lilli-putian uneasiness about his wife's conduct, and all the world knew this. " He professed it his own method to go his own way and to let madam go hers," said Lady Louisa. In a word, " Horace Walpole himself was generally supposed to be the son of Carr, Lord Hervey, and Sir Robert not to be ignorant of it."

There is no question about Sir Robert's sexual irregular-ities; indeed he is said to have affected a reputation for them, and from 1728 onwards he lived openly with Miss Catherine Skerritt, whom he married after Lady Walpole's death. Horace Walpole was born on September 24, 1717 (O.S.). Of the four children already born to the Walpoles, the youngest, a daughter, was then eleven years old. As the fifth child grew up, " one striking circumstance," says Lady Louisa, " was visible to the naked eye; no beings in human shape could resemble each other less than the two passing for father and son; and while their reverse of likeness provoked a malicious whisper, Sir Robert's marked neglect of Horace in his infancy tended to confirm it. A number of children, young Walpole one, were accustomed to meet and play together. Such of them as, like himself, lived to grow old, all united in declaring that no other boy within their knowledge was left so entirely in the hands of his mother, or seemed to have so little acquaintance with his father."

None the less, husband and wife behaved as if the child had come quite regularly into the world. Sir Robert's brother Horatio stood godfather at his christening and provided the name; Sir Robert's sister, Dolly, Lady Townshend, was godmother—although if Lady Mary Wortley is right, she and the boy's mother were anything but friends; and when the time for a tutor came, Horace went to be taught along with his cousins, the four sons of Lord Townshend by his second marriage.

But this schooling did not begin till 1725 when he was eight years old; and as he was not only a late-born child, and so naturally petted, but also extremely weak and delicate, the care of him (in his own words) " so engrossed the attention " of his mother "that compassion and tenderness became extreme fondness." Another circumstance may have added to this devotion. Carr, Lord Hervey, died in 1723 when Horace was six years old. Lady Walpole behaved to this youngest born of hers as if he were the child of a man for whom she had felt the tenderest affection; and in one way, if the truth be as Lady Louisa transmits the story, she had her reward. She saw the boy grow up to remind her of his father. We know little about Carr, Lord Hervey, Lord Bristol's son, but we know much about the remarkable family to which he belonged. Lady Mary Wortley Montagu said once that mankind was divided into men, women and Herveys. Horace Walpole was extremely unlike Sir Robert Walpole, Sir Robert's brother, Sir Robert's other sons and the whole clan of stout, broad-spoken, loud-voiced Walpoles. We cannot even suggest that he took after his mother, for the antiquary Cole, who often came to the Walpoles' house in Chelsea when he was a schoolboy friend of Horace's, remembered her as " a very lusty, well-looking woman." On the other hand he was extremely like the Herveys, not only in their lean physical delicacy but in a profusion of rather spiteful fine-pointed wit. He was bookish too from the first, like all the Herveys, unlike the Walpoles ; on the other hand, whereas his brother, Sir Edward Walpole, had a passion for music, Horace had no ear at all.

Lady Louisa believed it probable that Horace Walpole himself never suspected that any doubt hung over his birth —and he certainly grew up regarding Sir Robert as not only a father, but a very satisfactory father ; one whose " infinite good nature " never thwarted any of his children, and who was so important a person that he could " gratify the first vehement inclination ever expressed " by the youngest child. For at ten years old, Horace Walpole took it in his head " to long to see the King." Writing down his memories sixty years later, after a life spent in professing academic preference for a republic, he comments : " As I have never since felt any enthusiasm for royal persons, I must suppose that the female attendants in the family must have put it into my head." At all events Lady Walpole begged the Duchess of Kendal to obtain for her son the honour of kissing his Majesty's hand before George I set out for Hanover— on what was to prove his last journey. " A favour so unusual to be asked for a boy of ten years old, was still too slight to be refused to the wife of the First Minister for her darling child ; yet not being proper to be made a precedent, it was settled to be in private and at night."

Accordingly Lady Walpole took the boy to St. James's, at ten o'clock.

" Notice being given that the King was come down to

supper, Lady Walsingham (the Duchess of Kendal's daughter) took me alone into the Duchess' anteroom, where we found alone the King and her. I knelt down and kissed his hand. He said a few words to me, and my conductress led me back to my mother.

"The person of the King is as perfect in my memory as if I saw him but yesterday. It was that of an elderly man, rather pale, and exactly like his pictures and coins; not tall; of an aspect rather good than august; with a dark tie-wig, a plain coat, waistcoat and breeches of a snuff-coloured cloth, with stockings of the same colour, and a blue riband over all. So entirely was he my object that I do not believe I once looked at the Duchess; but as I could not avoid seeing her on entering the room, I remember that just beyond His Majesty stood a very tall, lean, ill-favoured old lady; but I did not retain the least idea of her features, nor know what the colour of her dress was."

The account is a good example of Walpole's manner; but for my present purpose, it is more important to note that when the news of George I's death reached Eton a few weeks later, Horace Walpole, walking in procession with the other boys to the proclamation of the successor, burst into a flood of tears: perhaps from gratitude for the condescension that had been shown him; but, says the old man, "I think they partly fell because I imagined it became the son of a Prime Minister to be more concerned than other boys."

For, from as far back as childish memory could go, Horace Walpole had been aware of his position as the son of the most powerful man in England. Sir Robert Walpole was no less than that for twenty years without interruption, from 1721 onwards—indeed up to the moment when Horace Walpole took his seat in Parliament; though the tide had turned then, and the young member's maiden speech was in defence of a fallen minister threatened with impeachment.

It was only then that the two began to be in any sort of intimate relation to each other; and the relation must be followed in detail. But it is necessary here to take into account one more aspect of the story. Horace Walpole had a great deal of the reticence which takes the form of hiding real emotions behind a screen of superficial chatter. But in a letter to his cousin Harry Conway, in which the circumstances made it necessary that he should drop this screen, there comes this phrase—" If ever I felt much for anything (which I know may be questioned) it was certainly for my mother. I look on you as my nearest relation by her and I think I can never do enough to show my gratitude and affection to her." That was written seven years after her death when he was twenty-seven. Two years earlier, when the threat to Sir Robert menaced all the Walpoles, Horace wrote—" If our family is to be the sacrifice that shall pamper discord, at least *the one, the part* of it that interested all my concerns, and must have suffered from our ruin, is safe, secure and above the rage of confusion; nothing in the world can touch her peace now."

These words hold a singular volume of emotion to flow from the pen of so flippant a young gentleman of five and twenty. The truth is, that he had been his mother's partisan; and though he nowhere says it, he had things to forgive Sir Robert. Lady Louisa is plain and not unfair about this: " The mortifications of his youth on his mother's account could not but be severe; for as she lived till he reached manhood, he must have known how completely she was overlooked and disregarded, though not ill-treated, by her husband; and before his tears for her loss were dried, he had the pang of seeing Miss Skerritt, the rival she hated, installed in her place."

The hatred is perhaps a matter of inference: Lady Walpole may have been as philosophic as her husband. But her son's feeling is beyond dispute. Sir Robert Walpole had early secured the Rangership of Richmond Park, and valued the opportunities it gave for his favourite sport of hunting with beagles; he had built himself a lodge in the New Park, and in this lodge he had installed Miss Skerritt, and used to go down there of a week-end, to the Court's full knowledge. Queen Caroline, never delicate, took the simplest view of these withdrawals, and Lord Hervey's *Memoirs* echo her; but Sir Robert himself says, and it is easily believable, that they gave him the chance to get some work done in his one free time, with no company but that of the woman who loved him. Miss Skerritt was a lady of good family and large fortune, who gave up her life to this remarkable man; and she was not by any means universally ostracized: Lady Mary Wortley in particular delighted in her society, and Richmond Lodge no doubt had its callers. But naturally Horace Walpole did not go there in his mother's lifetime; he did not willingly go there when Miss Skerritt became the second Lady Walpole, and reigned for a few months as its recognized mistress. Even four years after she also had died, he was still avoiding the place; but not completely, for Sir Robert was out of office and still in some danger. It is plain too that through all his youth Horace had found himself in growing revolt from the Walpoles as Walpoles, and drawn to his mother's kin. In 1741, just after the return from two years spent abroad, he writes to his cousin Harry Conway, son of Lady Hertford, Lady Walpole's sister: " I settled it yesterday with Miss Conway that you three are brothers and sister to me and that if you had been so, I could not love you better. I have so many cousins and uncles and aunts and bloods that grow in Norfolk that if I had portioned out my affections to them, as they say I should, what a modicum would have fallen to each. So, to avoid fractions, I love my family in you three, their representatives."

There is no word here of his own brothers and sisters.

We know nothing of the two sisters, both of whom died young. Sir Robert's eldest son Robert, afterwards Lord Orford, does not seem to have been acutely conscious of his junior's existence; but letters survive which make it plain that the second son, Edward, regarded Horace as a conceited puppy, and also, oddly enough, that he was jealous of his father's preference for him.

It had come to that. The child whom Sir Robert Walpole at first slighted began (if Lady Louisa was rightly informed) to earn his good opinion by successes at Eton and " proved that whether he had or had not a right to the name he went by, he was likely to do it honour." There is, however, no other evidence of this. It is true that as soon as Horace grew up, Sir Robert provided him with posts in the public service, and in 1741 caused him to be returned for the pocket borough of Callington in Cornwall. But George II's Prime Minister would have done as much for any son of his, whatever his capacities or incapacities. All we have to go on as to the relation which formed itself between father and son (to use the accepted terms) is the impression left by a hundred references in the son's letters; and these convey the sense of a growing intimacy, which yet was not exactly filial. If a distant namesake had been chosen to act as confidential secretary for the great minister, and had learnt day by day to understand, to admire and to love him, the result would have been conveyed in much the same language. There is no warmth of blood in the affection.

In short, if Horace Walpole seems to us on first acquaintance charming but cold-blooded, and not merely artificial but actually a little unnatural, I think the reason is that he grew up with a queer half-conscious perception of something not quite normal in what were apparently his closest relationships —with the single exception of his mother. When he lost her, he was left almost an alien amongst those of his own house; and perhaps something in his flippancy was defensive and was formed early. He had the craving for affection as well as for society ; and though he was never stinted of the second, he grew up rather starved of the other.

However, during the period of his boyhood, he had all that his mother could give him; and at his school he threw himself enthusiastically into friendships. Throughout his life he had a taste for making friends ; and though a good many of the ties which he formed were ended by definite estrangements, on the whole he kept more of his early attachments than most men find it possible to preserve.

He went to Eton, so he tells us, on April 26, 1727— being nearly six months short of ten years old. There is no indication that this age was thought specially early, or that he suffered by his separation from home. One thing is certain : he thoroughly enjoyed his schooldays, but after his own fashion. Looking back from the height of an undergraduate's wisdom, he decided that he "was never quite a schoolboy," and also that he was not sorry for it ; but this means no more than that he did not play cricket nor join in any "expedition against bargemen." What he did was what it amused him to do, and he did it to the top of his bent, trying his puppy teeth in debate with other young gentlemen who shared his taste for literature and particularly for poetry. Scores of Etonians have done the same in every decade, and they are no doubt doing it to-day. There is, however, this difference : Horace Walpole was able to avoid the violent delights of playing-fields without incurring moral reproach. He was a slacker without knowing it ; the gospel of salvation by athletics was not yet revealed. Indeed, at the age of not quite fifteen he was clearly a little conceited because he and his friend Charles Lyttelton (to whom his earliest extant letter is addressed) "could recollect a thousand passages which were something above the common rate of a school-boy's diversions." He even went so far as to disparage the heroism of those expeditions in which he took no part. " I can remember with no small satisfaction that we did not pass our time in gloriously beating great clowns who would patiently bear children's thumps for the collections which I think some of our contemporaries were so wise as to make for them afterwards."

Charles Lyttelton (" my dearest Charles " in the letters) was one of a " triumvirate," as they called themselves—the third being George Montagu, nephew of the Earl of Halifax. A Lyttelton and a Montagu were natural allies for the Prime Minister's son, and they were all on a footing of Christian names, Charles and George and Horry. But outside this triumvirate, or rather connected with it by the single link of Horace, there was a " quadruple alliance " of which we do not hear till its members were scattered to the Universities. One of them, Richard West, went to Oxford, the other three to Cambridge—Horace Walpole himself, Thomas Ashton and Thomas Gray. West, being son of the Irish Lord Chancellor and grandson of William III's panegyrist, Bishop Burnet, had at least some connection with the ruling Whig oligarchy, in which Sir Robert's son moved naturally ; but Ashton's father was an usher in Lancashire, and Gray's schooling was paid for by his mother out of the proceeds of a milliner's shop where she and her sister worked with their apprentices. In our day such parents could not have sent their boys to Eton, unless as holders of a King's scholarship, which neither Gray nor Ashton obtained ; the separation of youth into groups according to the income of their parents was much less exactly carried out in the eighteenth century than in our democratic age. Horace Walpole has often been accused of snobbishness, a defect specially common among boys at a public school, yet it is more than likely that Gray's circumstances were known and were commented upon by his schoolfellows. Nor was Gray distinguished enough in school-work to tempt even intellectual snobbery : Horace Walpole made his own discovery, and his passion for interchange of literary ideas had its best reward when he made close schoolboy friendship with the finest poet and the most richly stored mind of that age. It is proof of his intelligence that he realized his good fortune and made the most of it, submitting to a relation which from first to last had more than a touch of discipleship.

On the other hand his perception of Gray's merit might have been less keen had it not been heightened by a proprietary sense. He felt himself from the first a discoverer; and in later life he showed no sort of indulgence to the men for whom rival claims were set up, in opposition, as it were, to his and Eton's poet.

Unluckily the three letters that remain from his schoolboy days were all written to Lyttelton, who dropped out early from his list of intimates—entering the church, to be launched, as befitted his family, towards a deanery and a not too remote eventual bishopric. But we have several passages written later in retrospect, and they show a radiant picture. In 1736, he writes from Cambridge, to West at Oxford: " Gray is at Burnham " (in the house of his mother's kinsman, Mr. Rogers, admirably close to the famous beeches), " and what is surprising has not been at Eton. Could you live so near it without seeing it ? That dear scene of our quadruple alliance would furnish me with the most agreeable recollections."

These, as other passages show, were in the main literary.

" I can never forget the agreeable hours we have passed in reading Virgil and Horace; and I think they are topics will never grow slack."

On the other hand, Cambridge disappointed him. " We have not the least poetry stirring here. . . . I have been so used to the delicate food of Parnassus that I can never condescend to apply to the grosser studies of Alma Mater. . . . I am not against cultivating these studies as they are certainly useful, but then they quite neglect all polite literature, all knowledge of this world."

In short, Cambridge seemed to him more like school; Eton had been his real university. He had learnt a reasonable amount of Latin there, enough to enjoy Roman literature; Greek probably never got beyond being a task. As to mathematics, when he went to Cambridge, the blind Professor Saunderson had him in hand for a while, but sent him away, saying it would be robbery to take his money as he could never learn anything of the subject. But if he owed Cambridge very little, he owed Eton a great deal; it was there that he learnt to use his wits; and though he was never the kind of school-boy who develops a precocious sense of responsibility and exercises himself in this cramped field for government and command, he was already the delighted observer and critic of such endeavours. " Alexander at the head of the world never tasted the true pleasure that boys of his own age have enjoyed at the head of a school among their little intrigues, little schemes and policies: " so he wrote, not yet nineteen, to his contemporary George Montagu, praising the happiness of school days. With the adorable faculty for laughing at his own enthusiasms which is one of his great charms (because it never checked his genial flow of new adorations), he sketches his progress from one intellectual calf love to another—from the " *bergers* and *bergères*, *îles d'amour* and *batelières* " to something more seriously classical.

" Dear George, were not the playing fields at Eton food for all manner of flights ? No old maid's gown, though it had been tormented into all the fashions from King James to King George, ever underwent so many transformations as those poor plains have in my idea. At first I was contented with tending a visionary flock, and sighing some pastoral name to the echo of the cascade under the bridge. How happy should I have been to have had a kingdom only for the pleasure of being driven from it, and living disguised in an humble vale ! As I got further into Virgil and Clelia, I found myself transported from Arcadia to the garden of Italy; and saw

Windsor Castle in no other view than the *Capitoli immobile saxum.*"

"Clelia" means that he had begun by reading Madame de Scudéry. These sentimental French romances were then practically the only substitute for the novel of to-day; consequently, verse came in for a larger share of attention than now.

"Poetry I take it is as universally contagious as the small pox; everyone catches it once in their life at least, and the sooner the better," so West wrote from Oxford. A good many young people then wrote verse, who under the conditions of to-day would have tried their hand at prose fiction; and Walpole is probably one of them. Living when he did, and being what he was, he quite naturally set out to be a poet, having as yet no notion where his true vocation in literature lay—not even when he was preparing for it by these very clever epistles. Still, it is plain enough that from the first he was practising in its most elaborate form the art by which we know him. In March, 1735, he matriculated at Cambridge, and no sooner was he installed at King's than he sat down to write to Gray—still at Eton—an account of his journey "in the style of Addison's *Travels*"—very full of citation from the earlier Horace's *Journey to Brundisium*. We learn from it that Sir Robert's son set out in a coach and four to matriculate; that he slept a night at Hockerel, stayed three days at Newmarket, and on the last stage stopped at Lord Godolphin's house on the Gogmagog hills.

In May, 1736, we get a glimpse of the undergraduate just off on a jaunt to Oxford. Gray, writing to West, enjoys himself "in imagining the confusion you will be in when you hear that a coach and six is just stopped at Christchurch gates and desires to speak with you, with a huddle of things in it as different as ever met together in Noah's ark; a fat one and a lean one, and one that can say a little with his mouth and a great deal with his pen, and one that can neither speak nor write."

Who the fat friend was, Mr. Tovey, Gray's editor, cannot tell us; but the lean one had already impressed Gray with his volubility on paper. Gray's fine judgment at once distinguished where Walpole's talent lay, and in the first of his letters to Walpole there is nothing about poetry, but we have this charming piece of persiflage.

" Scandal (if I had any) is a merchandise you do not profess dealing in ; now and then indeed, and to oblige a friend, you may perhaps slip a little out of your packet, as a decayed gentlewoman would a piece of right Mechlin, or a little quantity of rum, but this only now and then, not to make a practice of it."

Gray was then writing from Cambridge in term time, and Walpole was away—being indeed more often out of residence than in it. Yet he was there, oddly enough, that summer in the long vacation and wrote on July 27, 1737, to Lyttelton, disparaging his own university by comparison with Oxford: " After seeing that charming place, I can hardly ask you to come to Cambridge."

Within a few days after this was written, there followed the event which really ended his youth. Lady Walpole died on August 20, a few months before her youngest and favourite son had completed his twentieth year. The only letter of this time which we have from Walpole himself referring to the occasion was written to Charles Lyttelton, on September 18, and it is chiefly concerned with her courage in facing the end. But to this intimate of boyhood he speaks freely : " You have often been witness to my happiness and by that may partly figure what I feel for losing so fond a mother. If my loss consisted solely in being deprived of one that loved me so much, it would feel lighter to me than it now does, for I doated on her."

The last word of the letter is poignant : " I am now got to Cambridge out of a house which I could not bear."—The house of course was Houghton, and though we have no direct description from Walpole himself of what passed there, yet a letter from Gray plainly echoes what Walpole had written, in that September while the wound was still green.

" We are now both at present, I imagine, in no very agreeable situation ; for my part I am under the misfortune of having nothing to do, but it is a misfortune which, thank my stars, I can pretty well bear. You are in a confusion of wine and roaring and hunting and tobacco, and heaven be praised you too can pretty well bear it."

It is plain that Sir Robert made no great pretence of lamentation and probably Horace foresaw what he cordially detested, the legitimized installation of Miss Skerritt in his mother's place. I do not think it mended matters that the second Lady Walpole died within a few months after the first.

CHAPTER II

THE GRAND TOUR WITH GRAY

AT this period there is a gap of eighteen months in the
long series of Walpole's correspondence. We can fill it
up to some extent by a letter to him from Gray, written in
August, 1738, to congratulate him on a new dignity—

"MY DEAR SIR,

I should say Mr. Inspector General of the Exports and
Imports."

Briefly, Horace Walpole, just before he came of age, had
through Sir Robert's paternal care received his first sinecure—
which in the following year was exchanged for the post of Usher
of the Exchequer—then reckoned worth £900 a year. He also
came into two other little places in the Exchequer, called Comp-
troller of the Pipe and Clerk of Escheats. These had been
held for him by deputy till his coming of age. Consequently
he was able as an old man to make this boast—" From that
time I lived on my own income, and travelled at my own
expense, nor did I during my father's life receive from him
but 250l. at different times ; which I say, not in derogation of
his extreme tenderness and goodness to me, but to show that I
was content with what he had given me, and that from the age
of twenty I was no charge to my family."

Leaving aside all comment on these protestations, it is
more to the present purpose that in 1739 Horace Walpole
became possessed of an income which enabled him to travel
at his own expense, and to travel lavishly ; and that his first
thought was to secure Gray's company. For this we are
deeply his debtor. In the first place, he brought it to pass that
the experiences of two clever youths in France and Italy, with

all the resources of society and sight-seeing open to them, were recorded by not one only, but by two of the best letter-writers of that age ; in the second, that Walpole's command of money enabled him to enrich Gray's experience to a degree that Gray's own means could never have permitted; and in the third, that a very clever and well-placed observer of persons and events had his mind enlarged for our advantage by the frequentation of a man of genius.

Say what we like about Horace Walpole, and admitting that his mouth was full of silver spoons, it is not to be forgotten that he chose his own friend, and in a sense his guide, with an insight that none of his preceptors was in the least likely to have shown for him.

The two young men who set out together for a first view of the continental countries were practically of the same age : Gray, some months the elder, being in his twenty-third year, Walpole in his twenty-second. They had long been friends, though the friendship had little colour of affection. Each had in his own way a dislike for expansion : Walpole avoided sentiment by volubility, Gray by an almost affected coldness of approach to all subjects. Yet we can note one movement that shows more than a taste for each other's society. On August 22, 1737, Gray was in the middle of an elaborate letter to West when he suddenly broke off. " While I write to you," the letter ends, " I have the bad news of Lady Walpole's death on Saturday night last. Forgive me if the thought of what my poor Horace must feel on that account obliges me to have done."

Gray was a mother's boy, as much as Horace Walpole was, and he knew what the loss of a mother meant. " My poor Horace " has a touch of intimacy which belongs, I think, to the inner mind. They were always either "Walpole" or "Gray," or " Dear Sir " (then usual as between undergraduates, for instance) to each other ; there is certainly no case in which Walpole speaks of his friend except by the surname.

Whatever its quality, the friendship was to be put to the severest test : for Gray travelled at Walpole's expense and in a manner as his dependent ; and his disposition was in no way one that made such a relation easy.   From first to last in their correspondence we are aware that Gray felt in himself a right of leadership, by superior ability, and by greater weight of metal ; and no doubt Walpole recognized this superiority, though by no means so clearly as in later life.   It is one thing to be convinced that your friend has remarkable talents, and quite another to find that all the world admits his genius. Then indeed you owe it to yourself to mark your critical sagacity by a certain deference ; but earlier in the development, other things count.   If Gray had the greater knowledge and weight, Walpole even at twenty-two was incomparably more a man of the world.   It is not in the least astonishing that in the end the two quarrelled ; it is greatly to their credit, more particularly to Walpole's, that the alliance lasted a full year and a half.   If he had behaved with less than a delicate consideration, that sensitive companion would soon have been gone ; and though looking back after Gray's death he took blame to himself for the breach between them, the letter in which he does so expresses regret and even confusion for faults which nine rich young men out of ten would have committed without the least awareness, then or thereafter, of any cause for self-reproach.

One fact, however, makes it plain that Walpole, in asking Gray to be his companion, considered much besides his own pleasure and convenience.   He thought things out for his friend and before leaving England executed a will under which in case he should die on the journey, Gray would inherit whatever he possessed.   It was all that he could do and possibly the inheritance might have been no great matter : but he knew Sir Robert well enough to be sure that this was the most effectual way of commending his friend to the Prime Minister's good offices.

However, all these speculations were far enough out of mind when the pair of them landed at Calais at five o'clock on Easter Day, 1739, after five hours' sail in a strong breeze " which pleased everybody mighty well," says Gray, " except myself who was extremely sick the whole time." We have no letter from Walpole till after they had reached Paris ; but later, among all the sights of Florence, he wrote to West: " To speak sincerely, Calais surprised me more than anything I have seen since." It was the first contact with a new world and even six months later, when he had seen Rome as well, he notes, " We did not cry out Lord ! half so much as at Calais which to this hour I look upon as one of the most surprising cities of the universe."

As Gray says, they " hardly saw anything there that was not so new and different from England that it surprised us agreeably." Next day, after a morning's sight-seeing—high mass in the great church, and a couple of convents—they set out by post-chaise for Boulogne. That vehicle had not then been introduced into England, so Gray describes it. " A strange sort of conveyance of much greater use than beauty, resembling an ill-shaped chariot, only with the door opening before instead of the side ; three horses draw it, one between the shafts, and the other two on each side, on one of which the postilion rides, and drives too. This vehicle will upon occasion, go fourscore miles a day, but Mr. Walpole, being in no hurry, chooses to make easy journies of it, and they are easy ones indeed ; for the motion is much like that of a sedan, we go about six miles an hour, and commonly change horses at the end of it : it is true they are no very graceful steeds, but they go well, and through roads which th y say are bad for France, but to me they secm gravel walks and bowling-greens ; in short it would be the finest travelling in the world, were it not for the inns, which are terrible places indeed."

At Paris, they got out of France to some extent. " The

minute we came" (it is still Gray who writes) " voilà Milors
Holdernesse, Conway and his brother; all stayed supper, and
till two o'clock in the morning, for here nobody ever sleeps;
it is not the way." Next day there was dinner at Lord
Holdernesse's (where they met the Abbé Prévost, not yet the
author of *Manon Lescaut*) and the theatre in the evening; next
day to that, Lord Conway's and the opera. Then came two
evenings at the *Comédie Française*, and so forth; by April 12,
Gray not yet three days in Paris, was writing:

" Mr. Walpole is gone out to supper at Lord Conway's,
and here I remain alone, though invited too. Do not think
I make a merit of writing to you preferably to a good supper;
for these three days we have been here, have actually given me
an aversion to eating in general. If hunger be the best sauce
to meat, the French are certainly the worst cooks in the world;
for what tables we have seen have been so delicately served,
and so profusely, that, after rising from one of them, one
imagines it impossible ever to eat again."

Of the two companions Gray was the one who interested
himself in matters of the table; his letters frequently return to
these subjects, which Walpole never mentions, except in later
life, to complain that he had the gout without deserving it.
But there they were, launched and enjoying themselves to the
top of their bent.

" Great part of our time is spent in seeing churches and
palaces full of fine pictures, etc., the quarter of which is not
yet exhausted. For my part" (says Gray), " I could entertain
myself this month merely with the common streets and the
people in them."

This sight-seeing was done in the mornings, and they had
a companion, Walpole's cousin, Harry Conway, a year or two
his junior, and his schoolfellow at Eton: though this, which
was to be the closest and most lasting of all his intimacies,
seems to have developed after school-days; and there is no
doubt that the affection took on a new degree of nearness after

Lady Walpole's death. These two, Lord Conway (afterwards Earl and then Marquis of Hertford) and Harry, afterwards General, and finally Field-Marshal Conway, were sons of her sister. Lord Conway, a good deal older than his brother, was a distinguished friend; but the two young men had been Horry and Harry to each other all their lives and were to be so till the end.

Conway, who, like all Horace Walpole's intimates, had literary tastes, gladly joined up with the new-comers. " Till we came," Gray writes, " he had not seen anything at all; for it is not the fashion here to have curiosity."

Whether Gray or his travelling companion was the better provided with this quality of curiosity, it would be hard to decide; but they needed some determination to indulge it.

" We had at first arrival an inundation of Visits pouring in upon us, for all the English are acquainted, and herd much together, and it is no easy Matter to disengage oneself from them, so that one sees but little of the French themselves. To be introduced to the People of high quality, it is absolutely necessary to be Master of the Language, for it is not to be imagined that they will take pains to understand anybody, or to correct a stranger's blunders. Another thing is, there is not a House where they don't play, nor is any one at all acceptable, unless they do so, a professed Gamester being the most advantageous character a Man can have at Paris."

It was not yet the moment when, as M. de Vogüe writes in his book on Juliette de l'Espinasse, " Paris discovered Europe and Europe discovered Paris." Twenty years later Walpole was to profit largely by the mutual discovery; but for the time being, the first of his letters, to West, after he had been three weeks abroad, shows him still, unwillingly, something of a tourist : " We have seen little of the people themselves who are not inclined to be propitious to strangers especially if they do not play and speak the language readily." It was settled, therefore, that the stay in Paris should come to an end when Lord Conway departed, and that the pair and Harry Conway with them should set out for Rheims, a provincial city in which Lord Conway had many acquaintances.

So off they set, about the end of May, and having established themselves in Rheims, fell severely to qualifying for parts in a society that spoke nothing but French.

"You must not wonder," says Walpole, writing to West on June 18, 1739, " if all my letters resemble dictionaries with French on one side and English on t'other : I deal in nothing else at present and talk a couple of words of each language alternately from morning to night."

They did not fall in love with Rheims or its great vine-covered plains—not even for the sake of its cathedral ; though Gray once more suggests compensations. "You have nothing to drink but the best champagne in the world and all sorts of provisions equally good." The provincial society impressed them by its stiffness ; an admirable letter from Gray describes the assemblies where everybody must sit down and play forty deals at quadrille without intermission and then must " rise up and eat of what they call the goûter which supplies the place of our tea. People take what they like and sit down again to play : after that they make little parties to go to the walks together and then all the company retire to their separate habitations." Nevertheless, they could on occasion improvise a supper or dance in one of the public gardens : violins were sent for, the fun went on till four o'clock when the gayest lady there proposed that " such as were weary should get into their coaches, and the rest of them should dance before them with the music in the van ; and in this manner we paraded through all the principal streets of the city and waked every body in it. Mr. Walpole had a mind to make a custom of the thing, and would have given a ball in the same manner next week ; but the women did not come into it ; so I believe it will drop, and they will return to their dull cards, and usual formalities."

The original scheme was that the party should go on from Rheims to Dijon, " a very splendid and very gay town," and then move into Provence—where they might have become discoverers of the Côte d'Azur.   But word came that George Montagu was on his way to join them, and with him another Etonian of the same flight—George Selwyn, who still passes for the wittiest man of that age.   Gray was ill pleased by the change as it postponed their travels till autumn ; and in fact it was September before the original three reached Dijon, which, according to Gray, made them regret the time they spent in Rheims ; but their stay was too short to enter into the society of the place.   They went on from there to Lyons which did not please them at all, but it was a necessary stage on the excursion which they had planned to Geneva.   Setting out on this in October, they took the road through Savoy on purpose to see the Grande Chartreuse ; and the Alps fairly went to Walpole's head.   He begins a kind of journal to West on the outward journey, before they had reached the Chartreuse.

" Precipices, mountains, torrents, wolves, rumblings, Salvator Rosa—the pomp of our park and the meekness of our palace !   Here we are, the lonely lords of glorious, desolate prospects.   I have kept a sort of resolution which I made, of not writing to you as long as I staid in France : I am now a quarter of an hour out of it, and write to you. Mind, 'tis three months since we heard from you.   I begin this letter among the clouds ; where I shall finish, my neighbour Heaven probably knows. . . .   But I am to undergo many transmigrations before I come to ' yours ever.'   Yesterday I was a shepherd of Dauphiné ; to-day an Alpine savage ; to-morrow a Carthusian monk ; and Friday a Swiss Calvinist."

Two days later, the sheet goes on at " Aix in Savoy."

" We are this minute come in here, and here's an awkward abbé this minute come in to us.   I asked him if he would sit down.   *Oui, oui, oui.*   He has ordered us a radish soup for supper, and has brought a chess-board to play with Mr. Conway. I have left 'em in the act, and am set down to write to you. Did you ever see anything like the prospect we saw yesterday? I never did. We rode three leagues to see the Grande Chartreuse; expected bad roads and the finest convent in the kingdom. We were disappointed pro-and con. The building is large and plain, and has nothing remarkable but its primitive simplicity; they entertained us in the neatest manner, with eggs, pickled salmon, dried fish, conserves, cheese, butter, grapes, and figs, and pressed us mightily to lie there. We tumbled into the hands of a laybrother, who, unluckily having the charge of the meal and bran, showed us little besides. . . . But the road, West, the road! winding round a prodigious mountain, and sur-rounded with others, all shagged with hanging woods, obscured with pines, or lost in clouds. Below, a torrent breaking through cliffs, and tumbling through fragments of rocks. Sheets of cascades forcing their silver speed down channelled precipices and hasting into the roughened river at the bottom. Now and then an old foot-bridge, with a broken rail, a leaning cross, a cottage, or the ruin of an hermitage. This sounds too bombast and too romantic to one that has not seen it, too cold for one that has. If I could send you my letter post between two lovely tempests that echoed each other's wrath, you might have some idea of this noble roaring scene, as you were reading it. Almost on the summit, upon a fine verdure, but without any prospect, stands the Chartreuse. We staid there two hours, rode back through this charming picture, wished for a painter, wished to be poets! Need I tell you we wished for you? Good night."

The first thing to observe about that passage is that by the age of twenty-two, Horace Walpole had completely mastered the art for which we prize him. The prose of his correspondence has the very accents of a talking voice: here the voice is hurried and excited, elsewhere it varies with his mood; but whatever the mood, it keeps the shifting intonation of talk. Some commentators have inclined to suggest that Walpole's letters are too good to be true, too well written to be natural; lacking in the spontaneousness which the best letter-writing should possess. Yet if one compares what Walpole wrote for print with what he wrote for a single reader, laboured artificiality will be found rather in the public utterance. It is quite true that he collected his letters for the press, and no doubt from a certain period, he wrote with a thought to their preservation. But by that time his art was formed; he wrote as he had always written, so that we can hear him saying it, one sentence hurrying on the heels of another. There is a letter from Gray and Walpole jointly to Ashton which puts the case amusingly about " the vast abundance and volubility of Mr. Walpole and his pen."

" He insists that it is not him but his pen that is so volubility, for although I am writing, as fast as I can drive, yet he is still chattering in vast abundance."

As for the excitement with which Horace Walpole related his first vision of mountain scenery, it is difficult to be sure whether it was an original or a borrowed emotion. His travelling companion was perhaps the first man in England who really had this passion at heart; and though at the moment Gray's letters expressed the same sort of feeling with less enthusiasm, his letters to West from Turin, the other side of the Alps, are chiefly concerned with retrospect. The first contact with Italian civilization had disappointed him: " I own I have not as yet anywhere met with their grand and simple works of Art that are to amaze one and whose sight one is to be the better for. But by those of Nature I am astonished even beyond expression. In our little journey up the Grande Chartreuse I do not remember to have gone ten paces without an exclamation that there was no restraining."

I have a feeling that these exclamations found their echo

in Horace Walpole's first volubility : all the more because
when he had to recount the actual crossing of the Alps, his
cry plainly comes from the heart :

" Such uncouth rocks, and such uncomely inhabitants !
My dear West, I hope I shall never see them again."

And, in point of fact, whereas in later life Gray con-
sistently explored whatever mountains he could reach, and
may be said to have discovered the Lake Country, Walpole
never moved a mile in quest of that form of the romantic.
Enough for him in the way of mountain prospect was the
steep side that falls from Richmond Park to the Thames
opposite Twickenham.

But in common fairness it should be allowed that
Walpole's Alpine journey was embittered to him by a reason
for which he is to be the better liked. They were travelling
when the roads were singularly unfrequented ; for, though
the plan had been to go down into Provence after the
journey to Geneva (where they left Conway), letters met them
at Lyons from Sir Robert, urging a visit to Italy instead ;
and both young men were more than willing. But it was
at the very end of October when they started, following the
route through Chambéry, and along the valley of the Arc,
till on the sixth day of their journey the mountain ascent
began : and here came tragedy.

They were in a narrow part of the road with a sheer drop
on the left and on the right a precipitous slope, pine clad ;
it was noonday with a bright sun ; Walpole had brought
with him " a little black spaniel of King Charles's breed ;
but the prettiest, fattest, dearest creature." He had let it
out of the chaise for air, " and it was waddling along close
to the head of the horses." " There darted out a young
wolf, seized poor dear Tory by the throat, and, before we
could possibly prevent it, sprung up the side of the rock and
carried him off. The postilion jumped off and struck at him
with his whip, but in vain. I saw it and screamed, but in

vain; for the road was so narrow, that the servants that were behind could not get by the chaise to shoot him."

Gray's account of the episode suggests a rather improbable danger: "If he had not been there and the creature had thought fit to lay hold of one of the horses, chaise, and we, and all must inevitably have tumbled about fifty fathoms perpendicular down the precipice." Walpole says only: "It was shocking to see anything one loved run away with to so horrid a death." From that time forward, mountains were never mentioned but with abhorrence: the Apennines completed what the Alps had begun, and six months later he writes to Conway "I am so surfeited with mountains and inns as if I had eat them." Their discomfort disgusted him; but it was not only the discomfort. "I have many to pass before I see England again, and no Tory to entertain me on the road." His taste in dogs was for lap-dogs, but he had a soft heart for them.

The actual crossing of Mont Cenis was accomplished a day after the tragedy. They slept at Lons-le-Bourg, and here, says Walpole, "we were obliged to quit our chaise which was taken all to pieces and loaded on mules, and we were carried in low arm-chairs on poles, swathed in beaver bonnets, beaver gloves, beaver stockings, muffs and bear-skins." Eight men did the carrying, and Gray's account of it is the more detailed.

"It was six miles to the top, where a plain opens itself about as many more in breadth, covered perpetually with very deep snow, and in the midst of that a great lake of unfathomable depth, from whence a river takes its rise, and tumbles over monstrous rocks quite down the other side of the mountain. The descent is six miles more, but infinitely more steep than the going up; and here the men perfectly fly down with you, stepping from stone to stone with incredible swiftness in places where none but they could go three paces without falling."

The whole distance was covered in five hours to Ferrière in Piedmont where they stopped, and heard " a new language spoken round about us." Evidently their Savoyard porters were French by tongue. They slept at Bossolens and on the eighth day reached Turin, where they stayed a fortnight and then posted on to Genoa, and found it so very fine that they were in fear of finding nothing finer. " We are fallen in love with the Mediterranean Sea and hold your lakes and your rivers in vast contempt," Gray writes, and says they spent most of their time, much to their hearts' content, " in cursing French music and architecture, and in singing the praises of Italy." In short, Italy captured both of them, and to the end of his days Horace Walpole was to look back on the year spent there as his happiest time. But Genoa was not the centre of his affections; Florence was Italy for him.

They got there after a journey through Tortona, Piacenza, Parma, Reggio and Modena, then to Bologna, where they spent twelve days in sight-seeing; and then crossed the Apennines to Florence. Here, says Gray, " Mr. Mann, the resident, has sent his servant to meet us at the gates, and conduct us to his house " (the Casa Ambrosio, now the Hotel *Grande Bretagne*). " He is the best and most obliging person in the world."

So began one of the oddest relationships of which literature holds record : Mr. Mann, whom we know by his later title of Sir Horace, is secure of immortality by the fact that for forty-five years he maintained one end of a correspondence which we possess in full—that is, if we care to exercise our privileges. But in practice we are all quite ready to believe Mr. Cunningham that Mann's half of the series may well be left to oblivion, and we know the gentleman not by what he wrote but by what was written to him. It is fair to say that letter after letter through the course of nearly half a century bears out what Gray—no way lavish with such expressions— said at the first encounter. Whether as Chargé d'Affaires or as Minister Plenipotentiary to the ducal court of Tuscany, he appears to have been certainly " the best and most obliging person in the world." Throughout all their long alliance Walpole never ceased to draw on his correspondent for good offices, not only to himself but to his acquaintance; but in return he never lost sight of any chance to serve Mann's interest, and, what is more truly the test, never ceased to be concerned for his health and happiness. If there be another example of such continued intimacy without personal contact, well then, that also goes to the credit of human nature. Anyhow the thing is so rare that it deserves consideration.

Walpole was one of the people who knew his own happiness when he had it, and so doubled his delight. It is for that power of enjoyment, of curiosity, of amusement, of appreciation, that we value his company so much after a hundred and fifty years; and this continued friendship was to be a living link with two things that were precious to him when he had them, yet, though things of passage, remained permanent in his memory—Italy and his youth. If he was constant in affection to Mann, it was not only for Mann's sake, but for love of these Italian days.

It was the height of spring time with him; nobody ever was younger than he when he wrote to West on February 27, 1740, after he had been more than two months a guest at Mann's house :

" Well, West, I have found a little unmasqued moment to write to you; but for this week I have been so muffled up in my domino, that I have not had the command of my elbows. But what have you been doing all the mornings ? Could you not write then ?—No, then I was masqued too ; I have done nothing but slip out of my domino into bed, and out of bed into my domino. The end of the Carnival is frantic bacchanalian ; all the morn one makes parties in masque to the shops and coffee-houses, and all the evening to the operas and balls. *Then I have danced, good gods ! How I have danced !*

. . . What makes masquerading more agreeable here than in England, is the great deference that is shown to the disguised. Here they do not catch at those little dirty opportunities of saying any ill-natured thing they know of you, do not abuse you because they may, or talk gross bawdy to a woman of quality."

Mann had an easy task in procuring a welcome for the great Minister's son : special notice was taken of him from the first. Gray writes to his mother, a week after their arrival : " Mr. Walpole is just come from being presented to the Electress Palatine Dowager ; she is a sister of the late Great Duke's ; a stately old lady, that never goes out but to church, and then she has guards, and eight horses to her coach. She received him with much ceremony, standing under a huge black canopy, and, after a few minutes' talking, she assured him of her good will, and dismissed him."

This sounds a little awe-inspiring, but Florentine society on the whole was not. Walpole writes :

" The freedom of the Carnival has given me opportunities to make several acquaintances ; and if I have not found them refined, learned, polished, like some other cities, yet they are civil, good-natured, and fond of the English. Their little partiality for themselves, opposed to the violent vanity of the French, makes them very amiable in my eyes."

In short, it was not only Italy that he fell in love with, but the Italians ; at least with the Italians as he found them in Florence. Elsewhere, he was no way so well pleased. They left Florence—he and Gray—towards the end of March because the Pope, Clement XII, had died, on February 6, and curious travellers could not miss the chance of being in Rome for the election of his successor. The Conclave was in full swing when they arrived on March 26 ; but there they found themselves in different and less easy conditions. "The English are numberless." Also, " though I am harmless in my nature, my name has some mystery in it " ; and rightly or wrongly the young man was persuaded that English correspondence was somehow made accessible to the Pretender, who was then living in Rome.

Indeed the first supplementary volume of letters published in 1918 by Dr. Paget Toynbee to complete his wife's great work, gives ground to believe that Horace Walpole's post-bag was worth watching : it suggests even that Sir Robert had a political motive in desiring that Horace should divert his tour from France to Italy. Through a series of letters to Mann, detail concerning the movements of the exiled Stuarts occupies the chief place ; and they are full of apprehensions of some expedition to be undertaken by one or other of the " Boys." Horace Walpole took kindly to the work of political reconnoitring ; he was zealous in his father's business ; he was zealous also, as he never ceased to be, for the interests of this friend at Florence, for whom he had already formed so eager an affection, and whom he sought to serve by assisting in what was Mann's chief duty—to watch for Jacobite conspiracy.

Over and above this main political concern—in which it is plain that Horace was so fully interested that he knew the names and movements of all the regular spies, and used ciphers to describe persons—there is a running account for Mann's benefit as to the day-to-day intrigues about the Papal election, given with the same light touch that was to be employed for nearly half a century in keeping the same correspondent posted on political affairs as they were seen from the neighbourhood of St. Stephens.

Gray does not appear in these letters ; the correspondence between Sir Robert's son and the English representative at Florence was kept private. But in the ordinary life of Rome these two travelling companions shared equally, as their best known letters make it plain.

They found a great deal to see and to describe at Rome : largely the gossip and rumours about the election, which dragged on its intrigues ; the rather gloomy state of a society divided between the " posterity of Popes " and " my ladies the countesses and marquises " of non-papal origin ; and, naturally, the antiquities and the works of art. They liked the sight-seeing better than the company.

" My dear Harry," Walpole writes to Conway, " how I like the inanimate part of Rome you will soon perceive at my arrival in England ; I am far gone in medals, lamps, idols, prints, &c., and all the small commodities to the purchase of which I can attain ; I would buy the Coliseum if I could : judge. My mornings are spent in the most agreeable manner ; my evenings ill enough. Roman conversations are dreadful things ! such untoward mawkins as the princesses ! and the princes are worse. Then the whole city is littered with French and German abbés, who make up a dismal contrast with the inhabitants. The Conclave is far from enlivening us ; its secrets don't transpire."

By the middle of May they were sick of it and " balancing in great uncertainty whether to go to Naples, or to stay here. . . . You know 'twould be provoking to have a Pope chosen just as one's back is turned." In June they stopped balancing and went off to Naples, where they spent nine or ten days and visited Herculaneum, whose remains excavation had only just begun to discover ; and Walpole had the advantage of Gray's already wide erudition in making this contact with Roman civilization of the second century after Christ. Then they journeyed back to Rome, found " the old eminences still cross and obstinate " and " a horrid thing called the *mal'aria* threatening to come on " ; so they packed their traps for Florence, and by July 9 were lodged again with Mann at his Casa in the Street of the Holy Apostles by the Bridge of the Trinity, and there Walpole settled in like a cat into his favourite armchair.

" I am happy here to a degree," he writes to Conway, " I am lodged with Mr. Mann, the best of creatures. I have a terreno all to myself, with an open gallery on the Arno, where I am now writing to you. Over against me is the famous Gallery; and, on the other hand, two fair bridges. Is not this charming and cool? The air is so serene, and so secure, that one sleeps with all the windows and door thrown open to the river, and only covered with a slight gauze to keep away the gnats. Lady Pomfret has a charming conversation once a week. She has taken a vast palace and a vast garden, which is vastly commode, especially for the cicisbeo-part of mankind, who have free indulgence to wander in pairs about the arbours. You know her daughters: Lady Sophia is still, nay she must be, the beauty she was: Lady Charlotte is much improved, and is the cleverest girl in the world; speaks the purest Tuscan, like any Florentine. The Princesse Craon has a constant pharoah and supper every night, where one is quite at one's ease. I am going into the country with her and the prince for a little while, to a villa of the Great Duke's. The people are good-humoured here and easy; and what makes me pleased with them, they are pleased with me. One loves to find people care for one, when they can have no view in it."

Perhaps it sharpened the edge of his enjoyment that he felt a limit set to it, and the same letter explains that both he and Conway had duties: " Let us see: you are to come back to stand for some place; that will be about April. 'Tis a sort of thing I should do, too; and then we should see one another, and that would be charming: but it is a sort of thing I have no mind to do: and then we shall not see one another, unless you would come hither—but that you cannot do: nay, I would not have you, for then I shall be gone.— So, there are many *ifs* that just signify nothing at all. Return I must sooner than I shall like."

Various small but significant indications in the letters show that his distaste for leaving was not simply an unwillingness to forgo pleasure, nor even to enter on the business of being a member of Parliament, which awaited him almost automatically, just as it awaited Conway, George Montagu, George Selwyn, and pretty nearly all the Eton boys of his set, though not of that other circle to which Gray and Ashton belonged. There was a permanent darkness in his mind, hinted at though never expressed. After he has set out all the attractions of Florence to Conway, he has this phrase : " You see how glad I am to have reasons for not returning ; I wish I had no better."

A couple of months later in September he writes again :

" As by the absence of the Great Duke, Florence is become in a manner a country town, you may imagine that we are not without démélés, but for a country town I believe there never were a set of people so peaceable, and such strangers to scandal. 'Tis the family of love, where everybody is paired, and for as constantly together as parroquets. Here nobody hangs or drowns themselves ; they are not ready to cut one another's throats about elections or parties ; don't think that wit consists in saying bald truths, or humour in getting drunk. But I shall give you no more of their characters, because I am so unfortunate as to think that their encomium consists in being the reverse of the English, who in general are either mad, or enough to make other people so."

Then he goes on to this younger cousin whom, as years went on, he treated as his elder and his hero.

" As I am convinced you love me, and as I am conscious you have one strong reason for it, I will own to you, that for my own peace you should wish me to remain here. I am so well within and without, that you would scarce know me : I am younger than ever, think of nothing but diverting myself, and live in a round of pleasures. We have operas, concerts, and balls, mornings and evenings. I dare not tell you all one's idlenesses : you would look so grave and senatorial, at hearing that one rises at eleven in the morning, goes to the opera at nine at night, to supper at one, and to bed at three. But literally here the evenings and nights are so charming and so warm, one can't avoid 'em."

The tone shifts here as he goes on. What begins with a plea for " My own peace " ends with a catalogue of diversions. Nevertheless, it is plain that not only Conway but all Walpole's friends knew that there was a sore place in his heart, and that his youth had only learnt to be happy when it got away from uncongenial surroundings. He wrote from Rome to Ashton, at a moment when some fear of banditti had made them feel prisoners till the Election should be over :

" I should not at all dislike my situation, if I were entirely at liberty and had nothing to call me to England. I shall but too soon miss there the peace I enjoy here ; I don't mention the pleasures I enjoy here, which are to be found in no other city in the world, but them I could give up to my friends with satisfaction. But I know the causes that drove me out of England, and I don't know that they are remedied. But adieu: when I leave Italy, I shall launch out into a life whose colour, I fear, will have more of black than of white."

In short, he disliked violently the coarse and riotous hilarity of the Houghton way of living ; and he had utterly resented Sir Robert's speedy marriage and installation of his mistress in the place of his mother. Yet none the less he was the Prime Minister's loyal and even ardent partisan; in March 1741, he writes gratefully to Conway for his account of the debate when a motion to " remove Sir Robert Walpole from his Majesty's presence and councils for ever " was defeated in both Houses. " I wrote last post to Sir Robert to wish him joy," he adds : " I hope he received my letter."

That sounds as if father and son were only very occasionally in communication.

The letter adds :

" Your account of Sir Robert's victory was so extremely well told that I made Gray translate it into French and have showed it to all that could taste it, or were inquisitive on the occasions."

This raises another aspect of Walpole's character, his conduct in a very difficult and delicate relation—which has been criticized, amongst others, by himself.

We do not know precisely the footing on which Gray accompanied Walpole. He travelled of course at Walpole's expense, and probably he was paid a salary. At least we do know that in Paris and elsewhere he had means to dress himself in the height of the fashion and did so with considerable attention to the details. But, salary or no, essentially one of these two friends and contemporaries was in the other's employment; none the less, the invitation came from Walpole, and Gray was, still more essentially, his guest. That famous philosopher, Brillat Savarin, has the fine saying that to invite a person means that you make yourself responsible for his happiness while he is your guest; and Walpole's responsibility in this kind had been extended over close on two years before it came to an end.

There is no trace at all of any friction in the letters written from Florence after the pair returned there. It is true, Gray would have liked to stay longer at Herculaneum; and about Rome, he writes from Florence (to his by no means sympathetic father).

" Finding no likelihood of a Pope yet these three months, and quite wearied with the formal assemblies and little society of that great city, Mr. Walpole determined to return hither, to spend the summer, where he imagines he shall pass his time more agreeably than in the tedious expectation of what, when it happens, will only be a great show. For my own part, I give up the thoughts of all that with but little regret; but the city itself I do not part with so easily, which alone has amusements for whole years."

However, Walpole was entitled to think that Gray as well as he could pass his time very agreeably at Florence: and in point of fact the two young men were very good company to each other. Gray was fully able to take interest in Walpole's verse-making, for that went on. He writes to West: "You have seen an epistle to Mr. Ashton that seems to me full of spirit and thought and a good deal of poetic fire." It should be noted here that Gray himself so far was writing all his poetry in Latin.

In July the two friends were sending, as was often their practice, a joint letter to West; and in October, Walpole begins thus:

"DEAR WEST,

T'other night as we (you know who we are) were walking on the charming bridge, just before going to a wedding assembly, we said, 'Lord, I wish, just as we are got into the room, they would call us out, and say, West is arrived. We would make him dress instantly, and carry him back to the entertainment. How he would stare and wonder at a thousand things, that no longer strike us as odd.' Would you not?"

The whole of this long letter is "a sketch of our employments," which manifestly were taken gaily. But as the winter wore on, there were signs of tedium. On January 2, 1741, Gray tells his father: "We still continue constant at Florence, one of the dullest cities in Italy." There were projects then of an excursion to Venice, but Walpole had taken a horror of post-chaises; what is more, he had grown lax about sight-seeing, and preferred amusements that were less to Gray's taste, and perhaps that Gray did not approve.

At all events we come finally to the eve of their departure from Florence, and in a letter to West, Gray makes it plain enough—though between the lines—that he no longer felt his company valued; that he found the need to make allowances for "others," and that the need had been impressed upon him in a disagreeable school.

FLORENCE, *April* 21, 1741.

"I know not what degree of satisfaction it will give you to be told that we shall set out from hence the 24th of this month, and not stop above a fortnight at any place in our way. This I feel, that you are the principal pleasure I have to hope for in my own country. Try at least to make me imagine myself not indifferent to you; for I must own I have the vanity of desiring to be esteemed by somebody, and would choose that somebody should be one whom I esteem as much as I do you. As I am recommending myself to your love, methinks I ought to send you my picture (for I am no more what I was, some circumstances excepted, which I hope I need not particularize to you); you must add then, to your former idea, two years of age, reasonable quantity of dulness, a great deal of silence, and something that rather resembles, than is, thinking; a confused notion of many strange and fine things that have swum before my eyes for some time, a want of love for general society, indeed an inability to it. On the good side you may add a sensibility for what others feel, and indulgence for their faults and weaknesses, a love of truth, and detestation of every thing else. Then you are to deduct a little impertinence, a little laughter, a great deal of pride, and some spirits. These are all the alterations I know of, you may perhaps find more. Think not that I have been obliged for this reformation of manners to reason or reflection, but to a severer schoolmistress, Experience. One has little merit in learning her lessons, for one cannot well help it; but they are more useful than others, and imprint themselves in the very heart."

When these fires were smouldering in that sluggish yet passionate temper, it is not surprising that some chance fanned them into flame. The pair set out from Florence, crossed the Apennines again, and as Walpole now hated Italian mountains, inns and post-chaises, he was probably intolerably pettish. The road lay through Bologna and Modena to Reggio where they were to see the fair : and at Reggio the companionship ended. I do not for an instant believe the story that Walpole opened one of Gray's letters to see if it contained disparaging remarks about himself ; in the first place he would never have done it : in the second place, had he done it, Gray would never have forgiven him. The truth is that the relation of dependency became intolerable once pleasure in each other's company was ended. We shall never know what precisely brought matters to a head, but Walpole's own account written nearly thirty years later to Mason, Gray's biographer, is very candid concerning the underlying causes.

" I am conscious, that in the beginning of the difference between Gray and me, the fault was mine. I was too young, too fond of my own diversions, nay, I do not doubt, too much intoxicated by indulgence, vanity, and the insolence of my situation, as a Prime Minister's son, not to have been inattentive and insensible to the feelings of one I thought below me ; of one, I blush to say it, that I knew was obliged to me ; of one whom presumption and folly perhaps made me deem not my superior *then* in parts, though I have since felt my infinite inferiority to him. I treated him insolently : he loved me, and I did not think he did. I reproached him with the difference between us, when he acted from conviction of knowing he was my superior. I often disregarded his wishes of seeing places, which I would not quit other amusements to visit, though I offered to send him to them without me. Forgive me, if I say that his temper was not conciliating ; at the same time that I will confess to you that he acted a more friendly part, had I had the sense to take advantage of it—he freely told me of my faults. I declared I did not desire to hear them, nor would correct them. You will not wonder that with the dignity of his spirit, and the obstinate carelessness of mine, the breach must have grown wider, till we became incompatible."

There is this to be observed. Gray left Reggio for Venice, travelling with Mr. John Chute and a younger Englishman, Francis Whithed, who were friends of Mann's and of Walpole's. These two resumed a close intimacy with Walpole after they had returned to England ; and there is not the least suggestion anywhere that these very likeable gentlemen felt that Gray, who was also still their friend, had been scurvily treated.

Meanwhile, Walpole, staying on by himself at Reggio, came near to afflict Gray with a formidable regret ; for he was seized with a quinsy and very nearly died. By good luck Joseph Spence, Pope's friend, the Professor of Poetry at Oxford, chanced to be in Reggio ; Walpole had met him in the previous year at Florence, and had corresponded with him from there ; they had renewed the acquaintance at Reggio, so that naturally Walpole, finding himself seriously ill, sent for this fellow-countryman, who took charge. But for this stroke of good fortune, Spence considered that Mr. Walpole, " who is one of the best natured and most sensible young gentlemen that England affords, would have in all probability fallen a sacrifice to this disorder."

By May 10 the invalid was able to write West an account of Reggio and its fair, to which " come all the nobility of Lombardy and all the broken dialects of Genoa, Milan, Venice, Bologna, etc. . . . You never heard such a ridiculous confusion of tongues. All the morning one goes to the fair undressed, as to the walks of Tunbridge ; 'tis just in that manner, with lotteries, raffles, etc."

In default of Gray he attached himself to Spence, and to Lord Lincoln whom Spence was bear-leading, and went with them to Venice : thence, still with them, to Genoa and by sea to Antibes, whence they explored the South of France through Toulon and Marseilles to Toulouse and so came back to Paris by Orleans and reached Dover on September 12, 1741.

CHAPTER III

ENTERING PARLIAMENT

THERE was good reason why Horace Walpole should
have made some haste to get back to England. At the
general election held in 1741 he was returned as member for
Callington in Cornwall, a seat which was part of Sir Robert's
property. The election had notably weakened the First
Minister's hold on the House of Commons ; and he was,
since 1739, in the disagreeable position of conducting a
European War into which popular clamour had forced him
against his own wish and judgment.

Manifestly it was the son's business to be at hand supporting his father by vote on any critical occasion : it was only
what the code of the age would have demanded of any gentleman indebted to another for a seat. What is more, Horace
Walpole was undoubtedly a firm believer in Sir Robert's
value to the nation as director of its fortunes ; yet he behaved
as if the seat were his natural appanage, carrying no obligation,
and as if the Minister's tenure of power were entirely indifferent
to his supporter.

We have nothing to help us beyond the unstable bog of
conjecture : between May 10 and September there is a total
blank in his correspondence. All that we do know, from the
passages already quoted, is that he felt a strong distaste for
returning to England, and that the prospects of parliamentary
life did not touch his imagination. He was still very young ;
a man at five and twenty who has never had to do anything
but please himself is hardly grown up ; he had certainly not
outgrown his affectations, and one of these which never
wholly left Horace Walpole was a sort of contempt for the

serious affairs of life. Indeed, he was never seriously concerned for anything except when his affections were engaged ;
and up to this period of his life it would be too much to say
that he had affection for Sir Robert.

He was proud of him ; he would have felt lessened by the
great man's overthrow. But the real excuse for his tardiness
is, I think, that he did not seriously conceive the possibility of
such an event. The Prime Minister was threatened ; so for
that matter was the Hanoverian dynasty ; but for as long as he
could remember, his father, Sir Robert, had ruled in the name
of a Hanoverian King. The conception of power naturally
alternating between parties in the State had not yet become
clearly formed in England ; and for the last twenty years it
had been completely pushed aside by Sir Robert's dominating
will. It is true that in the spring of 1741 the Motions to
remove Walpole had made the menace concrete, but the son
was then remote from all that could drive home the reality ;
and when he at last reached English soil the first signs were
of reassurance. " At Dover I found the benefit of the
motions having miscarried last year, for they respected Sir
Robert's son even in the person of his trunks."

He found, too, England such as twenty years of Sir
Robert's administration had made it.

" The country-town (and you will believe me, who, you
know, am not prejudiced) delights me : the populousness, the
ease, the gaiety, and well-dressed everybody amaze me.
Canterbury, which on my setting out I thought deplorable,
is a paradise to Modena, Reggio, Parma, &c. I had before
discovered that there was nowhere but in England the distinction of *middling people* ; I perceive now, that there is peculiar
to us *middling houses* : how snug they are ! "

That letter, at a halt on the road, was written from
Sittingbourne in Kent to Mann at Florence on September 13.
It is the opening of a series that was to reach five hundred
and extend over forty years ; but if the frequency of the out-

set had been maintained, five thousand would have been nearer the mark; he wrote at first every few days to this friend, who was truly an intimate. Undoubtedly if we had the whole of this letter we should know more of the writer's feelings. It goes on:

"I write to-night because I have time; to-morrow I get to London just as the post goes. Sir R. is at Houghton."

Then follow asterisks which indicate that a passage has been omitted by the editor, Mrs. Paget Toynbee, as "unfit for publication." The letters to Mann are, with the exception of half a dozen to his cousin Henry Conway, the only record of Horace Walpole's life from 1741 up to Sir Robert's death in 1745, and, as is well known, he soon perceived their interest as a memoir of the times and asked Mann to keep all and return them periodically. They were copied under his direction, with certain omissions; and the originals were destroyed. Publication was made from the copies, which are still in the possession of Lord Waldegrave. All earlier editors in printing from them omitted certain passages which Walpole left in; Mrs. Toynbee was the first to indicate where these omissions are; and her carefulness makes it possible to affirm that Horace Walpole, on his return to England, but before he had met Sir Robert, used some expressions in regard to him which it is thought better to withhold.

It is important to note this; for from the time when they met onwards, there is not a word written by the younger man about the elder which departs from the tone of affection and admiration. Part of the second letter is lost, including the date; but it was written about a fortnight after the first and shows that Horace Walpole was installed with his father at 10, Downing Street— a house which was originally offered by George I to Sir Robert as a personal gift in perpetuity; but the Minister preferred to accept it as First Lord of the Treasury, and so made himself the first of a long succession of official occupants.—The letter says:

"I had written and sealed my letter, but have since received another from you, dated September 24. I read Sir Robert your account of Corsica; he seems to like hearing any account sent this way—indeed, they seem to have more superficial relations in general than I could have believed."

The next, written on October 8, begins with what we know now to have been an intimation of approaching break-up.— "I have been very near sealing this letter with black wax." Sir Robert had come back very ill on Sunday night from his lodge in the New Park at Richmond where he still liked to spend his week-ends. Although danger was counted to be past when the letter was written, and another on October 13 says "Sir Robert is quite recovered," that of October 19 gives a vivid and melancholy contrast. Some words are missing; all these early letters are damaged to a degree which shows that the idea of preserving the series had not yet occurred to anyone; but a small conjectural addition is easy.

"[He who never woke till he] was called in the morning, and was asleep as soon as his head touched the pillow, for I have frequently known him snore ere they had drawn his curtains, now never sleeps above an hour without waking; and he, who at dinner always forgot he was Minister, and was more gay and thoughtless than all his company, now sits without speaking, and with his eyes fixed for an hour together. Judge if this is the Sir R. you knew."

Nevertheless, there is no trace of gloom about the correspondence. The virtuoso was "fitting up an apartment in Downing Street"; all his cases of treasures had come through from the Customs House, and he was "up to head and ears in dirt, straw, and unpacking," but radiant, for "Are you not glad? every individual is safe and undamaged." His virtuosoship made him good company for the sick man, who was collector almost as much as sportsman and had filled Houghton with costlinesses. So Mann's good offices are requested—the first of a regiment of such requests—to

57

negotiate for the purchase of two pictures ; a Madonna and Child, by Domenichino, in the Palazzo Zambeccari, at Bologna. The other by Correggio, " in a convent at Parma, and reckoned the second best of that hand in the world. . . . Sir R. would not scruple at any price, for he has of neither hand. The convent is poor : the Zambeccari collection is to be sold, though, when I inquired after this picture, they would not set a price."

There was a lull in politics during the interim recess ; meantime London provided a vast deal of gossip and gaiety. Plays did not win Mr. Walpole's approval.

" Nothing was ever so bad as the actors except the company. There is much in vogue a Mrs. Woffington, a bad actress ; but she has life."

The young gentleman was a bad critic, and he never became a good one ; but he had no superior at describing balls, and the great event was one given by Sir Thomas Robinson of Rokeby in honour of " a little girl of the Duke of Richmond's "—Lady Emily Lennox, second in a family of beautiful sisters, all of whom figure largely in every memoir of Walpole's period. It was a household into which he was welcomed and of which he never said an unkind word. The ball began at eight and had one hundred and ninety-seven people present, which was counted a surprising number, especially as it was " so well conducted that nobody felt a crowd."

" Except Lady Ancram, no married woman danced ; so, you see, in England, we do not foot it till five-and-fifty. The beauties were the Duke of Richmond's two daughters, and their mother, still handsomer than they : the Duke sat by his wife all night, kissing her hand : how this must sound in the ears of Florentine *cicisbè's*, cock or hen ! "

The elder of the two daughters was fated to make a runaway match with Walpole's friend, Henry Fox ; the second married the Earl of Kildare, who became the Duke of

Leinster, and Lord Edward Fitzgerald was their son. Lady Sarah Lennox, the most beautiful of all, who turned the young head of King George III, and finally became the mother of the Napier heroes, was still in the nursery.

After the ball, it was the royal birthday.

"I was in a great taking about my clothes, they came from Paris, and did not arrive till nine o'clock of the birthday morning. I was obliged to send one of the King's messengers for them and Lord Holderness's suit to Dover. There were nineteen suits came with them. Do you know I was in such a fright lest they should get into the news, and took up the *Craftsman* with fear and trembling."

The young man was certainly making the most of his position in Downing Street; but I wonder if in those times the Opposition papers would have made capital out of this use of a King's Messenger. Pulteney and the rest might have looked forward to an early day in power, and preferred to let it be a handy precedent.

Meantime Mann was kept busy with commissions.

"I find I cannot live without Stosch's intaglio of the Gladiator, with the vase, upon a granite. You know I offered him fifty pounds; I think, rather than not have it, I would give a hundred. What will he do if the Spaniards should come to Florence? Should he be driven to straits, perhaps he would part with his Meleager too. You see I am as eager about baubles as if I were going to Louis [a dealer] at the Palazzo Vecchio! You can't think what a closet I have fitted up; such a mixture of French gaiety and Roman virtù! you would be in love with it: I have not rested till it was finished: I long to have you see it. Now I am angry that I did not buy the Hermaphrodite; the man would have sold it for twenty-five sequins: do buy it for me."

A letter from Conway, the friend who was nearest to his affections, helps to complete the portrait of Horace Walpole as a young man. They had still not met, as Conway was in the country : and so assurances are given :

"You won't find me much altered, I believe ; at least, outwardly. I am not grown a bit shorter, or a bit fatter, but am just the same long lean creature as usual. Then I talk no French, but to my footman ; nor Italian, but to myself. What inward alterations may have happened to me, you will discover best ; for you know 'tis said, one never knows that one's self. I will answer, that the part of it that belongs to you, has not suffered the least change—I took care of that."

To say that it did not suffer change at any time would be too much ; but the intimacy was constant ; though as the years went by and the younger cousin held high posts of responsibility in war and peace, his idle elder slipped more and more into the position of an admiring junior. But at this moment they were both very young, and one of them at least full of affectations. The letter goes on—

"For virtù, I have a little to entertain you : it is my sole pleasure.—I am neither young enough nor old enough to be in love."

This philosopher was just turned four and twenty ; he was indeed, as he says of himself twenty years later, writing to the same Conway, "an absurd young man." It is part of youth's habitual pose—when youth poses—to insist on being unhappy, and although Horace Walpole does not go beyond a mild melancholy here because he is not breaking his heart for anyone, nor likely to break it, he does suggest— though in very moderate phrase—what was a real affliction. Things were not altogether happy at 10, Downing Street :

"As I do not love living *en famille* so much as you (but then indeed my family is not like yours), I am hurried about getting myself a house ; for I have so long lived single, that I do not much take to being confined with my own family."

His own family included notably the second brother Edward, who was openly jealous of his junior, in whom the

From a painting by N. Hone   *National Portrait Gallery*

HORACE WALPOLE 4th EARL OF ORFORD

elder (as appears from an angry letter written by him after Sir Robert's death) detected " a confidence and presumption of some kind of superiority.—You have assumed to yourself," Sir Edward went on, " a preeminence from an imaginary disparity between us in point of abilities and character." The letter, which was written in 1745, after the two brothers had been for three years in the House of Commons together, is known to us only by the fragment from it quoted in a long reply which Horace Walpole wrote and kept but never sent. It is not difficult to believe that the elder brother had some ground for thinking that the younger man gave himself airs : and if he had in the least degree a jealous temper, society, which did not pamper the elder but spoilt the younger, gave plenty of occasion for jealousy. Yet if we can trust Horace Walpole's testimony, the sharpest resentment was of Sir Robert's partiality. Long afterwards—thirty years afterwards—he wrote to Mason, who, referring to Walpole in his Life of Gray, had used the words, " Sir Robert's favourite son."

" Alas, if I ever was so, I was not so thus early ! Nor, were I so, would I for the world have such a word dropped ; it would stab my living brother to the soul, who, I have often said, adored his father and of all his children loved him the best."

This phrase conveys at least something like a recognition that special favour did go to the young man, in the last years when he was the fallen Minister's constant companion ; it recognizes too, with the generosity which Horace Walpole often showed in retrospect, that if his brother, Sir Edward, was jealous, this fault was allied to a real devotion. But jealousy is soon roused, and does not take long to make itself felt ; and though all this was only brewing in November, 1741, when the complaint of family discord was written to Conway, still no doubt the discomforts were already real, and there was as yet no offset.

But once Parliament met, there was an end to the talk of a separate establishment. Horace Walpole found himself plunged into the thick of one of the most exciting things in the world, a real fight in the House of Commons.

That is a true description, I think, even in these times of limited liabilities, and true even for the most half-hearted adherent. But when Horace Walpole came in, the fight raged against one man, and that man his father—still the stoutest champion there, yet fighting now with the odds against him; and the stake was by no means limited. Impeachment was well within the possibilities; the hunt was up in good earnest. We track the movement of it from day to day in the letters to Mann.

Parliament met on December 1, merely to choose a Speaker —unanimously; but a division was foreseen on the election of his Deputy. " The Court " still counted on a majority of forty and " a good majority like a good sum of money soon makes itself bigger." The Court meant Sir Robert; for needless to say, in those times the King made no pretence of indifference. Then came the King's speech, and there was a division in the Lords against the Address of thanks. " Lord Chesterfield made a very fine speech all levelled at the House of Commons "; but the Court's majority was forty-one. In the Commons no division was taken, but Pulteney attacked, and Sir Robert " with as much health, and as much spirit, as much force and command as ever, answered him for an hour and offered to second a motion for a day to examine the State of the Nation ". Pulteney moved it, Sir Robert did second it, and this ordeal was fixed for a day in January, six weeks ahead. Honours seemed to rest with the old warrior; but next day on one of the election petitions—cach of which was simply a trial of party strength—the Court's majority dropped to seven. Horace Walpole chose to be witty about it :

" The Opposition triumphs highly, and with reason ; one

or two such victories, as Pyrrhus, the member for Macedon, said, will be the ruin of us. I look upon it now, that the question is, Downing Street or the Tower; will you come and see a body, if one should happen to lodge at the latter? There are a thousand pretty things to amuse you; the lions, the armoury, the crown, King Harry's cod-piece, and the axe that beheaded Anna Bullen. I design to make interest for the room where the two princes were smothered; in the long winter evenings when one wants company (for I don't suppose that many people will frequent me then), one may sit and scribble verses against Crouch-back'd Richard, and dirges on the sweet babes. If I die there, and have my body thrown into a wood, I am too old to be buried by robin redbreasts, am not I?"

That was only the young man attitudinizing: he was so far only playing with the idea of defeat. Next week he had defeat to chronicle, though only on a matter of no more importance than the choice of a Chairman of Committee. "The Opposition carried their man by a majority of four— 242 as against 238—the greatest number, I believe, that ever *lost* a question. You have no idea of their huzza! unless you can conceive how people must triumph after defeats for twenty years together. . . . It was not very pleasant to be stared in the face to see how one bore it—you can guess at my bearing it, who interest myself so little about anything."

He had not yet stopped posing: but what follows is real. "Sir R. is in great spirits, and still sanguine. I have so little experience, that I shall not be amazed at whatever scenes follow. My dear child, we have triumphed twenty years; is it strange that fortune should at last forsake us; or ought we not always to expect it, especially in this kingdom? They talk loudly of the year *forty-one*, and promise themselves all the confusions that began a hundred years ago from the same date. I hope they prognosticate wrong; but should it be so, I can be happy in other places. One reflection I shall have, very sweet, though very melancholy ; that if our family is to be the sacrifice that shall first pamper discord, at least *the one, the part* of it that interested all my concerns, and must have suffered from our ruin, is safe, secure, and above the rage of confusion : nothing in this world can touch her peace now ! "

Naturally the pack that had been blooded ran the hunt hard ; they tried to make the House sit on Saturday, to deny the Prime Minister his weekly air and exercise. A wrangle over the Westminster Election went on till half-past four in the morning—" the longest day that ever was known. I say nothing of myself, for I could but just speak when I came away ; but Sir Robert was as well as ever, and spoke with as much spirit as ever, at four o'clock. This way they will not kill him ; I will not answer for any other. As he came out, Whitehead, the author of *Manners*, and agent, with one Carey, a surgeon, for the Opposition, said ' Damn him, how well he looks ! ' "

There is a new tone here of genuine affection and admiration :

" Sir Robert is very sanguine : I hope, for his sake and his honour, and for the nation's peace, that he will get the better ; but the moment he has the majority secure, I shall be very earnest with him to resign. He has a constitution to last some years, and enjoy some repose ; and for my own part (and both my brothers agree with me in it), we wish most heartily to see an end of his ministry. If I can judge of them by myself, those who want to be in our situation do not wish to see it brought about more than we do."

There followed a recess of three weeks, filled with letters about gossip, foreign affairs and virtù ; then we get back to the battle as reported to Mann.

Friday, Jan. 22, 1742.

" Don't wonder that I missed writing to you yesterday, my constant day : you will pity me when you hear I was shut up in the House of Commons till one in the morning. I came away more dead than alive, and was forced to leave Sir R. at supper with my brothers : he was still alive and in spirits. He says he is younger than me, and indeed I think so, in spite of his forty years more. My head aches to-night, but we rose early : and if I don't write to-night, when shall I find a moment to spare ? Now you want to know what we did last night ; stay, I will tell you presently."

Briefly, after two days of routine business, there had come Pulteney's famous motion which took the generalized form of proposing a Secret Committee of twenty-one to sit and examine persons and papers. But at least one supporter blundered out that he should vote for it as a committee of accusation.

" Sir Robert immediately rose, and protested that he should not have spoken, but for what he had heard last ; but that now, he must take it to himself. He pourtrayed the malice of the Opposition, who, for twenty years, had not been able to touch him, and were now reduced to this infamous shift. He defied them to accuse him, and only desired that if they should, it might be in an open and fair manner ; desired no favour, but to be acquainted with his accusation. He spoke of Mr. Doddington, who had called his administration infamous, as of a person of great self-mortification, who, for sixteen years, had condescended to bear part of the odium. For Mr. Pulteney, who had just spoken a second time, Sir R. said, he had begun the debate with great calmness, but give him his due, he had made amends for it in the end. In short, never was innocence so triumphant."

It was triumph by a narrow margin : they defeated the motion by three.

" When the debate was over, Mr. Pulteney owned that he had never heard so fine a debate on our side ; and said to Sir Robert, ' Well, nobody can do what you can ! ' ' Yes,'

replied Sir R., ' Yonge did better.' Mr. Pulteney answered,
' It was fine, but not of that weight with what you said.'
They all allow it ; and now their plan is to persuade Sir
Robert to retire with honour. All that evening there was a
report about the town, that he and my uncle were to be sent to
the Tower, and people hired windows in the City to see him
pass by—but for this time I believe we shall not exhibit so
historical a parade."

It was, however, the end of a great career. After some
other narrow divisions, the Minister was urged by his family
and friends to resign. A final defeat in one of the election
petitions settled it. " When you receive this, there will be no
longer a Sir Robert Walpole," Horace wrote to Mann on
February 4, 1742 ; " you must know him for the future as the
Earl of Orford. That other envied name expires with his
Ministry." Power passed to the rival party, which was
identified with the Prince of Wales's Opposition Court. " It
was understood from the heads of the party that nothing more
was to be pursued against him." But within less than a week
there was talk of no less than an impeachment ; the King's
favour to the fallen man, shown not merely by attention to
himself but by giving his illegitimate child by Miss Skerritt
the rank and title of an Earl's daughter, infuriated the rabble
of his opponents. He, meanwhile, after taking his seat in the
Lords went quietly to his retirement at Richmond, where he
had lived so long with Miss Skerritt ; and Horace Walpole,
his own mother's partisan, had therefore always avoided the
place. But he wrote to Mann :

" Our Earl is still at Richmond : I have not been there
yet ; I shall go once or twice ; for however little inclination
I have to it, I would not be thought to grow cool just now.
You know I am above such dirtiness, and you are sensible
that my coolness is of much longer standing."

Indeed, danger was still serious, and the new Coalition
moved for a Secret Committee to inquire into the conduct of

the last twenty years. " There was not a man of our party that did not expect to lose it by at least fifteen or twenty, but, to our great amazement, and their as great confusion, we threw out the motion, by a majority of 244 against 242."

In ordinary fair play that should have been the end, but there was no temper of fair play ; and on March 23 a new motion, different only in form, was introduced, proposing a committee to inquire into the conduct of Lord Orford for the past ten years, and " half the term was voted by the same House of Commons that had refused inquiry into the whole." On this motion Horace Walpole made his maiden speech, of which he sent the text to Mann. It is enough perhaps to quote one paragraph from this discourse, which had the distinction of receiving a compliment from Cornet William Pitt, whose fame was already formidable.

" While the attempts for this inquiry were made in general terms, I should have thought it presumption in me to stand up and defend measures in which so many abler men have been engaged, and which, consequently, they could so much better support ; but when the attack grows more personal, it grows my duty to oppose it more particularly, lest I be suspected of an ingratitude which my heart disdains. But I think, Sir, I cannot be suspected of that, unless my not having abilities to defend my father can be construed into a desire not to defend him."

The letters are a better service to the accused man than the speech was, for I defy anyone to read them without conceiving a liking for Sir Robert. In April there was talk of an adjournment to give the Secret Committee time to meet.

" Their object is returned from Houghton in great health and greater spirits. They are extremely angry with him for laughing at their power. The concourse to him is as great as ever ; so is the rage against him. All this week the mob has been carrying about his effigies in procession, and to the Tower. The chiefs of the Opposition have been so mean as to give these mobs money for bonfires, particularly the Earls of Lichfield, Westmorland, Denbigh, and Stanhope : the servants of these last got one of these figures, chalked out a place for the heart, and shot at it. You will laugh at me, who, the other day, meeting one of these mobs, drove up to it to see what was the matter : the first thing I beheld was a mawkin, in a chair, with three footmen, and a label on the breast, inscribed ' Lady Mary.' "

Such savagery, which did not even spare the " poor girl " as Horace calls her who " must be *created* an earl's daughter and bear the flirts of impertinent real quality " defeated itself in an England which Sir Robert Walpole, more than any one, had trained to lenity. Even while the Secret Committee, packed with partisans against him, was sitting, public opinion had a sure instinct. " It has not been the fashion to desert the Earl and his friends : he has had more concourse, more professions, and has still, than in the height of his power."

By July the whole proceedings had faded out into futility : the last attempt was to pass a Bill giving indemnity to any witness, however deep his own guilt, who would prove that Walpole had been aware of his misdeeds. This precious measure was passed by the Commons, but the Lords threw it out, and a motion in the Commons, to declare that this was " an obstruction of justice," failed to pass by some fifty votes.

It does not seem clear that the new Government really wished to push matters to extremes. Yet some years later, Horace Walpole, discussing his own pedigree and its complement of illustrious sufferers, writes : " The good Lord of Bath (Pulteney) whom I saw in Richmond Gardens this evening, did, I believe, intend to ennoble my genealogy with another execution."

Lord Orford himself took matters very easily, and the Letters have a delightful story which illustrates English character as well as that of this most typical Englishman.

" The few people that are left in town have been much

diverted with an adventure that has befallen the new ministers. Last Sunday the Duke of Newcastle gave them a dinner at Claremont, where their servants got so drunk, that when they came to the inn over against the gate of New Park, the coachman, who was the only remaining fragment of their suite, tumbled off the box, and there they were planted. There were Lord Bath, Lord Carteret, Lord Limerick, and Harry Furnese in the coach : they asked the inn-keeper if he could contrive no way to convey them to town. 'No,' he said, ' not he, unless it was to get Lord Orford's coachman to drive them.' They demurred ; but Lord Cartetet said, ' Oh, I dare say, Lord Orford will willingly let us have him.' So they sent, and he drove them home."

The story is resumed in another letter :

" Lord Orford has been at Court again to-day : Lord Carteret came up to thank him for his coachman ; the Duke of Newcastle standing by. My father said, ' My Lord, whenever the Duke is near overturning you, you have nothing to do but to send to me, and I will save you.' The Duke said to Lord Carteret, ' Do you know, my Lord, that the venison you eat that day came out of New Park ? ' Lord Orford laughed, and said, ' So, you see I am made to kill the fatted calf for the return of the prodigals ! ' "

But Horace Walpole did not take matters so lightly. He was passionately concerned, and twenty years later, when he was always ready to go to the House of Commons, " find his old corner under the window and laugh," it amused him to think how little indifferent he had once been. " To a man without ambition or interestedness, politicians are canaille. Nothing appears to be more ridiculous in my life than my having ever loved their squabbles, and at an age when I loved better things too."

With all respect to his memory, this is the language of affectation : and he was much more likeable in politics when he was passionately his father's partisan. As for the " better things " of which he spoke in 1762, they probably mean literature and art; and there are times when other things swamp these. In the middle of the secret proceedings against Lord Orford, Horace wrote to West:

" 'Tis an age most unpoetical. 'Tis even a test of wit to dislike poetry. . . . I do not think an author would be universally commended for any production in verse, unless it were an Ode to the Secret Committee, with rhymes of liberty and property, nation and administration."

While the Committee's inquiry was still proceeding, West passed out of Walpole's life, dying untimely at twenty-six; and the reconciliation with Gray was still distant. Few men could be more suggestible than this volatile person, and beyond doubt Sir Robert's influence at this time outweighed all others. It was allied to the taste for virtù; in the letters to Mann, inquiries after the Domenichino which had been ordered for Houghton alternate with reports on the political crisis.

There was still some talk of a separate establishment for the young man who in June, 1742, was bidding farewell to Downing Street—

" I am writing to you in one of the charming rooms towards the Park: it is a delightful evening, and I am willing to enjoy this sweet corner while I may, for we are soon to quit it. . . . Sir Robert goes into a small house of his own in Arlington Street, opposite to where we formerly lived. Whither I shall travel is yet uncertain: he is for my living with him; but then I shall be cooped—and besides, I never found that people loved one another the less for living assunder."

Yet, in point of fact, father and son, if father and son they were, were never asunder till death made the separation. In Arlington Street Sir Robert went into a " middling house which has long been his and was let: he has another, a small one next to it for me, and they are laid together." This suited the young man well enough ; but Houghton was no way to his taste. To receive letters, he says, " will be my only entertainment, for I neither hunt, brew, drink, nor reap." Yet it was evidently not so bad when he got there, and the old man's delight was contagious, and characteristic.

" The other night, as soon as he had gone through showing Mr. Ellis the house, ' Well,' said he, ' here I am to enjoy it, and my Lord of Bath may kiss my . . .' "

The statesman, satiated with power, was quite sincere in his enjoyment. Horace writes again on January, 1743, when they were back in London :

" Sir Robert's health is now drunk at all the clubs in the city ; they are for having him made a duke, and placed again at the head of the Treasury ; but I believe nothing could prevail on him to return thither. He says he will keep the 12th of February—the day he resigned—with his family as long as he lives."

Even at Houghton Horace could admire this philosophy.

" We are quite alone " (in July of that year). " You never saw anything so unlike as being here five months out of place, to the congresses of a fortnight in place ; but you know the *Justum et tenacem propositi virum* can amuse himself without *Civium ardor !* " But he adds with that engaging frankness which makes much of his charm : " As I have not so much dignity of character to fill up my time, I should like a little more company."

We know exactly how they lived at Houghton. The family consisted of the Earl, Horace with his half-sister, Lady Mary, Mrs. Leneve, an elderly kinswoman who acted as housekeeper, and her daughter. The other personage was a successor to the vanished Tory—Patapan, of whom there is much discourse. He was of noble Italian origin and had entered on his position at Florence as a pampered companion. Here is a sketch in a letter to Mann, but addressed to Chute, then in Florence, for Chute had seen Houghton.

" My love to Mr. Chute : tell him, as he looks on the east front of Houghton, to tap under the two windows in the left-hand wing, up stairs, close to the colonnade—there are Patapan and I, at this instant, writing to you ; there we are almost every morning, or in the library ; the evenings, we walk till dark ; then Lady Mary, Miss Leneve, and I play at comet ; the Earl, Mrs. Leneve, and whoever is here, discourse ; *car telle est notre vie !* "

An air of resignation pervades that letter, but it did not always prevail. Houghton grew less endurable, not more, when it had the company which Norfolk afforded. In August, 1743, he pours out his heart to the same Mr. Chute :

" Indeed, my dear Sir, you certainly did not use to be stupid, and till you give me more substantial proof that you are so, I shall not believe it. As for your temperate diet and milk bringing about such a metamorphosis, I hold it impossible. I have such lamentable proofs every day before my eyes of the stupefying qualities of beef, ale, and wine, that I have contracted a most religious veneration for your spiritual nourriture. Only imagine that I here every day see men, who are mountains of roast beef, and only seem just roughly hewn out into the outlines of human form, like the giant-rock at Pratolino. I shudder when I see them brandish their knives in act to carve, and look on them as savages that devour one another. I should not stare at all more than I do, if yonder Alderman at the lower end of the table was to stick his fork into his neighbour's jolly cheek, and cut a brave slice of brown and fat. Why, I'll swear I see no difference between a country gentleman and a sirloin ; whenever the first laughs, or the latter is cut, there run out just the same streams of gravy ! Indeed, the sirloin does not ask quite so many questions. I have an Aunt here, a family piece of goods, an old remnant of inquisitive hospitality and economy, who, to all intents and purposes, is as beefy as her neighbours. She

72

wore me so down yesterday with interrogatories, that I dreamt all night she was at my ear with ' who's ' and ' why's,' and ' when's ' and ' where's,' till at last in my very sleep I cried out, ' For God in heaven's sake, Madam, ask me no more questions ! '

" Oh ! my dear Sir, don't you find that nine parts in ten of the world are of no use but to make you wish yourself with that tenth part ? . . . They say there is no English word for *ennui* ; I think you may translate it most literally by what is called ' entertaining people,' and ' doing the honours ' ; that is, you sit an hour with somebody you don't know and don't care for, talk about the wind and the weather, and ask a thousand foolish questions, which all begin with, ' I think you live a good deal in the country,' or ' I think you don't love ' this thing or that. Oh ! 'tis dreadful ! "

In London things took a brighter cast ; at all events the spectacle had its humours : and a passage in his letter of November 1, 1742, to Mann helps us to realize what a change was made by Sir Robert's fall from power. We, in spite of ourselves, conceive of the King's surroundings as somehow outside of party dissensions : but in those days people went to Court or stayed away as a demonstration of party allegiance ; and those who paid court to the Prince of Wales at Carlton House avoided his father. Here is what Walpole said about the King's levee and the Drawing-room after the change :

" There were so many new faces that I scarce knew where I was ; I should have taken it for Carlton House, or my Lady Mayoress's visiting-day, only the people did not seem enough at home, but rather as admitted to see the King dine in public. 'Tis quite ridiculous to see the numbers of old ladies, who, from being wives of Patriots, have not been dressed these twenty years ; out they come in all the accoutrements that were in use in Queen Anne's days. Then the joy and awkward jollity of them is inexpressible ! They titter, and wherever you meet them, are always going to court, and looking at their watches an hour before the time. I met several on the Birthday, (for I did not arrive time enough to make clothes) and they were dressed in all the colours of the rainbow : they seem to have said to themselves twenty years ago, ' Well, if ever I go to court again, I will have a pink and silver, or a blue and silver ' and they keep their resolutions."

A year later it was a delight to the young man to observe in Arlington Street, where Carteret and Pelham also had their houses, that " of the three levees in this street, the greatest is in this house, as my Lord Carteret told them the other day ; ' I know you all go to Lord Orford : he has more company than any of us—do you think I can't go to him too ? ' "

With the New Year, what was said in jest grew earnest. Carteret, as Secretary of State, was responsible for carrying the unpopular measures necessary to maintain the contingent of Hanoverian troops ; the war had taken a threatening turn ; and by January 24, 1744, " the whole world, nay the Prince himself, allows that if Lord Orford had not come to town, the Hanoverian troops had been lost." Yet there was actually a preparation for invasion from Dunkirk, bringing the young Pretender with it. Weather once again helped the English fleet and by March the danger was over; Horace Walpole was always something of an alarmist, yet his letters for this year are less nervous than usual on public grounds ; but he had one subject for personal anxiety which was to last many years : Harry Conway, closest of all to his affection, was with the army on the continent.

But then came 1745, and the old man at Arlington Street was dying and through all February Horace Walpole was " either continually in his room or obliged to see multitudes of people." The last descriptive word is written on March 4.

" How dismal a prospect for him, with the possession of the greatest understanding in the world, not the least impaired, to lie without any use of it ! for to keep him from pains and restlessness, he takes so much opiate, that he is scarce awake four hours of the four-and-twenty ; but I will say no more of this."

When the next letter was written, Lord Orford had been dead ten days ; Mann, to whom it was addressed, was in some danger, for the Spaniards were threatening Tuscany, and Horace Walpole was all the more keenly aware of his impotence to help. " All my interest and significance are buried in my father's grave."

It is not a selfish expression : his concern for Mann's position was very real. But it sets out the truth sharply. Till then he had been a great man's son commanding powerful influences. Thenceforward, for what he was to be, he must depend on his own resources. These of course included the places with which his father had established him for life, and also a considerable inheritance—eight thousand pounds : not large indeed for the son of a man so reputed for wealth, but Sir Robert had been a great spender. It left Horace Walpole adequately endowed for life in the society of his time, but no more than adequately. He was of course rich as compared with the literary men who were among his associates ; he could even in a small way play the Mæcenas. But if he had money enough for his whims and for his generosities, it is because he was careful ; yet he was never too careful to open his purse wide on a fair occasion.

One incident—or rather, one demonstration of his willingness—belongs to the period while he was still in attendance on his father ; and it may close this chapter, for it tells a great deal of his nature as a young man.

Harry Conway, who was then five and twenty, had fallen in love with Lady Caroline Fitzroy, the Duke of Grafton's daughter. Horace Walpole, his elder by two years, knew and disapproved of the attachment ; he thought it imprudent, for Conway had very small private means. Now, in July, 1844, Conway wrote to his friend that he thought of breaking off the engagement : and Horace felt and said that this put him in a difficult position. His known wishes and opinions were so strong against the alliance that he could not advise a breach without seeming to be prompted by his own prejudice; and he had a scruple against advising a line of action which, although it answered his own desire, might be held to make against Conway's credit; for this, it may be said without exaggeration, was first and last Horace Walpole's chief concern in the world. He decided therefore to lessen so far as he could the obstacles to this marriage; so, after recalling the fact that Lady Caroline had shown her disposition most clearly by refusing good matches for the young soldier, he puts his proposal:

" My dearest Harry, you must see why I don't care to say more on this head. My wishing it could be right for you to break off with her (for, without it is right, I would not have you on any account take such a step) makes it impossible for me to advise it; and, therefore, I am sure you will forgive my declining an act of friendship which your having put in my power gives me the greatest satisfaction. But it does put something else in my power, which I am sure nothing can make me decline, and for which I have long wanted an opportunity. Nothing could prevent my being unhappy at the smallness of your fortune, but its throwing it into my way to offer you to share mine. As mine is so precarious, by depending on so bad a constitution, I can only offer you the immediate use of it. I do that most sincerely. My places still (though my Lord Walpole has cut off three hundred pounds a year to save himself the trouble of signing his name ten times for once) bring me in nearly two thousand pounds a year. I have no debts, no connections; indeed no way to dispose of it particularly. By living with my father, I have little real use for a quarter of it. I have always flung it away all in the most idle manner; but my dear Harry, idle as I am, and thoughtless, I have sense enough to have real pleasure in denying myself baubles, and in saving a very good income to make a

man happy, for whom I have a just esteem and most sincere
friendship. I know the difficulties any gentleman and man
of spirit must struggle with, even in having such an offer
made him, much more in accepting it. I hope you will allow
there are some in making it. But hear me : if there is any
such thing as friendship in the world, these are the opportunities of exerting it, and it can't be exerted without it is
accepted. I must talk of myself to prove to you that it will
be right for you to accept it. I am sensible of having more
follies and weaknesses, and fewer real good qualities, than
most men. I sometimes reflect on this, though I own, too
seldom. I always want to begin acting like a man, and a
sensible one, which I think I might be if I would. Can I
begin better, than by taking care of my fortune for one I love ?
You have seen (I have seen you have) that I am fickle, and
foolishly fond of twenty new people ; but I don't really love
them—I have always loved you constantly : I am willing to
convince you and the world, what I have always told you, that
I loved you better than anybody. If I ever felt much for
anything (which I know may be questioned), it was certainly
for my mother. I look on you as my nearest relation by her,
and I think I can never do enough to show my gratitude and
affection for her. For these reasons, don't deny me what I
have set my heart on—the making your fortune easy to
you. . . ."

The offer was not accepted ; and later, Conway made a
marriage that gave his friend complete satisfaction. But the
memory of this early proof of friendship must have had its
effect on the relations between the two throughout life : for
an honester, kinder and more delicate letter could not be
written by one brother to another.

One more small trait must be added to complete the
picture of Horace Walpole at the period of his father's death.
He was writing to Mann, who had more reasons than one to
condole with him, and whose guest, Chute, was also under a

bereavement. "You have nothing but misfortunes of your friends to lament," he says. "If it would not sound ridiculously, though, I assure you, I am far from feeling it lightly, I would tell you of poor Patapan's death : he died about ten days ago."

Before that there had been hardly a letter to Mann without mention of "his Patapanic Majesty" or the like : after this reticent epitaph, not another word. Walpole was notably constant in his devotion to the creatures with which he surrounded himself; and he never came to feel the parting lightly when their days were numbered, nor could he ever bring himself to quicken the end. Madame du Deffand knew well what she was doing when she left him, in his old age, the care of her cross and pampered Tonton, who bit everybody, including Horace Walpole himself.

CHAPTER IV

THE JACOBITE RISING

WHEN Horace Walpole faced the world entirely on his own account after Lord Orford's death, he had certainly no cause for uneasiness. That phrase to Mann, " All my interest and significance are buried in my father's grave," is more picturesque than accurate. It is true that close contact with a great source of power was no longer easily at his command ; but there is no proof that he ever sought power or cared about access to it. Otherwise his position was securely established ; he had his seat in parliament, his places for life, and moreover he had already, in his own right, a reputation. Scarcely three months after he had begun his chronicle to Florence, Mann wrote to his brother Galfridus, a member of the House of Commons : " Mr. Walpole's letters are full of wit : don't they adore him in England ? " Horace on hearing this replied :

" Not at all—and I don't wonder at them ; for if I have any wit in my letters, which I do not at all take for granted, it is ten to one that I have none out of my letters. A thousand people can write, that cannot talk ; and besides you know, (or I conclude so, from the little one hears stirring,) that numbers of the English have wit, who don't care to produce it. . . . Oh ! there are a thousand other reasons I could give you, why I am not in the least in fashion. I came over in an ill season : it is a million to one that nobody thinks a declining old minister's son has wit. . . . Indeed, if I were disposed to brag, I could quote two or three half-pay officers, and an old aunt or two, who laugh

79

prodigiously at everything I say; but till they are allowed judges, I will not brag of such authorities."

But four years later he takes a different line with George Montagu, his Eton schoolfellow and member of the Trium-virate, who had grown up into a virtuoso like Horace himself.

"Dear George,—I cannot help thinking you laugh at me when you say such very civil things of my letters, and yet, coming from you, I would fain not have it all flattery:

> So much the more, as, from a little elf,
> I've had a high opinion of myself,
> Though sickly, slender, and not large of limb.

With this modest possession, you may be sure I like to have you commend me, whom, after I have done with myself, I admire of all men living."

A year later, he renews his remonstrance—no doubt, rather half-heartedly; but what he writes, contains the root of the matter:

"Don't commend me: you don't know what hurt it will do me; you will make me a pains taking man, and I had rather be dull without any trouble. From partiality to me, you won't allow my letters to be letters. Jesus! It sounds as if I wrote them to be fine, and to have them printed, which might be very well for Mr. Pope, who having wrote pieces carefully, which ought to be laboured, could carry off the affectation of having studied things that have no excuse but their being wrote flying. Therefore if you have a mind I should write you news, don't make me think about it; I shall be so long turning my periods, that what I tell you will cease to be news."

That is a perfectly sound theory of the art of letter-writing, as indeed was to be expected. Horace Walpole was a great reader, but he read in the main to gratify his curiosity; none of his many judgments in poetry, fiction or the drama give reason to credit him with that discernment which only comes from a gift for enjoying the best. What he loved, what gave him real artistic pleasure, was the work of writers whose talent had affinity with his o-/n: above all, Madame de Sévigné and Grammont—social chroniclers. One essential in such writing is lively movement.

There are of course letters concerned with the mind's inner history, which of necessity move slow, which are ponderings gradually crystallized : but not such were the letters that Walpole wanted to read or to write. " Of all people living I know," Gray told him, " you are the least a friend to letters spun out of one's own brains, with all the toil and restraint that attends sentimental productions." His were written (we know it on the unimpeachable authority of Richard Bentley who stayed for long periods in his house) " with the greatest ease imaginable, with company in the room, and even talking to other people at the time." Letter writing was indeed to Horace Walpole a form of conversation : but it was something more—a duty of friendship, though as he says to Mann " it is one of the first duties that the very best people let perish out of their rubric." It meant, no doubt, keeping in touch ; but it meant also, and chiefly, doing your friend the service of giving him news at a period when the supply of that commodity was not so copiously provided as nowadays.

But, being as he was, a student of all social chronicles, it was not long before he perceived that the series of letters to Mann which he had begun on a simple instinct of friendliness was certain to have value as a vivid contemporary record ; and he took steps, as we have seen, systematically to recover what he wrote, and kept it together under his own control—a proceeding for which we are infinitely his debtors. None the less, he wrote always to Mann as to an individual, not to the public—though, as years went on, the individual withered and grew impersonal : so that this

main series of his correspondence has not the quality of
what he wrote to Conway, or to George Montagu, where
a keen sense of his correspondent's personality pervades the
whole.

But to return to the spring of the year 1745 : This gifted
young gentleman, rising eight and twenty, had to consider
how to settle himself down to his liking. He turned round
and round in that part of the universe which he frequented,
like a cat or a dog looking for the most convenient position.
But whereas cat or dog obeys dumb ancestral promptings,
Horace Walpole was as exempt from instincts as a human
being can attain to being. He was a bundle of vagaries
and there was a touch of originality about them; he did
at all events very clearly think out for himself what he liked
and why he liked it.

One form of settlement, and the most obvious of all,
he seems to have ruled out from the first : I cannot find the
least indication that he even thought of marriage—at least
not till he was in the seventies. There is a tradition, to
which Mr. Lewis Melville gives credit, that in his young days
at Florence he became engaged (or wished to become engaged)
to Lady Sophia Fermor. I can only say that the references
to this lady—and there are many—in his letters give no hint
of any such episode. What he does imply plainly (in a
letter to Conway) is that there were love passages in those
Florentine days between her and the young Lord Lincoln,
then doing the grand tour in company with Mr. Spence.
It is plain also that he watched with keen and sympathetic
interest the progress of this lady's young beauty; and that
he was not only interested but delighted when it was rumoured
that Carteret, of all men, had chosen her to be his wife.
For although Carteret had been one of the colleagues whom
Sir Robert had cast out, and was thenceforward part of the
opposition, and indeed Sir Robert's successor in power,
Horace Walpole counted him among the most distinguished

figures of his age. He notes with a sort of approving pride the young wife's devotion to a husband thirty years her elder; and finally when premature death left Lord Granville (as Carteret then was) for the second time a widower, his comment on it is no less impersonal than it is sincere in pity.

We are not without light upon his theories as to the subject of matrimony. Writing to Mann at the end of 1743, he comments on the marriage of Mann's sister to a gentleman whose fortune was scanty.

" But your sister was in love, and must consequently be happy to have him. Yet I own I cannot much felicitate anybody that marries for love. It is bad enough to marry; but to marry where one loves, ten times worse. It is so charming at first, that the decay of inclination renders it infinitely more disagreeable afterwards."

Practice in these matters is of course much more interesting than theory, and if I could throw any clear light on Horace Walpole's sexual history, it would be, by current standards, a biographer's first duty to communicate all the succulent details. Unhappily none are in my reach. The passage just quoted does at least suggest that the young man was not without experience of the charming beginnings to which he refers, even if he had (at twenty-six) to trust somewhat to report and observation for the phenomena of subsequent decay. Otherwise the evidence is rather negative. Horace Walpole did not look like a man of strong passions; but then neither did Lord Hervey, brother to the man whom Lady Louisa Stuart held to be Horace Walpole's true father. Yet Queen Caroline, a very plain-spoken lady, was continually rallying Lord Hervey about his " visits to London to his nasty *guenipes.*" Nobody in that plain-spoken age seems to have brought any such charge against Horace. If they accused him of anything, it was of an absurd partiality for the society of old ladies. The letters show beyond dispute that he loved also the company and the spectacle of beautiful women; but he never wanted to establish any one of them, young or old, in permanence at his hearthside.

There was a philosophy at the back of this which he had formulated even at this early age.

"I always travel without company," he writes to Mann in August, 1744, "for then I take my own hours and my own humours, which I don't think the most tractable to shut up in a coach with anybody else. You know St. Evremont's rule for conquering the passions, was to indulge them; mine for keeping my temper in order, is never to leave it too long with another person. I have found out that it will have its own way, but I must make it take its way by itself."

Then he goes on to meditations which forecast with surprising exactness the kind of nest that he would make out for himself, after a few preliminary turnings and scratchings. A year before, he had been writing to the same Mann as a determined Londoner.

"Were I a physician, I would prescribe nothing but *recipe ccclxv drachm. Londin.* Would you know why I like London so much? Why, if the world must consist of so many fools as it does, I choose to take them in the gross, and not made into separate pills, as they are prepared in the country. Besides, there is no being alone in the country: questions grow there, and that unpleasant Christian commodity, neighbours. Oh, they are all good Samaritans, and do so pour balms and nostrums upon one, if one has but the toothache, or a journey to take, that they break one's head."

But in 1744—when he was still speculating in the abstract, and the country meant Houghton with company not of his choosing—his maturer thought came down to this—

"If I had a house of my own in the country, and could live there now and then alone, or frequently changing my company, I am persuaded I should like it; at least, I fancy

I should; for when one begins to reflect why one don't like the country, I believe one grows near liking to reflect in it.'

It is not often that a young man knows so clearly the sort of life that will suit him. But for a while yet, Walpole was to remain what Gray called him, "the perpetual Londoner." Events in 1745 made him seriously concerned to know whether he would be able to call any house in England his own. Within a few weeks after Lord Orford's death the European war for which his opponents had been so eager, and which he so long staved off, took a turn threatening for England : the Allies were defeated at Fontenoy with heavy loss by the French under Marshal Saxe. George Montagu lost a brother, and there were also fears of an invasion of Tuscany by the Spanish, which brought Mann's fortunes into question. Horace Walpole had only the consolation that his hero Conway earned distinction. But in truth such solace was little to his mind.

"I can't but think," he told Conway, "we were at least as happy and great when all the young Pitts and Lytteltons were pelting oratory at my father for rolling out a twenty years peace, and not envying the trophies which he passed by every day in Westminster Hall."

By the end of July the bulletin to Mann was full of prospects of invasions. "Not five thousand men in the island and not above fourteen or fifteen ships at home." It was almost serious enough to decide him against allowing Mr. Chute—still with Mann at Florence—to buy a bronze eagle that had been found in the precincts of Caracalla's bath at Rome. "Would it not be folly to be buying curiosities now ? how can I tell that I shall have anything in the world to pay for it, by the time it is bought ? You may present these reasons to Mr. Chute ; if he laughs at them, why then, he will buy the eagle for me."

Mr. Chute did laugh at them, the eagle was destined to

be one of Walpole's glories; but for the rest of the year there was much solicitude as to how it should be sent across a hostile Europe, and seas that the English fleet could not command. By September matters had got past jesting: the Young Pretender was in Scotland and on his way to Edinburgh: before the month was out, he had routed Cope at Prestonpans; and till the 20th of December the letters have little in them but news of rebellion's progress. The tide turned then in England, but Scotland was still unsubdued: nevertheless gossip had begun to fill most of the pages even before April 25, when the battle of Culloden is announced. It is a bad period in the correspondence: we miss all the gaiety, and the irony is forced: for they were the letters of a very nervous gentleman. Ten years later, when other rumours spread, Horace Walpole writes: "I took all my fears out in the Rebellion: I was frightened enough then: I will never have another panic."

Like other people in that state, he was all for stern measures, and the despatch of General Hawley to the scene is quoted with exultation: "Frequent and sudden executions are his passion." Later, when his normal feelings had free play, he recognized Hawley for the butcher that he was; and his descriptions of the State trials which wound up the affair are among the masterpieces and generous in temper. These passages are long, but since nothing could give a better example of his peculiar gift, or better illustrate the temper of the times, some at least shall be given, beginning with the letter to Mann, written from Arlington Street on August 1, 1746.

"I am this moment come from the conclusion of the greatest and most melancholy scene I ever yet saw. You will easily guess it was the Trials of the rebel Lords. . . . A coronation is a puppet-show, and all the splendour of it idle; but this sight at once feasted one's eyes and engaged all one's passions. It began last Monday; three parts of

Westminster Hall were inclosed with galleries, and hung
with scarlet; and the whole ceremony was conducted with
the most awful solemnity and decency, except in the one
point of leaving the prisoners at the bar, amidst the idle
curiosity of some crowd, and even with the witnesses who
had sworn against them, while the Lords adjourned to their
own House to consult. . . . I had armed myself with all
the resolution I could, with the thought of their crimes and
of the danger past, and was assisted by the sight of the Marquis
of Lothian in weepers for his son who fell at Culloden—but
the first appearance of the prisoners shocked me, their
behaviour melted me. Lord Kilmarnock and Lord Cromartie
are both past forty, but look younger. Lord Kilmarnock
is tall and slender, with an extreme fine person; his behaviour
a most just mixture between dignity and submission; if in
anything to be reprehended, a little affected, and his hair
too exactly dressed for a man in his situation; but when
I say this, it is not to find fault with him, but to show how
little fault there was to be found. Lord Cromartie is an
indifferent figure, appeared much dejected, and rather sullen:
he dropped a few tears the first day, and swooned as soon
as he got back to his cell. For Lord Balmerino, he is the
most natural brave old fellow I ever saw: the highest intrepidity, even to indifference. At the bar he behaved like
a soldier and a man; in the intervals of form, with carelessness
and humour. He pressed extremely to have his wife, his
pretty Peggy, with him in the Tower. Lady Cromartie only
sees her husband through the grate, not choosing to be shut
up with him, as she thinks she can serve him better by her
intercession without: she is big with child and very handsome; so are their daughters. When they were to be brought
from the Tower in separate coaches, there was some dispute
in which the axe must go—old Balmerino cried, 'Come,
come, put it with me!' At the bar, he plays with his fingers
upon the axe, while he talks to the gentleman-gaoler, and

one day somebody coming up to listen, he took the blade and held it like a fan between their faces. During the trial, a little boy was near him, but not tall enough to see; he made room for the child and placed him near himself.

When the trial began, the two Earls pleaded guilty; Balmerino not guilty, saying he could prove his not being at the taking of the Castle of Carlisle, as was laid in the indictment. . . . Then some witnesses were examined, whom afterwards the old hero shook cordially by the hand. The Lords withdrew to their House, and returning, demanded of the judges, whether one point not being proved, though all the rest were, the indictment was false? to which they unanimously answered in the negative. Then the Lord High Steward asked the Peers severally, whether Lord Balmerino was guilty. All said 'guilty upon honour,' and then adjourned, the prisoner having begged pardon for giving them so much trouble. While the Lords were withdrawn, the Solicitor-General Murray (brother of the Pretender's minister) officiously and insolently went up to Lord Balmerino, and asked him, how he could give the Lords so much trouble, when his solicitor had informed him that his plea could be of no use to him? Balmerino asked the bystanders who this person was? and being told, he said, 'Oh, Mr. Murray. I am extremely glad to see you; I have been with several of your relations; the good lady, your mother, was of great use to us at Perth.' Are not you charmed with this speech? How just it was. As he went away, he said, ' They call me Jacobite; I am no more a Jacobite than any that tried me: but if the Great Mogul had set up his standard, I should have followed it, for I could not starve.' . . .

. . . Great intercession is made for the two Earls: Duke Hamilton, who has never been at Court, designs to kiss the King's hand, and ask Lord Kilmarnock's life. The King is much inclined to some mercy; but the Duke [of Cumberland], who has not so much of Cæsar after a victory, as in gaining it, is for the utmost severity. It was lately proposed in the city to present him with the freedom of some company; one of the aldermen said aloud, 'Then let it be the *Butchers*.' . . ."

August 12. "Lord Cromartie is reprieved : the Prince [of Wales] asked his life, and his wife made great intercession. Duke Hamilton's intercession for Lord Kilmarnock has rather hurried him to the block : he and Lord Balmerino are to die next Monday. Lord Kilmarnock, with the greatest nobleness of soul, desired to have Lord Cromartie preferred to himself for pardon, if there could be but one saved ; and Lord Balmerino laments that himself and Lord Lovat were not taken at the same time ; ' for then,' says he, ' we might have been sacrificed, and these other two brave men escaped.' Indeed Lord Cromartie does not much deserve the epithet ; for he wept whenever his execution was mentioned. Balmerino is jolly with his pretty Peggy. There is a remarkable story of him at the battle of Dunblain, where the Duke of Argyll, his colonel, answered for him, on his being suspected. He behaved well ; but as soon as we had gained the victory, went off with his troop to the Pretender ; protesting that he had never feared death but that day, as he had been fighting against his conscience. Popularity has changed sides since the year '15, for now the City and the generality are very angry that so many rebels have been pardoned."

(August 16. To George Montagu.) "I have been this morning at the Tower, and passed under the new heads at Temple Bar, where people make a trade of letting spying-glasses at half-penny a look. Old Lovat arrived last night. I saw Murray, Lord Derwentwater, Lord Traquair, Lord Cromartie and his son, and the Lord Provost at their respective windows. The other two wretched Lords are in dismal towers, and they have stopped up one of old Balmerino's windows because he talked to the populace ; and now he has only one, which looks directly upon all the scaffolding.

They brought in the death-warrant at his dinner. His wife fainted. He said, 'Lieutenant, with your damned warrant you have spoiled my lady's stomach.' . . . It will be difficult to make you believe to what heights of affectation or extravagance my Lady Townshend carries her passion for my Lord Kilmarnock, whom she never saw but at the bar of his trial, and was smitten with his falling shoulders. She has been under his windows; sends messages to him; has got his dog and his snuff-box; has taken lodgings out of town for to-morrow and Monday night, and then goes to Greenwich; forswears conversing with the bloody English, and has taken a French master. She insisted on Lord Hervey's promising her he would not sleep a whole night for my Lord Kilmarnock, 'and in return,' says she, 'never trust me more if I am not as yellow as a jonquil for him.' She said gravely t'other day, 'Since I saw my Lord Kilmarnock, I really think no more of Sir Harry Nisbett than if there were no such man in the world.' But of all her flights, yesterday was the strongest. George Selwyn dined with her, and not thinking of her affliction so serious as she pretends, talked rather jokingly of the execution. She burst into a flood of tears and rage; told him she now believed all his father and mother had said of him; and with a thousand other reproaches flung upstairs. George coolly took Mrs. Dorcas, her woman, and made her sit down to finish the bottle: 'And pray, sir,' said Dorcas, 'do you think my lady will be prevailed upon to let me go and see the execution? I have a friend that has promised to take care of me, and I can lie in the Tower the night before.'"

August 21. "I came from town the day after the execution of the rebel Lords: I was not at it, but had two persons come to me directly who were at the next house to the scaffold: and I saw another who was upon it, so that you may depend on my accounts.

Just before they came out of the Tower, Lord Balmerino

drank a bumper to King James's health. As the clock struck ten they came forth on foot, Lord Kilmarnock all in black, his hair unpowdered in a bag, supported by Forster, the great Presbyterian, and by Mr. Home, a young clergyman, his friend. Lord Balmerino followed, alone, in a blue coat, turned up with red, (his rebellious regimentals), a flannel waistcoat, and his shroud beneath; their hearses following. They were conducted to a house near the scaffold: the room forwards had benches for spectators; in the second Lord Kilmarnock was put, and in the third backwards Lord Balmerino: all three chambers hung with black. Here they parted! Balmerino embraced the other, and said, 'My Lord, I wish I could suffer for both!' He had scarce left him, before he desired again to see him, and then asked him, 'My Lord Kilmarnock, do you know anything of the resolution taken in our army, the day before the battle of Culloden, to put the English prisoners to death?' He replied, 'My lord, I was not present; but since I came hither, I have had all the reason in the world to believe that there was such order taken; and I hear the Duke has the pocket-book with the order.' Balmerino answered, 'It was a lie raised to excuse their barbarity to us.'—Take notice, that the Duke's charging this on Lord Kilmarnock (certainly on misinformation) decided this unhappy man's fate! The most now pretended is, that it would have come to Lord Kilmarnock's turn to have given the word for the slaughter, as lieutenant-general, with the patent for which he was immediately drawn into the rebellion after having been staggered by his wife, her mother, his own poverty, and the defeat of Cope. He remained an hour and a half in the house, and shed tears. At last he came to the scaffold, certainly much terrified, but with a resolution which prevented his behaving in the least meanly or unlike a gentleman. He took no notice of the crowd, only to desire that the baize might be lifted up from the rails, that the mob might see the spectacle. He stood and prayed sometime with Forster, who wept over him, exhorted and encouraged him. He delivered a long speech to the Sheriff, and with a noble manliness stuck to the recantation he had made at his trial; declaring he wished that all who embarked in the same cause might meet the same fate. He then took off his bag, coat and waistcoat, with great composure, and after some trouble put on a napkin-cap, and then several times tried the block; the executioner, who was in white, with a white apron, out of tenderness concealing the axe behind himself. At last the Earl knelt down, with a visible unwillingness to depart, and after five minutes dropped his handkerchief, the signal, and his head was cut off at once, only hanging by a bit of skin, and was received in a scarlet cloth by four of the undertaker's men kneeling, who wrapped it up and put it into the coffin with the body: orders having been given not to expose the heads, as used to be the custom.

The scaffold was immediately new-strewed with saw-dust, the block new-covered, the executioner new-dressed, and a new axe brought. Then came old Balmerino, treading with the air of a general. As soon as he mounted the scaffold, he read the inscription on his coffin, as he did again after-wards: he then surveyed the spectators, who were in amazing numbers, even upon masts of ships in the river; and pulling out his spectacles read a treasonable speech, which he delivered to the Sheriff, and said, the young Pretender was so sweet a Prince, that flesh and blood could not resist following him; and lying down to try the block, he said, ' If I had a thousand lives, I would lay them all down here in the same cause.' He said, if he had not taken the sacrament the day before, he would have knocked down Williamson, the lieutenant of the Tower, for his ill usage of him. He took the axe and felt it, and asked the headsman how many blows he had given Lord Kilmarnock; and gave him three guineas. Two clergymen, who attended him, coming up, he said,

' No, gentlemen, I believe you have already done me all the service you can.' Then he went to the corner of the scaffold, and called very loud for the warder, to give him his perriwig, which he took off, and put on a night-cap of Scotch plaid, and then pulled off his coat and waistcoat and lay down; but being told he was on the wrong side, vaulted round, and immediately gave the sign by tossing up his arm, as if he were giving the signal for battle. He received three blows, but the first certainly took away all sensation. He was not quarter of an hour on the scaffold; Lord Kilmarnock above half a one. Balmerino certainly died with the intrepidity of a hero, but with the insensibility of one too. As he walked from his prison to execution, seeing every window and top of house filled with spectators, he cried out, ' Look, look, how they are all piled up like rotten oranges ! '

My Lady Townshend, who fell in love with Lord Kilmarnock at his trial, will go nowhere to dinner, for fear of meeting with a rebel-pie; she says, everybody is so bloody-minded, that they eat rebels ! The Prince of Wales, whose intercession saved Lord Cromartie, says he did it in return for old Sir William Gordon (Lady Cromartie's father), coming down out of his death-bed to vote against my father in the Chippenham election. If his Royal Highness had not countenanced inveteracy like that of Sir Gordon, he would have had no occasion to exert his gratitude now in favour of rebels."

Other letters describe the trial and execution of old Lord Lovat and they are not less good, in the same vein. But one more quotation shall illustrate the temper of that age. George Selwyn, Walpole's fellow-Etonian, was not only a wit but much beloved; and a great part of his life was devoted with the utmost tenderness to a small girl who may have been his daughter, but probably was the Duke of Queensberry's. Nevertheless, for this humane and amiable gentleman, the finest sight in ordinary life was a hanging;

executions in the grand manner were the climax of experience, and Walpole tells of him at this period that he " thinks always *à la tête tranchée*," and when he went to his dentist, said he would drop his handkerchief as a signal for the operation to begin. Yet it seems that this trait in him raised objections : Walpole told Conway—" Some women were scolding him for going to see the execution, and asked him, how he could be such a barbarian to see the head cut off ? ' Nay,' says he, ' if that was such a crime, I am sure I have made amends, for I went to see it sewed on again.' When he was at the undertaker's, as soon as they had stitched him together, and were going to put the body into the coffin, George, in my Lord Chancellor's voice, said, ' My Lord Lovat, your lordship may rise.' "

It was a strong-stomached generation.

CHAPTER V

THE BEGINNING OF STRAWBERRY HILL

SO soon as the rebellion and its attendant excitements were done with, Horace Walpole carried out his plan of getting himself a retreat in the country—" for take notice," he says to Mann writing from it, " I put this place upon myself for the country." It was however a small house within the precincts of Windsor Castle, and had this advantage, it was near Gray's summer resort at Burnham Beeches.

For Gray had come back into the story. The reconciliation had been brought about by the two men themselves in the autumn of 1745. Walpole took the first step, writing to propose it. Gray, when he next came to London, wrote a note on his arrival " and immediately received a very civil answer." The account which he gives to Wharton—who knew that the meeting was to take place—gives a lively picture of Walpole, but in doing so, shows us clearly enough a rather prickly defensive attitude in Gray.

" I went the following evening to see *the Party* (as Mrs. Foible says) and was something abashed at his Confidence; he came to meet me, kiss'd me on both Sides with all the Ease of one, who receives an Acquaintance just come out of the Country, squatted me into a Fauteuil; begun to talk of the Town & this & that t'other, & continued with little interruption for three Hours, when I took my Leave very indifferently pleased, but treated with wondrous Good-breeding. I supped with him next night (as he desired). Ashton was there, whose formalities tickled me inwardly."

There follows a contemptuous description of Ashton, who had been the intimate of both, and still was Walpole's;

95

Gray was the quicker of the two to dismiss this pompous person. Then the letter goes on:

"Next morning I breakfasted alone with Mr. W.; when he had all the éclaircissement I ever expected & I left him far better satisfied, than I had been hitherto. When I return I shall see him again."

It is a fair construction of this to say that Walpole's good will had won over a somewhat morose and sensitive nature, and had regained him a companionship that he did right to value. A notable passage in a letter from Gray, written two years later, speaks of some estrangement between Walpole and a third person—presumably Ashton—which a meeting had failed to remedy.

"I should have expected everything from such an explanation; for it is a tenet with me (a simple one, you'll perhaps say) that if ever two people, who love one another, come to breaking, it is for want of a timely éclaircissement, a full and precise one, without witnesses or mediators, and without reserving any one disagreeable circumstance for the mind to brood upon in silence."

Undoubtedly the *éclaircissement* in Gray's own case had been full and frank. In October, 1746, Chute and his friend Whithed returned to England after their long stay in Italy. Gray first heard of it from Walpole, with whom he was by then on such terms that he had almost forgotten there had been a notorious breach, for he wrote to Chute:

"My God! Mr. Chute in England? What, and have you seen him, and did he say nothing to you? not a word of me? such was my conversation, when I first heard news so surprising, with a person, that (when I reflect) it is indeed no great wonder you did not much interrogate concerning me, as you knew nothing of what has passed of late."

And in a following letter, there is this:

"Yes, we are together again. It is about a year, I believe, since he wrote to me, to offer it, and there has been (particularly of late), in appearance, the same kindness and confidence as of old. What were his motives, I cannot yet guess. What were mine, you will imagine and perhaps blame me. However, as yet I neither repent, nor rejoice over-much, but I am pleased. He is full, I assure you, of your Panegyric. Never anybody had half so much wit, as Mr. Chute (which is saying everything with him, you know) and Mr. Wh^d is the finest young man that ever was imported."

The advent of these returned travellers was admirably calculated to help on the renewed friendship; Gray liked Chute no less than Walpole did, who for his part set it down that " Mr. Chute has absolutely more wit, knowledge and good nature than to their great surprise ever met in one man." A couple of months after their arrival Chute and Whithed fetched Gray out of his retirement; he writes to Wharton —" I have been in town flaunting about at public places with my two Italianized Friends. The World itself has some attraction in it to a Solitary of six years standing, and agreeable well meaning people of Sense (thank Heaven there are so few of them) are my peculiar Magnet."

I am not sure that this description exactly fitted Gray's conception of Horace Walpole; perhaps he was not quite sure of the " Sense," perhaps not of the " well-meaning " (oddly chosen word). On the other hand, there is no doubt that after two years of their renewed intercourse Walpole found that the six years' seclusion had infected the " Solitary" with an unpleasing cast of thought. " I agree with you absolutely in your opinion about Gray," he writes to their fellow-Etonian, George Montagu, perhaps the most like-minded with him of all his friends, " he is the worst company in the world. From a melancholy turn, from living reclusely, and from a little too much dignity, he never converses easily; all his words are measured and chosen, and formed into sentences; his writings are admirable; he himself is not agreeable."

But Horace Walpole was far too intelligent to cut himself off from intercourse with so admirable a writer, for the excellent reason that he was himself being rapidly drawn towards writing for the public. In truth, the two were held together by common interests rather than by mutual liking. Walpole, knowing the value of what he received, went to Gray for critical advice, which it is plain was given with a cool enjoyment of the task and no reluctance to fault-finding ; while Gray, though a self-sufficing worker, came more and more to treat Walpole as his first audience—an intermediary to that publicity which he was always shy of seeking, and which, through Walpole, could be induced to seek him.

A letter from Cambridge, written by Gray a couple of months after the reconciliation, makes it plain that the friendship was now instinctively concentrating on the ties created by literature.

" This comes du fond de ma cellule to salute Mr. H. W. not so much him that visits and votes, and goes to White's and to Court, as the H. W. in his rural capacity, snug in his tub on Windsor-hill, and brooding over folios of his own creation ; him that can slip away, like a pregnant beauty (but a little oftener), into the country, be brought to bed perhaps of twins, and whisk to town again the week after, with a face as if nothing had happened."

What follows makes it clear that Walpole had been confiding to Gray all his literary projects—including one which he did not carry out till five years later, the proposed " Memoirs of the Reign of George I."

" Among the little folks, my godsons and daughters," Gray writes, " I cannot choose but enquire more particularly after the health of one; I mean (without a figure) the Memoires. Do they grow ? Do they unite, and hold up their heads, and dress themselves ? Do they begin to think of making their appearance in the world, that is to say, fifty years hence, to make posterity stare, and all good people cross themselves."

Literary confidences were to be mutual; Gray sends " a scene in a tragedy "—his long meditated " Agrippina." " If it don't make you cry it will make you laugh; and so it moves some passion, that I take to be enough." We have not Walpole's answer; but another letter from Gray in January shows that he had been appreciative—and also that he enjoyed the correspondence. " I write to you with equal pleasure," Gray answers, " though not with equal spirits or equal plenty of material." He has no gossip and can only go on with encouragement about the *Memoirs*. " You need not fear but posterity will ever be glad to know the absurdity of their ancestors."

There is also more about " Agrippina "—a work which never saw completion, and which would scarcely have given to Walpole proof demonstrative that his recaptured friend was indeed a poet of genius. But we have to remember that he was already acquainted with the " Ode on a Distant Prospect of Eton College " of which in October, 1746 (the time of Chute's reappearance), he sent a copy to Conway. Yet his comment—" You will immediately conclude out of good breeding that it is mine and that it is charming," indicates sufficiently that Gray had not yet—perhaps not even in Horace Walpole's mind—taken definitive rank. No doubt also, Walpole had seen the earlier " Ode to Spring," written in 1742 during the period of their estrangement. Further, very soon after we find mention of the Eton Ode, Walpole's household became associated for ever with what is at least a minor masterpiece of Gray's. In February, 1747, Gray received the account of a domestic tragedy; Walpole's cat had come to an untimely end, attempting to poach goldfish out of a glass jar which was among the ornaments of Arlington Street; and, as the world knows, he answered with a poem, to which his letter had this prelude:

"As one ought to be particularly careful to avoid blunders in a compliment of condolence, it would be a sensible satisfaction to me (before I testify my sorrow, and the sincere part I take in your misfortune) to know for certain who it is I lament. I knew Zara and Selima (Selima was it ? or Fatima ?), or rather I knew them both together; for I cannot justly say which was which. Then as to your handsome Cat, the name you distinguish her by, I am no less at a loss, as well knowing one's handsome cat is always the cat one likes best; or if one be alive and the other dead, it is usually the latter that is the handsomest. Besides, if the point were never so clear, I hope you do not think me so ill-bred or so imprudent as to forfeit all my interest in the survivor; oh no! I would rather seem to mistake, and imagine to be sure it must be the tabby one that had met with this sad accident. . . . Heigh ho! ᵀ feel (as you to be sure have done long since) that I have very little to say, at least in prose. Somebody will be the better for it; I do not mean you, but your Cat, feue Mademoiselle Sélime, whom I am about to immortalize for one week or fortnight, as follows . . ."

As a result of this, before the end of the year, Gray was on his way to a first appearance in print. Walpole, an active go-between, had given the two odes and Selima to Dodsley for his *Poetical Miscellany* that appeared in 1748. In this collection was included also an ode by West, and moreover, that Epistle to Thomas Ashton which Horace Walpole had composed in Italy, and which Gray had praised in a letter to West.

There had been some coyness about this "publication" of the Epistle; but Gray says, writing after the volume had reached him—

"You know I was of the publishing side, and thought your reasons against it none; for though, as Mr. Chute said extremely well, the still small voice of Poetry was not made to be heard in a crowd; yet satire will be heard, for all

A GREAT ORIENTAL BOWL

This is the large blue and white tub that stood in
"the Cloister" by the front door. In it was drowned
the cat, as sung by Gray.

the audience are by nature her friends ; especially when she appears in the spirit of Dryden, with his strength, and often with his versification, such as you have caught in those lines on the Royal Unction, on the Papal Dominion, and Convents of both Sexes ; on Henry VIII and Charles II, for these are to me the shining parts of your Epistle. There are many lines I could wish corrected, and some blotted out, but beauties enough to atone for a thousand worse faults than these."

One may fairly say then that the two, who had set out together to see Europe, set out also together—and once more by Walpole's initiative—on this new adventure of commencing author, though they were to travel very different roads.

Indeed, in so far as Horace Walpole was a writer of poems or of books, I cannot bring myself to take him very seriously. Except as a letter writer we know him only by one creation—but that is illustrious. He is the creator of Strawberry Hill ; few houses in all England have been known by name to so many millions of people ; and it is very odd to consider why. I doubt if Hatfield or Chatsworth is so widely celebrated. Abbotsford no doubt has been, but then Abbotsford became a place of pilgrimage, the centre of a national cult. Walpole, on the other hand, was universally known in a very small exclusive society and (except in the corresponding society of Paris) nowhere outside it ; Scott's reputation was diffused over all Europe and America. What is more, though Scott's and Walpole's houses were alike architecturally deplorable, nobody took Strawberry Hill seriously. It was a freak ; but a freak so characteristic of the time that its name lives like Ranelagh and Vauxhall, surrounded by airy notions of old world elegance—completely unclouded by that Gothic gloom which its creator believed himself to have achieved.

Yet this is anticipation. He went to Strawberry Hill

looking for a better realization of what he had aspired to realize at Windsor—a retreat where he could retire and live his own life, so placed that the hermit could at any moment slough his chrysalis and turn back into a butterfly. Three months after he had established himself at Windsor, Harry Conway chaffed him and wanted to know if he had " really grown a philosopher."

" Really I believe not," was the answer, " for I shall refer you to my practice rather than to my doctrine, and have really acquired what they only pretend to seek, content. So far, indeed, I was a philosopher even when I lived in town, for then I was content too ; and all the difference I can conceive between those two opposite doctors was, that Aristippus loved London, and Diogenes Windsor ; and if your master the Duke, whom I certainly prefer to Alexander, and who certainly can intercept more sunshine " (the Duke of Cumberland was of earth-shaking bulk) " would but stand out of my way, which he is extremely in, while he lives in the Park here, I should love my little tub of forty pounds a year, more than my palace *dans la rue des ministres*, with all my pictures and bronzes, which you ridiculously imagine I have encumbered myself with in my solitude. Solitude it is, as to the tub itself, for no soul lives in it with me; though I could easily give you room at the butt-end of it, and with vast pleasure ; but George Montagu, who perhaps is a philosopher too, though I am not sure of Pythagoras's silent sect, lives but two barrels off; and Ashton, a Christian philosopher of our acquaintance, at the foot of the hill."

But the tub only held him for a year. On June 5, 1747, a letter to Mann announces a general election—in which his own part is so easy " that I shall have no trouble, not even the dignity of being carried in triumph, like the lost sheep, on a porter's shoulders ; but may retire to a little new farm that I have taken just out of Twickenham. The house is so small, that I can send it you in a letter to look at ; the prospect is as delightful as possible, commanding the river, the town, and Richmond Park; and being situated on a hill descends to the Thames through two or three little meadows, where I have some Turkish sheep and two cows, all studied in their colours for becoming the view."

It lay just off the road from Twickenham to Hampton Court, which bounded it on the landward side; another highway ran along between it and the Thames; but no houses then broke, as they now do, the view of the great river. A letter to Conway gives us his first raptures, in an enchanted and enchanting piece of writing, calling it, " the prettiest bauble you ever saw."

" It is set in in enamelled meadows, with filigree hedges:

> A small Euphrates through the piece is roll'd,
> And little finches wave their wings in gold.

Two delightful roads, that you would call dusty, supply me continually with coaches and chaises; barges as solemn as Barons of the Exchequer move under my window; Richmond Hill and Ham walks bound my prospect; but, thank God! the Thames is between me and the Duchess of Queensberry. Dowagers as plenty as flounders inhabit all around, and Pope's ghost is just now skimming under my window by a most poetical moonlight. I have about land enough to keep such a farm as Noah's, when he set up in the ark with a pair of each kind; but my cottage is rather cleaner than I believe his was after they had been cooped up together forty days."

Of course he exaggerates the smallness—or perhaps made Houghton his standard; it was an ordinary square little two-storied house with four windows on each side; its door on' the north led almost on to the inner road; but east, south and west, it saw green fields and trees. However, though at the time he had no guess of this, it was tiny enough compared with what it was to grow to; the oddest germ from which should spread a freakish growth, part sham monastery, part would-be Gothic castle.

The name came later, and it was not an invention; he discovered "Strawberry Hill" in the lease of his new possession.

"I like to be there better than I have liked being anywhere since I came to England," he wrote to Mann with an unusual touch of emotionalism. For the returned Italians, Chute and Whithed, had put him upon plans of returning to Italy. "I sigh after Florence, and wind up all my prospects with the thought of returning there. I have days when I even set about contriving a scheme for going to you, and though I don't love to put you upon expecting me, I cannot help telling you that I wish more than ever to be with you again. I can truly say that I never was happy but at Florence, and you must allow that it is very natural to wish to be happy once more."

But Italy never saw him more; and the real anchor that held him to England was Strawberry. House and man grew indivisible. It provided him with an occupation for his lifetime.

He began with the outdoor: "Planting and fowls and cows and sheep are my whole business." George Montagu had supplied a fine strain of bantams, and by 1748 there were seven and twenty from the original veterans. That year, he ran down to spend his Christmas alone, ("Did you ever know a more absolute country-gentleman?") and found not only several of his honeysuckles out, but "literally a blossom upon a nectarine-tree." Planting was in full swing; he had got four more acres ("which makes my territory prodigious in a situation where land is so scarce, and villas as abundant as formerly at Tivoli and Baiæ") and was proposing "a terrace the whole breadth of my garden on the brow of a natural hill, with meadows at the foot, and commanding the river, the village, Richmond-hill, and the park, and part of Kingston."

But by summer the house had begun to tempt him with projects. He let George Montagu, a kindred spirit, know that at Cheneys, a seat of the Bedford family, were piteous fragments of an old Tudor dwelling—unroofed but still having " beautiful arms in painted glass in the windows . . . I propose making a push and begging them of the Duke of Bedford. They would be magnificent for Strawberry-Castle."

For the " little plaything house " that he had bought from Mrs. Chenevix, the toy woman, was beginning to become the toy castle; it was to have a frowning martial skyline (in stucco). " Did I tell you that I have found a text in Deuteronomy to authorize my future battlements? ' When thou buildest thy new house, then shalt thou make a battlement for thy roof, that thou bring not blood upon thy house, if any man fall from thence.' "

By November, Mann also was charged to pick up old painted glass arms or anything that Italy could offer " for a little Gothic castle " to be built at Strawberry Hill; and for the next forty years, the British representative at Florence kept sending one *trouvaille* after another to enrich what grew to be a vast and most oddly assorted collection of objects of *virtu*.

The lord of Strawberry liked to confide his projects to the sympathetic, but as a rule he did not desire company; though he lost no time in advising Conway (who had just, to his admiring cousin's delight, married the widowed Lady Ailesbury) that there was room for a married couple, and that his half-sister and her husband Charles Churchill had already been his guests. " But there are very few I ask to come here and fewer still that I wish to see here," he adds, sincerely enough. For in another way the place was not only occupation but made another of his chief occupations possible. This urban rusticity gave him the means of solitude when he wanted it, and this meant more and more the means of getting books written as well as letters. The itch for print grew on him with startling rapidity.

He began with it as a kind of extension to his connoisseurship. At the end of 1747 he brought out an edition of Lady Mary Wortley's *Eclogues* : for his dislike of the lady did not prevent him from admiring her writings. At the same time he was compiling the first of his own works, a description of the pictures at Houghton, intended for a " slight memorial " of the great place, for whose glory he foresaw a near end. The first Lord Orford had left to his successor a mountain of debts and moreover this new owner of Houghton was already a dying man.

In 1750 Walpole was tempted to break down his rule of solitude and take in an inmate who would help in the castle building. This was Richard Bentley, son of the great scholar— no scholar himself but a clever draughtsman and designer. Walpole was seized by one of his sudden enthusiasms and wrote to George Montagu : " He has more sense, judgment and wit, more tact, and more misfortunes than I have ever met in any man." So began, in 1750, an intimacy which lasted ten years ; and second only to Walpole's own is the mark left by Richard Bentley on what was once Mrs. Chenevix's dwelling. He had very soon gothicized its modest staircase with a surprising balustrade and animal figures.

The association of these two while it lasted was characteristic. Bentley was a man of many gifts, something of a writer, something of an artist, something of a wit, and Horace Walpole, who loved dabbling in many pursuits, loved perhaps even more assisting others to dabble. He submitted indeed constantly to Gray's criticism, which was always slightly astringent, and never outspoken in praise ; and he says, probably with truth, in a letter to Mason that though Gray was " far from an agreeable confidant to self-love," yet " he had always more satisfaction in communicating anything to him, though sure to be mortified, than in being

flattered by people whose judgments he did not respect."
On the other hand, he did not dislike praise from clever
folk, and Bentley probably was not sparing of it; at all
events he entered with gusto into all the connoisseur's delights
and he gave the virtuoso full occasion to exercise himself in
constructive criticism. Walpole not only prided himself on
being an amateur in letters; he loved to have dealings with
other amateurs to whom he could offer suggestions without
finding himself rebuffed by trained competence. Moreover,
in a frugal way, he liked to be a patron. He liked giving
help to deserving talent. Hobbes's saying that benevolence
is a love of power and delight in the exercise of it might
apply justly to many of Horace Walpole's activities—though
by no means to all. Letters to his deputy, Mr. Bedford,
show us that he did a considerable deal of almsgiving by
stealth; and he certainly did not plume himself on these
movements of compassion. But he no less certainly had
the harmless vanity which is pleased by the successful launch-
ing of a protégé; and with it there went the corresponding
shortness of temper. He very easily grew impatient with
Bentley when Bentley did not make the most of such
opportunities as were offered to him by his patron's benevolent
zeal. Worse still: Bentley had a wife. It is always easier
for a patron to help an unmarried man, and Mrs. Bentley
was in Horace Walpole's opinion more than usually detri-
mental; he could not forgive Bentley's obstinacy in letting
her get in the way. On the whole the Bentley alliance was
not a great success. It brought out Walpole's foibles
rather than his qualities, it showed him in his most supercilious
aspect.

But in all other relations the man was now perhaps at
his most likeable; unless indeed one has a preference for
what he was when quite old, and preoccupied with a touching
devotion to the young. He was at his best—it is not surprising—when he was concerned with his enjoyments, not

with his afflictions ; and at this time the world was so full of a number of things that he managed to be much happier than any of the several kings who came under his observation. He deserves some credit for his felicity, and Gray, that austere judge, gave it to him. " I congratulate you on your happiness and seem to understand it," he wrote. " The receipt is obvious ; it is only ' Have something to do ' ; but how few can apply it." That was written later in 1757, when they were both forty ; but there is no great difference in Horace Walpole (though there was in Gray) between the man of thirty and the man of forty. Whether at thirty or at forty, he could have said with truth—as he did say later, looking back regretfully in a time when serious and untoward business had been thrust upon him—" I was never quarter of an hour without occupation."

There was, to begin with, Strawberry ; the bantams to be fed, plantings to be seen to, this or that addition to be made in the house ; there was the whole business of connoisseurship. Then there was always some book or other in progress, and these books for the most part involved a great deal of research ; he was an antiquarian who knew how to popularize, and make the result of his huntings not only accessible but readable. And there was also—what concerns us most—his vast and growing correspondence. If he was idle—and he tells us that his friends thought him idle, that most of his contemporaries were serious young men (like Harry Conway) who blamed him because he would sooner spend an hour with George Selwyn than attend to politics—well, if he was idle, it was to our profit. His mind was always busy, always lying in wait for some incident, some trait of character, some witty saying that could make material for a letter. He was no more idle when he spent half the night playing loo than a landscape painter is when he strolls about the countryside simply looking round him. His sketch-book was out of sight but never out of mind.

And of course it was not only at loo tables and masquerades that he hunted material for our diversion. He was for some twenty-five years a member of Parliament, on the easiest terms. There was a choice of boroughs in the family. Just after he had become lord of Strawberry, a general election came on. King's Lynn which had been Sir Robert's seat was vacant; but the elder Horatio Walpole's son (who figures in the letters unattractively) was available. "Pigwiggin is to be chosen for Lynn whither I would not go because I must have gone: I go to Callington again, whither I don't go."

Or as another letter puts the indignant comment of his friends, they stood for constituencies, he sat for his. None of the rough and tumble of electioneering disturbed his elegance. In a sense he was not an active member of the House of Commons, but he seems to have been assiduous in his attendance. None of his letters mention his having spoken, after the maiden speech in defence of Sir Robert; but there is a passage in one, written after he had ceased to be a member, that describes how he went down to the House at a moment of political excitement (chiefly to hear Charles Fox), and to his surprise felt a "palpitation as if I were coming down with the intention of making a speech there." That seems to imply repeated experience. But, even nowadays, speech-making is by no means the first duty of an ordinary member of parliament, and in the eighteenth century debate was left to a very few performers. A member's business was to vote—and even more than that, to be there; to assist by his presence in the affair of governing the country, guided in part no doubt by argument but still more by those mysterious influences which are called the temper of the House, the tradition of the place, the atmosphere of Parliament, and so forth. He was there much more to inform himself in the public interest than to inform others. This duty Horace Walpole sedulously discharged—and contrived to discharge it without neglecting any of the other opportunities for acquiring information. Here is a letter to Bentley—written in 1755 when the gentleman of thirty-eight felt some need to excuse himself; but it is a picture of him any time in the reign of George II.

"You know how late I used to rise: it is worse and worse: I stay late at debates and committees; for, with all our tranquillity and my indifference, I think I am never out of the House of Commons; from thence, it is the fashion of the winter to go to vast assemblies, which are followed by vast suppers, and those by balls. Last week I was from two at noon till ten at night at the House; I came home, dined, new-dressed myself entirely, went to a ball at Lord Holdernesse's, and stayed till five in the morning. What an abominable young creature! But why may not I be so? Old Haslang dances at sixty-five; my Lady Rochford without stays, and her husband the new groom of the stole, dance. In short, when Secretaries of State, Cabinet Councillors, Foreign Ministers, dance like the universal ballet in the Rehearsal, why should not I—see them? In short, the true definition of me is that I am a dancing senator—Not that I do dance, or do anything by being a senator; but I go to balls, and to the House of Commons—to look on; and you will believe me when I tell you, that I really think the former the more serious occupation of the two; at least the performers are most in earnest. What men say to women, is at least as sincere as what they say to their country."

There were of course other times when the House of Commons itself, not the balls, kept him till four or five in the morning; in either case, he was there chiefly as a looker on—but always with the same alert note-taking intelligence. Thanks to him, more perhaps than to any other, the people of that age are alive to us—and we may agree with him that the people of the ballrooms are as interesting as the parliamentary performers.

There was, for instance, the Duchess of Queensberry—to whom Phœbus himself, according to Prior's fancy, could not refuse a favour—

> " Kitty at heart's desire
> Obtained his chariot for a day
> And set the world afire."

In 1729, when Sir Robert Walpole's power was at its height, but with all the wits against it, this inimitable *frondeuse* ostentatiously canvassed everybody in the King's drawing-room for subscriptions to the " Beggar's Opera," in which everybody took the highwayman, MacHeath, to represent the Prime Minister. She was banished from the court for this supreme insolence ; but after close on twenty years had passed she thought it time to come back.

" Nobody gave in to it. At last, in 1747 she snatched at the opportunity of her son being obliged to the King for a regiment in the Dutch Service, and would not let him go to thank, till they sent for her too."

A few months later she was giving a masquerade and trying to get the King to it ; but he would not go. Heaven knows how he would have been treated. Walpole went of course (though he must " own that it is wondrous foolish to dress oneself out in a becoming dress in *cold blood*") and he found that the Duchess " had stuck up orders about dancing, as you see at public bowling greens, turned half the company out at twelve, kept these she liked to supper, and in short contrived to do an agreeable thing in the rudest manner imaginable ; besides having dressed her husband in a Scotch plaid which is just now one of the things in the world that is reckoned most unpopular,"—not unnaturally, two years after plaid and claymore had been worn in rebellion at the gates of Derby.

But the great lady's vitality and prolonged charm got the better of Horace Walpole's disapproval. He might write to Conway in his first description of Strawberry Hill, " Thank

God ! the Thames is between me and the Duchess of Queensberry." That was in 1747 when he was thirty ; but in 1771
when he was fifty-five and she, heaven knows what age, he
crossed the Thames one day to call on her, found her out
driving and left this epigram—

> " To many a Kitty, love his car
> Will for a day engage,
> But Prior's Kitty, ever fair,
> Obtained it for an age."

" She is still figuring in the world," he wrote to Mann, " not
only by giving frequent balls, but really by her beauty." Her
clothes were fantastic. At the French Ambassador's ball
in 1773 she " had a round gown of rose colour with a man's
cape which with the stomacher and sleeves was all trimmed
with mother-of-pearl earrings. This Pindaric gown was a
sudden thought to surprise the Duke, with whom she had
dined in another dress." Yet she could carry things off.
A month or two later that same season she " was in a new
pink lutestring and looked more blooming than the maccaro-
nesses. One should sooner take her for a young beauty of
an old-fashioned century than for an antiquated goddess of
this age—I mean, by twilight."

Having kept her dancing spirits till the sixties, "she died
in 1777 of a surfeit of cherries." They were a great race,
the nobilities of Horace Walpole's generation.

Chief among his friends were the family of Charles II's
grandson, the second Duke of Richmond ; and no lady of
that age was more celebrated than the Duke's youngest
daughter, Lady Sarah Lennox, who turned the head of
George III, and was seriously expected to be his Queen.

Yet not even Lady Sarah's beauty made such a talk in
London as rose about the two Miss Gunnings when they
burst upon the town in the summer of 1751. Walpole
wrote :

" These are two Irish Girls, of no fortune, who are declared the handsomest women alive. I think their being two so handsome and both such perfect figures is their chief excellence, for singly I have seen much handsomer women than either; however, they can't walk in the park, or go to Vauxhall, but such mobs follow them that they are generally driven away."

Early in the next year he tells Mann:

" The event that has made most noise since my last, is the extempore wedding of the youngest of the two Gunnings, who have made so vehement a noise. Lord Coventry, a grave young lord, of the remains of the patriot breed, has long dangled after the eldest, virtuously with regard to her virtue, not very honourably with regard to his own credit. About six weeks ago Duke Hamilton, the very reverse of the Earl, hot, debauched, extravagant, and equally damaged in his fortune and person, fell in love with the youngest at the Masquerade, and determined to marry her in the spring. About a fortnight since, at an immense assembly at my Lord Chesterfield's, made to show the house, which is really most magnificent, Duke Hamilton made violent love at one end of the room, while he was playing at pharaoh at the other end; that is, he saw neither the bank nor his own cards, which were of three hundred pounds each; he soon lost a thousand. I own I was so little a professor in love, that I thought all this parade looked ill for the poor girl; and could not conceive, if he was so much engaged with his mistress as to disregard such sums, why he played at all. However, two nights afterwards, being left alone with her while her mother and sister were at Bedford House, he found himself so impatient, that he sent for a parson. The doctor refused to perform the ceremony without licence or ring; the Duke swore he would send for the Archbishop —at last they were married with a ring of the bed-curtain, at half an hour after twelve at night, at Mayfair chapel. The Scotch are enraged; the women mad that so much beauty has had its effect; and what is most silly, my Lord Coventry declares that now he will marry the other."

A month later, March 23, 1752—

" The world is still mad about the Gunnings; the Duchess of Hamilton was presented on Friday; the crowd was so great, that even the noble mob in the drawing-room clambered upon chairs and tables to look at her. There are mobs at their doors to see them get into their chairs; and people go early to get places at the theatres when it is known they will be there."

Lord Coventry carried out his intention, and Lady Coventry was the standard of beauty while her life lasted. Every year there was a beauty announced that was to be " handsomer than my lady Coventry." " But I have known one threatened with such every summer for these seven years and they are always addled by winter," Walpole writes in 1759. The rage of curiosity for all that concerned her was incurable; a shoemaker at Worcester made two guineas and a half by showing a shoe that he was making for her at a penny a time. But she had neither wit nor breeding to match her beauty, and her descent on Paris was a failure, as she spoke no French, her lord very little—" just enough to show how ill-bred he is." In England she continually blundered but people forgave her—even George II himself.

" The King asked her if she was not sorry that there are no Masquerades this year—(for you must know we have sacrificed them to the idol earthquake)—she said, no, she was tired of them; she was surfeited with most sights; there was but one left that she wanted to see—and that was a Coronation! The old man told it himself at supper to his family with a great deal of good-humour."

She herself had an easy temper and, if scandal was right, as easy a virtue. Lord Bolingbroke was credited with her favours, and the Duke of Cumberland " appeared in form with her at the causeway in Hyde Park; it is the new office where all lovers now are entered." That was in 1756. Three years later her ascendancy began to be challenged—so at least Horace Walpole considered, for the challenger was his niece, Maria Walpole, Sir Edward's natural daughter, who had just made a great match with Lord Waldegrave. That summer while the two beauties, challenged and challenger, were in the Park, a mob gathered about them insultingly; and the King thereupon provided a guard to attend Lady Coventry on her outings; she walked with two sergeants bearing halberds before her, she herself parading between her husband and Lord Pembroke, a declared admirer.

But the end of her triumph was near; all the other entries in 1759 and 1760 speak of her swift decline, though when Lord Ferrers was tried by his peers for murdering his servant, " to the amazement of everybody Lady Coventry was there; and what surprised me much more, looked as well as ever. I sat next but one to her, and should not have asked her if she had been ill—yet they are positive she has few weeks to live. She and Lord Bolingbroke seemed to have different thoughts, and were acting over all the old comedy of eyes."

Autumn saw the end of it.

" The charming Countess is dead at last; and as if the whole history of both sisters was to be extraordinary, the Duchess of Hamilton is in a consumption too, and going abroad directly. Perhaps you may see the remains of these prodigies."

A few days later he writes to Mann, assuming that the surviving sister was on her road to Florence:

" I think the Duchess will not answer your expectation. She never was so handsome as Lady Coventry, and now is a skeleton. It is hard upon a standard beauty, when she travels in a deep consumption. Poor Lady Coventry concluded her short race with the same attention to her looks. She lay constantly on a couch, with a pocket glass in her hand; and when that told her how great the change was, she took to her bed the last fortnight, had no light in her room but the lamp of a tea-kettle, and at last took things in through the curtains of her bed, without suffering them to be undrawn. The mob, who never quitted curiosity about her, went to the number of ten thousand, only to see her coffin."

Rumour ran that she had died of the cult of beauty ; he notes of another pretty woman that she was dying, " killed like Lady Coventry and others by white lead, of which she could never be broken." But no doubt the illness was consumption, with which the younger sister too was touched —not fatally. Her story is even more amazing, though she never created the same enthusiasm—as was not surprising from what is told here :

" Duke Hamilton is the abstract of Scotch pride ; he and the Duchess at their own house walk in to dinner before their company, sit together at the upper end of their own table, eat off the same plate, and drink to nobody beneath the rank of Earl—would not one wonder how they could get anybody either above or below that rank to dine with them at all ? "

Hamilton, however, did not last long, and upon his decease another Duke—of Bridgewater—was eager to replace him ; but the widowed beauty refused him and married a soldier, Colonel Campbell, who was remotely heir to the dukedom of Argyll. She lived to see him succeed to it ; she lived to see two of her sons by the first husband become in succession Dukes of Hamilton ; and two of her sons by the Campbell succeeded each other as Dukes of Argyll. Horace Walpole did not foresee all this, but it was no wonder he should write in 1759 :

" What an extraordinary fate is attached to those two women ! Who could have believed that a Gunning would unite the two great houses of Campbell and Hamilton ? For my part, I expect to see my Lady Coventry Queen of Prussia. I would not venture to marry either of them these thirty years, for fear of being shuffled out of the world *prematurely*, to make room for the rest of their adventures."

There is another beauty whose story runs through the correspondence—but it is less admirable. Miss Elizabeth Chudleigh, one of the Maids of Honour to the Princess of Wales, figures conspicuously in the account of a subscription masquerade which the Royalties attended. She was " Iphigenia but so naked that you would have taken her for Andromeda." Cunningham quotes from a contemporary letter the saying that " the high priest might easily inspect the entrails of the victim," and that " the Maids of Honour (not of maids the strictest) were so offended that they would not speak to her."

George the Second, though near seventy, " had a hankering " after her; bestowed on her a watch from one of the booths at another public masquerade, " which cost him five and thirty guineas—actually disbursed out of his private purse and not charged on the civil list." Walpole thought this rather paltry for a reigning king, but as he says elsewhere " the monarch is never less generous than when he has a mind to be so; the only present he ever made my father was a large diamond, cracked quite through. Once or twice in his younger and gallant days he has brought out a handful of maimed topazes or amethysts and given them to be raffled for by the Maids of Honour." He bestowed what was no doubt more precious on Miss Chudleigh, when at the drawing-room " against all precedent he kissed her in the circle, saying he had appointed her mother housekeeper at Windsor and hoped she would not think a kiss too great a reward for his obeying her commands." However, Miss Chudleigh had already disposed of her charms, by a private marriage to Augustus Hervey, second son of Lord Hervey, Queen Caroline's favourite; she even had two children by him while still a Maid of Honour; and later, the marriage being unavowed, she, as Walpole says, " lived very publicly with the Duke of Kingston," whose bounty enabled her to give very sumptuous entertainments ; at one there were " pyramids and temples of strawberries and cherries : you would have thought she was kept by Vertumnus."

All went well with her through George II's reign and for several years of his successor's—except that occasional infidelities of her Duke caused public display of her anguish. But in 1767 she was still " keeping off age by sticking roses and sweet peas in her hair." Trouble came to her two years later when Augustus Hervey, twenty years after his marriage, proceeded against Miss Chudleigh for divorce, in order that he might marry a physician's daughter at Bath. However, all the witnesses of her marriage and the two children of it being dead, she swore in Doctors Commons that there had been no marriage, and forthwith proceeded to marry her Duke who had " kept her openly for about five and thirty years and who by this means would recover half his fortune which he had lavished on her ! " This devoted lover died in 1773, leaving his whole fortune, seventeen thousand a year, to the lady. But then fate turned ; it became necessary to decide whether she was duchess or countess—for Augustus Hervey had succeeded to the Earldom of Bristol—and the result was a famous trial in the House of Lords. Her peers found her guilty of bigamy, reduced her to the rank of countess and then let her disappear. " She must be fifty-five or six," Walpole writes. " She and her mother were my playfellows when we lived at Chelsea and her father was Deputy Governor of the College."

However in the heyday of her career, she was none of his playfellows ; merely one of the notorieties whose vagaries he observed and noted, in the circle to which he and they belonged ; they made good paragraphs for his letters, which, as he said to Mann in 1749, were " nothing but gossiping gazettes," though Mann like George Montagu said " such extravagant things of them."

Naturally, the famous and notorious ladies had their male counterparts; the clubs provided him with much matter. For instance, in 1750, when he was in bed at Arlington Street, there came actually an earthquake; not much of an earthquake; " so gentle you could have stroked it," George Montagu said; still there was " a great vibration and roaring "; bells jingled and a couple of old houses fell down.

" A parson, who came into White's, and heard bets laid on whether it was an earthquake or the blowing up of powder-mills, went away exceedingly scandalized, and said, ' I protest, they are such an impious set of people, that I believe if the last trumpet was to sound, they would bet puppet-show against Judgment.' "

They certainly would bet on almost anything, and a paragraph appeared in the press saying that when a man dropped down dead at the door of White's and was carried in—" the club immediately made bets whether he was dead or not, and when they were going to bleed him, the wagerers for his death interposed, and said it would affect the fairness of the bet."

Then there were the surprising marriages, of which the Duke of Hamilton's midnight spousals to the younger Gunning are only a mild example. Mr. Keith who officiated on that occasion was the occupant of Mayfair Chapel and specialized in such contingencies. Legislation was proposed to prevent these unceremonious unions, and Mr. Keith, as Walpole tells Montagu, was very angry. " G—d d——n the bishops ! " said he, " so they will hinder my marrying. Well, let 'em; but I'll be revenged ! I'll buy two or three acres of ground, and, by G—d ! I'll underbury them all ! "

But perhaps the completest example of the eighteenth-century tone will be found in a letter to Bentley written on January 9, 1755, concerning the " extraordinary death of Lord Montford ":

" He himself, with all his judgment in bets, I think would have betted any man in England against himself for self-murder; yet after having been supposed the sharpest genius of his time, he, by all that appears, shot himself on the distress of his circumstances; an apoplectic disposition, I believe, concurring either to lower his spirits, or to alarm them. Ever since Miss —— lived with him, either from liking her himself, as some think, or to tempt her to marry his Lilliputian figure, he has squandered vast sums at Horseheath, and in living. He lost twelve hundred a-year by Lord Albemarle's death, and four by Lord Gage's the same day. He asked immediately for the government of Virginia or the Foxhounds and pressed for an answer with an eagerness that surprised the Duke of Newcastle, who never had a notion of pinning down the relief of his own or any other man's wants to a day. Yet that seems to have been the case of Montford, who determined to throw the die of life and death, Tuesday was sennight, on the answer he was to receive from court; which did not prove favourable. He consulted indirectly, and at last pretty directly, several people on the easiest method of finishing life; and seems to have thought that he had been too explicit; for he invited company to dinner for the day after his death, and ordered a supper at White's, where he supped too, the night before. He played at whist till one in the morning; it was New Year's morning; Lord Robert Bertie drank to him a happy New Year; he clapped his hand strangely to his eyes! In the morning he had a lawyer and three witnesses, and executed his Will, which he made them read twice over, paragraph by paragraph; and then asking the lawyer if that will would stand good, though a man were to shoot himself? And being assured it would, he said, ' Pray stay while I step into next room ';—went into next room and shot himself. He clapped the pistol so close to his head, that they heard no report. The housekeeper heard him fall, and, thinking he had a fit, ran up with drops, and found his skull and brains shot about the room! . . . I feel for the distress this man must have felt, before he decided on so desperate an action. I knew him but little; but he was good-natured and agreeable enough, and had the most compendious understanding I ever knew. He had affected a finesse in money matters beyond what he deserved, and aimed at reducing even natural affections to a kind of calculation, like Demoivre's. He was asked, soon after his daughter's marriage, if she was with child: he replied, ' upon my word, I don't know! I have no bet upon it.' "

The same letter goes on to say that insurance brokers had begun to insure against suicide—though not beyond £300; and that a man having taken out such an insurance invited the insurers to dine at a tavern where they met several other persons.

" After dinner he said to the life-and-death brokers, ' Gentlemen, it is fit that you should be acquainted with the company; these honest men are tradesmen, to whom I was in debt, without any means of paying, but by your assistance; and now I am your humble servant.' He pulled out a pistol and shot himself."

These are a few traits of the time. But no picture of the age would be complete without its highwayman. Walpole was robbed in Hyde Park at the beginning of November, 1749, as he was driving back from Holland House by moonlight. The episode nearly was serious; by an accident one of the two men, McLean, though a veteran performer, let off his pistol and singed Walpole's face; the ball passed through the roof of the chariot, missing his head by an inch. Mr. McLean was taken in the following June. Walpole did not appear against him, it was unnecessary. " Still " (he says), " I am honourably mentioned in a Grub-Street ballad for not having contributed to his sentence. There are as many prints and pamphlets about him as about the earthquake. The first Sunday after his condemnation, three thousand people went to see him; he fainted away twice with the heat of his cell. You can't conceive the ridiculous rage there is of going to Newgate; and the prints that are published of the malefactors, and the memoirs of their lives and deaths set forth with as much parade as—as—Marshal Turenne's—we have no Generals worth making a parallel."

Things were pretty brisk in the trade; that autumn as Horace Walpole sat in his dining-room at Arlington Street before eleven at night, he heard the cry of " Stop, thief! " A highwayman had attacked a post-chaise in Piccadilly, fifty yards off, opposite where the Ritz Hotel now stands; the robber was pursued, rode over the watchman, almost killed him and escaped.

This topic does not cease throughout the letters; but it has periodic prominence, coinciding with the close of a war. Especially in the period after Great Britain had abandoned the struggle to retain America, Walpole and his friends could not stir out of their houses at Richmond and Twickenham without an armed guard. He was stopped as he drove to a card party at the Duchess of Montrose's house and had the presence of mind to conceal his watch but gave up his purse. When it was over he endeavoured to reassure his companion, Lady Browne, saying: " There, that is all; you see there is nothing in it "; nor could he understand why she continued apprehensive, till she explained her fears of what might happen when the highwayman investigated the purse. It contained only bad money, and she carried it to proffer on such an occasion.

It is only right to note that after the Seven Years War Walpole was asked to use influence with Grenville, then (in 1763) head of the Treasury, so that worn-out soldiers should more easily find admission to the hospitals. He wrote to his correspondent:

" I lamented the sufferings of our brave soldiers and have tried in vain to suggest little plans for their relief;

methodize if you please your plan, and it shall not be lost for lack of solicitation; we swarm with highwaymen who have been heroes. We own our safety to them, consequently we owe them a return of preservation."

He was a typical Englishman of the eighteenth century, but of the type which leads opinion and alters it; above all he was a hundred years before his time in humanity. The Slave Trade had revolted him.

" We have been sitting," he writes in 1750, " this fortnight on the African Company; *we*, the British Senate, that temple of liberty, and bulwark of Protestant Christianity, have this fortnight been pondering methods to make more effectual that horrid traffic of selling negroes. It has appeared to us that six-and-forty thousand of these wretches are sold every year to our plantations alone!—it chills one's blood. I would not have to say that I voted in it for the continent of America! The destruction of the miserable inhabitants by the Spaniards was but a momentary misfortune, that flowed from the discovery of the New World, compared to this lasting havoc which it brought upon Africa. We reproach Spain, and yet do not even pretend the nonsense of butchering these poor creatures for the good of their souls! "

But all these general traits only suggest the background to Horace Walpole's life. Another chapter must sketch its main occupations, from the first period of it, and his chief companions.

CHAPTER VI

THE LOOKER-ON AND THE SPECTACLE

WALPOLE'S long life is so devoid of incident that one cannot easily plot it out into divisions. His youth and education : his foreign tour : his first years in Parliament and intimacy with Sir Robert Walpole up to the statesman's death : these are clear enough. But from his twenty-eighth year—when Lord Orford died—to his eightieth, summer and winter succeed each other, and each finds him much as he was before. There are no brusque happenings. His retirement from Parliament meant little more than a change of habits. Indeed the only two dates important for his personal history are 1765, when he went to France and formed that singular attachment to an old blind lady which coloured his life from the time he was forty-eight till he was sixty-three ; and 1789, when at seventy-two, he met the two young Miss Berrys and was made perhaps happier than he had ever been, by a passionate devotion.

Yet he himself, looking back when he was far on in the sixties, divided his life into three periods, of which the middle one was the most brilliant and exciting. Those were the years in which he saw England under the elder Pitt's inspiration dominate the world. He disliked war, but he loved to see his country triumph ; for all his affectation of indifference, he had a fine faculty of admiration ; and in the other two periods of his inactive but most observant life, the spectacle of affairs gave this talent no nourishment. Yet there was a difference. The period after Chatham's retirement was darkened by humiliations in America for which East Indian triumphs did not console him. He was sore in these years, and bitter : his pride suffered the more because it had been pampered. Such words would be too strong to describe his state of mind in what he called the " sixteen unfortunate and inglorious years " (from 1741 to 1757) that followed the removal of Sir Robert Walpole from power. For one thing —at least, so soon as the Jacobite rebellion was no longer an urgent menace—he was not sorry to see the failure of those who had belittled " the name in the world most venerable to me." For another, he was young, he was still new to the excitement of parliamentary scenes ; he admired Pulteney's talent, he thought Carteret a great man. But from the time when these brilliant performers lost control, and Henry Pelham shared the power with that fumbling personage, his brother, the Duke of Newcastle, Horace Walpole complained of boredom. He was always ready to quote Sir Robert's maxim *Quieta non movere*, always ready to praise the advantages of a quiet life ; but when he could write to Mann in November, 1751, on the House's reassembling, " We are not likely to have one division this session —nay, I think, not a debate," plainly such peace approached lethargy. He is far from his most likeable when he has to deal with Pelham ; his ironic letter to Bentley about England's loss when Pelham died in 1754 sounds hardly decent ; and we are tempted to remember that Pelham was the minister to whom Horace Walpole had, unsuccessfully, applied for a favour—namely, that the patent for a place which he shared with his brother, Sir Edward, should be made tenable for both their lives and not only for that of the elder brother.

Yet Englishmen had been thankful for the quiet time to which Sir Robert Walpole had accustomed them and which Pelham had the credit of restoring. " How shocking it will be," cries Horace, " if things should go on just as they are ! I mean by that, how mortifying if it is discovered, that when all the world thought Mr. Pelham did and could alone

maintain the calm and carry on the government, even he was
not necessary, and that it was the calm and the government
that carried on themselves ! "

He did not believe that it would prove to do so ; he
believed that the resulting confusion would " make a party " ;
for, as one of the latter notes added by himself admits, " Mr.
Walpole, when young, loved faction." And in the full glee
of factiousness, he wrote to Mann :

" Mr. Pelham is dead ! all that calm, that supineness, of
which I have lately talked to you so much, is at an end !
there is no heir to such luck as his."

It is plain enough that the commentator was enjoying
himself : indeed he ended his letter—" As a person who loves
to write history better than to act it, you will easily believe
that I confine my sensations on the occasion chiefly to observation—at least, my care that posterity may know all about it
prevents my indulging any immoderate grief."

Such a happening as the unexpected death of an in-
dispensable Minister set the pot a-boiling as Horace Walpole
loved to see it boil. When George Montagu wondered that
Strawberry was forsaken in the month of June, that Walpole
had been these last eight days in London amid dust and stinks
instead of seringa, roses, battlements and niches, he had to
be reminded that the castle-builder had " another Gothic
passion, which is for squabbles in the Witanagemot." When
a new House of Commons came to be elected in 1753,
" I think," Walpole wrote, " the spirit is as great now they
are all on one side as when parties ran the highest." For a
time there was dullness. " I who love to ride in the whirl-
wind cannot record the yawns of such an age," was the
chronicler's disgusted comment to Bentley. But things soon
changed with a vengeance. That Parliament held Pitt and
held Fox. The former of these two champions was never
on any terms of intimacy with Horace Walpole : Henry
Fox was his close friend ; but it was Pitt, not Fox, who stirred

this dilettante politician to enthusiasm. War with France threatened from April, 1755, onwards: there were fears of invasion; in July, Admiral Boscawen attacked a French squadron off the American coast. Yet although there was fighting in America both by land and sea, no definite declaration of war had come from France. It was in Parliament that war raged; for Pitt had broken away from the Duke of Newcastle, who had however secured the support of Fox. On November 14 there was a great Parliamentary engagement; the House sat from before two in the afternoon till a quarter to five in the morning discussing the treaties by which England was engaged in formidable obligations for the sake of the King's duchy of Hanover. Walpole wrote an account of it to Conway who was then in Ireland as Chief Secretary to the Lord Lieutenant. One famous passage must be quoted:

"There was a young Mr. Hamilton who spoke for the first time, and was at once perfection: his speech was set, and full of antithesis, but those antitheses were full of argument: indeed his speech was the most argumentative of the whole day; and he broke through the regularity of his own composition, answered other people, and fell into his own track again with the greatest ease. His figure is advantageous, his voice strong and clear, his manner spirited, and the whole with the ease of an established speaker. You will ask, what could be beyond this? Nothing, but what was beyond what ever was, and that was Pitt! He spoke at past one, for an hour and thirty-five minutes: there was more humour, wit, vivacity, finer language, more boldness, in short, more astonishing perfections, than even you, who are used to him, can conceive. He was not abusive, yet very attacking on all sides: he ridiculed my Lord Hillsborough, crushed poor Sir George, terrified the Attorney, lashed my Lord Granville, painted my Lord of Newcastle, attacked Mr. Fox, and even hinted up to the Duke (of Cumberland)."

Many have read this description, but not all remember the conclusion, which concerns the reporter himself:

" My Lord Talbot was neuter ; he and I were of a party : my opinion was strongly with the opposition ; I could not vote for the treaties ; I would not vote against Mr. Fox. It is ridiculous perhaps, at the end of such a debate, to give an account of my own silence ; and as it is of very little consequence what I did, so it is very unlike me to justify myself. You know how much I hate *professions* of integrity ; and my pride is generally too great to care what the generality of people say of me : but your heart is good enough to make me wish you should think well of mine."

Nothing could be more characteristic of the period and of the man. Horace Walpole had no constituents to concern themselves as to how he voted : he was, as he said, " a whig in grain," but there were at this moment properly speaking no parties. A vote might be given from principle, and he detested the treaties which might draw on war. Again, votes might be given for interest ; but, as he prided himself on saying, he wanted nothing and was content with the provision which he owed to his father. Again, a vote might be given for friendship and though he admired Pitt and agreed with him, he was the friend of Mr. Fox. So between one thing and another he sat, listened, enjoyed, no doubt cheered, but did not vote. At least during the quarter of a century that he served in parliament, and perhaps during all his life, his attention was more engrossed by politics than by any other theme ; but in political life he was always the looker on. What he actually did in the political field was seldom done from any political reason.

The odd part of it, to our ideas, is that Pitt was still a member of the administration which he was attacking. However, that was settled a few days later by a group of dismissals. Pitt's disgrace did not mend matters for the Court party ; he now was on the warpath in full panoply.

"His antagonists endeavoured to disarm him, but as fast as they deprived him of one weapon, he finds a better; I never suspected him of such an universal armoury—I knew he had a Gorgon's head, composed of bayonets and pistols, but little thought that he could tickle to death with a feather. On the first debate on these famous treaties, last Wednesday, Hume Campbell, whom the Duke of Newcastle had retained as the most abusive counsel he could find against Pitt (and hereafter perhaps against Fox), attacked the former for *eternal invectives*. Oh! since the last philippic of Billingsgate memory you never heard such an invective as Pitt returned —Hume Campbell was annihilated! Pitt like an angry wasp, seems to have left his sting in the wound, and has since assumed a style of delicate ridicule and repartee. But think how charming a ridicule must that be that lasts and rises, flash after flash, for an hour and a half! Some day or other, perhaps you will see some of the glittering splinters that I gathered up. I have written under his print these lines, which are not only full as just as the original, but have not the tautology of *loftiness* and *majesty*:

> ' Three orators in distant ages born,
>   Greece, Italy and England did adorn;
>   The first in loftiness of thought surpass'd,
>   The next in language, but in both the last:
>   The power of Nature could no farther go;
>   To make a third, she join'd the former two.'

Indeed, we have wanted such an entertainment to enliven and make the fatigue supportable. We sat on Wednesday till ten at night; on Friday till past three in the morning; on Monday till between nine and ten. We have profusion of orators, and many very great, which is surprising so soon after the leaden age of the late Right Honourable Henry Saturnus!" (Pelham). "The majorities are as great as in Saturnus's *golden age*."

Then follows a contemptuous detail of the new appointment : " our very changes change " : and after half a dozen names, he adds :

" The other parts by the comedians ; I don't repeat their names, because perhaps the fellow that to-day is designed to act Guildenstern, may to-morrow be destined to play *half* the part of the second grave-digger.

With regard to the invasion, which you are so glad to be allowed to fear, I must tell you that it has quite gone out of fashion again, and I really believe was dressed up for a vehicle (as the apothecaries call it) to make us swallow the treaties. All along the coast of France they are much more afraid of an invasion than we are."

But within a matter of nine months after, England had lost Minorca, and was seeking satisfaction by preparing to shoot Admiral Byng whom it held responsible because he had avoided an action ; there was disaster in America ; and the country was raging to have Mr. Pitt in power and the Duke of Newcastle out. They got Mr. Pitt in, and from the end of 1756 a new era commenced.—All the fluctuations of these uncertain movements, the gradual effect of strong popular feeling on the court, and the impediments to action produced by personal friendships, we can follow in the letters.

They are, I think, a far more valuable contribution to history than those *Memoirs* which in these years he was compiling, as his chief literary concern. Gray had seen them, of course : so had George Montagu, who prophesied that one day his papers would be seized. On that head he wrote to Montagu that as dinner was proceeding in his house " word was brought that one of the King's messengers was at the door. . . . Every drop of ink in my pen ran cold, Algernon Sidney danced before my eyes." It was in fact a frequent obsession with Horace Walpole to dream of martyrdom for some kind of leze-majesty ; however, the messenger proved to be merely reporting for orders to a Minister, who was one of his guests.

Most of what he was writing in this first of his political periods had to do with politics—squibs in the " World " and the like. But on the whole, he was at this time much less a writer than he became later on. In fact, outside of the squabbles in the Witanagemot, his chief concern was Strawberry, which grew and grew under the auspices of a sort of Committee of Taste.

Bentley was one of its chief members, but the importunacy of creditors constrained this clever but erratic gentleman to seek an abode in the island of Jersey, and he became chiefly a corresponding member. The most constant of all was Chute, who had a regular bedroom of his own, on the upper floor, hung with red paper, and with prints " framed in a new manner invented by Lord Cardigan . . . with black and white borders printed." In the miniature tower, bequeathed to Walpole by the previous occupants, the Chenevixes, was a " charming closet " with two windows, one facing on the garden, the other on the " beautiful prospect " across the Thames to Richmond Park. The closet was Mr. Chute's College of Arms, for he was the authority on heraldry ; it had two presses with books of heraldry and antiquities ; it had also, for Horace Walpole's own special delight, Madame de Sevigné's Letters " and any French books that related to her and her acquaintance."

Chute, who had the great merit of being willingly available, was almost always Walpole's companion in those excursions to the famous mansions and beauty spots of England, which almost always were described in long letters to the absent Bentley, marooned on his Channel Island. But the man to whom Horace Walpole described his enthusiasms with most rapture, and the man of all others whose company he seems to have desired, was George Montagu. There was a vein of eccentricity in this friend. For while he had lived in town, he had become almost inaccessible to his acquaintance ; when he settled and gave himself up to country squirehood, he became as popular as if he was standing for the county; it was always hard to induce him to pay a visit, the letters are full of complaints on this score; but when he did come he was enchanted and enchanting. "The weather grows fine," Walpole wrote to Bentley in March, 1754, "I carried George Montagu thither, who was in raptures and screamed, and hooped, and hollaed, and danced, and crossed himself a thousand times over." The only grievance was that he could never be got there to see it in full glory, in all its "greenth, blueth, gloomth, honeysuckle and seringa-hood." Again and again efforts were made to get this friend to settle himself near by. In 1755 the sister who kept house for him died and Horace Walpole wrote a letter which is in notable contrast to his usual tone.

"Nobody living feels more for you than I do: nobody knows better either the goodness or tenderness of your heart, or the real value of the person you have lost.

If you can listen yet to any advice, let me recommend to you to give up all thoughts of Greatworth; you will never be able to support life there any more: let me look out for some little box for you in my neighbourhood. You can live nowhere where you will be more beloved; and you will there always have it in your power to enjoy company or solitude, as you like. I have long wished to get you so far back into the world, and now it is become absolutely necessary for your health and peace. I will say no more, lest too long a letter should be either troublesome or make you think it necessary to answer; but do not, till you find it more agreeable to vent your grief this way than in any other."

That may sound to us as formal as the opening "My dear Sir,"—but there is no mistaking the sincerity; and only a nature capable of strong attachment and ardently desirous of affection would so estimate his friend's loss.

Horace Walpole never had the luck to get for a permanent

stand-by this companionship which he so greatly desired. The two men remained close friends, delighted when they met, yet only meeting at long intervals : and nobody else has left us words which spoke so feelingly of Horace Walpole's kindness or so justly praised the value that lay behind his connoisseurship. But in the end, through some queer lonely streak in Montagu's nature, they drifted out of touch, and that in a period of Walpole's life when he had most need of congenial companionship.

This softer side of him is shown much in another relationship. Sir Horace Mann's brother Galfridus was a friend for his own sake and for his brother's. Walpole had it in his power to serve him by getting him one of the contracts for army clothing ; and when Galfridus Mann fell into a consumption, the letters to Florence are full of details of his suffering, recorded by one who evidently hated to see anything suffer. If his own brother had been in the case, he could not have shown a more poignant and active concern—which was rendered the sharper because he thought that the sick man's wife was cruelly inconsiderate. But Horace Walpole was not lenient to the wives of the men he liked : it is not easy to believe that either Mrs. Bentley, whom he habitually called Tisiphone, or Mrs. Galfridus Mann, " that little white fiend," were altogether such hell-cats as he painted them. None the less, his kindness was real. It is true the virtuoso in him found a good deal of consolation for Mann's death in devising a suitable monument and epitaph ; but long years after, we find him watching with delight the successful appearance of " Gal's " son in the world, and missing no chance to convey his interest and approbation to the Minister in Florence who had been concerned for the lad's upbringing. In the same way, though he often rapped Bentley over the knuckles in a way that savoured too much of the patron, far-off years found him making provision for the little Bentleys.

Of course the softest of all soft places in his heart was kept for Harry Conway, " whom nature designed for a hero of romance " and with whom happily his hero-worshipper had almost always occasion to sympathize by rejoicing. At the battle of Laffelt, where the Duke of Cumberland was defeated, Conway distinguished himself by personal bravery ; and late in that year to Walpole's delight he married a charming widow, Lady Ailesbury, of the great Campbell house, daughter to the fourth Duke of Argyll. They had one child, Anna, who in the end of the story became heiress to most of what Horace Walpole had to leave. She was indeed always in a manner part of his family. When she was three years old, he was already put in charge of her, for Conway and his wife had to go to Ireland, to join his regiment. It was an odd charge to be undertaken by a fashionable and most worldly gentleman of five and thirty ; but many passages in the letters show that when Horace Walpole was staying at a country house he was oftenest to be found running races and playing games with the children. This child certainly was made much of. There is an amusing letter from him to Conway concerning " his wife " as he calls her, and the installation provided in Arlington Street.

" I flatter myself she is quite contented with the easy footing we live upon ; separate beds, dining in her dressing-room when she is out of humour, and a little toad-eater that I have got for her, and whose pockets and bosom I have never examined, to see if she brought any *billets doux*. . . . If you should happen to want to know any more particulars, she is quite well, has walked in the Park every morning, or has the chariot, as she chooses ; and in short one would think that I or she were much older than we really are, for I grow exceedingly fond of her."

However, if truth discloses that Horace Walpole had an affectionate and even sentimental side, truth has also to admit that the qualities by which he has survived were not those which made him kind to children and sick people. It is the wit and the worldling that we value.

One would have liked to be at Strawberry on July 10, 1754, when Chute came down to stay, bringing Gray with him : there was no doubt much talk of literature among the three gentlemen, all aged about thirty-seven. Or a fortnight later when Montagu and his brother the Colonel came and " screamed with approbation through the whole Cu gamut," inspecting plantations, and Poyang, the pond where goldfish bred abundantly, and the latest embellishments to library windows, battlements and God knows what. Yet perhaps it would have been even better to look in at Christmas of that year. Walpole was quite alone, busy putting up his books (" thanks to arches and pinnacles, and pierced columns I shall not appear scantily provided "). But in a day or two he expected Gilly Williams, George Selwyn and Dick Edgecumbe. " You will allow," he says to Bentley, " that when I do admit anybody within my cloister I choose them well." These were indeed the choice spirits of clubland, and they figure together in a famous Conversation-piece painted by Sir Joshua for Horace Walpole which hung at Strawberry Hill. Their gathering there at Christmas and at Easter became a kind of custom.

They were all of course in Parliament and in place. But the familiarity with politics of one of them may be judged from an episode during the confusions when Pitt began to break away from the Duke of Newcastle. Someone met Edgecumbe and asked him with great importance if he knew whether Mr. Pitt was out. " Edgecumbe, who thinks nothing important that is not to be decided by dice " (and who consequently had never once thought of Pitt's political state), answered ' Yes.' ' Ay, how do you know ? ' ' Why, I called at his door just now and his porter told me so.' "

George James—" Gilly "—Williams comes down to us with high repute as a wit; but he survives really by his association with Selwyn, who in his turn is remembered by the innumerable quotations of his witticisms and references to traits of his character in the literature of that age. I do not know one of them more characteristic of all that life than what Walpole wrote to George Montagu about the events of a Sunday night in June, 1757.

He was just come back to Arlington Street from White's, about half-past twelve (for he was never of the late sitters) and was undressing to step into bed, when he heard his footman Harry whose bedroom faced the street roar out, "Stop, thief," and run down stairs. "I ran after him. Don't be frightened; I have not lost one enamel, nor bronze, nor have been shot through the head again." The attempt was on the house of a neighbour who had gone out of town and locked up his doors. A lady from an adjoining house had heard noises, and screamed out "Watch," which scared off two fellows posted to look out. "Down came I, and with a posse of chairmen and watchmen found the third fellow in the area of Mr. Freeman's house. Mayhap you have seen all this in the papers, little thinking who commanded the detachment. Harry fetched a blunderbuss to invite the thief up. One of the chairmen who was drunk, cried, 'Give me the blunderbuss, I'll shoot him!' But as the general's head was a little cooler, he prevented military execution and took the prisoner without bloodshed, intending to make his triumphal entry into the metropolis of Twickenham with his captive tied to the wheels of his post chaise. I find my style rises so much with the recollection of my victory, that I don't know how to descend to tell you that the enemy was a carpenter, and had a leather apron on. The next step was to share my glory with my friends. I despatched a courier to White's for George Selwyn, who, you know, loves nothing upon earth so well as a criminal, except the execution of him. It happened very luckily that the drawer, who received my message, has very lately been robbed himself, and had the wound fresh in his memory. He stalked up into the clubroom, stopped short, and with a hollow trembling voice said, ' Mr. Selwyn! Mr. Walpole's compliments to you, and he has got a house-breaker for you! ' "

Immediately gentlemen poured out into St. James's Street and round the corner to Arlington Street (opposite to where is now the door of the Ritz), and found Horace Walpole and his company mounting guard over the area railings. Then having procured the keys, they marched into the house to search for more of the gang.

" Col. Seabright with his drawn sword went first, and then I, exactly the figure of Robinson Crusoe, with a candle and a lanthorn in my hand, a carbine upon my shoulder, my hair wet and about my ears, and in a linen night-gown and slippers. We found the kitchen shutters forced, but not finished ; and in the area a tremendous bag of tools, a hammer large enough for the hand of Jael, and six chisels ! "

Such was London in 1752. It is a pity that we have not Selwyn's account of it. The truth is that Selwyn's recorded sayings are disappointing : one of the few exceptions is his observation to Walpole when Pelham's household goods were being sold. " Lord," says he, " how many toads have been eaten off those plates." He excelled, it seems, at uttering veiled impertinences with a glance " from the very summit of the whites of his demure eyes " ; or as another phrase of Walpole's sketches the same trick—which Reynolds has painted—" George Selwyn, hearing some people at Arthur's t'other night lamenting the distracted state of the country, joined in the discourse with the whites of his eyes and his prim mouth."

This mixture of " strange and dismal ways," and of a taste for vaults and executions, with " infinite fun and humour " as Walpole put it, made Selwyn the delight of his age. But these typical clubmen were never intimates of Walpole's in the same way that Chute and Montagu were—

still less comparable to Conway. They did not share his essential tastes for literature, for history, and for connoisseurship. Above all they were perplexed by his passion for the society of old ladies—their own tastes being quite other. Indeed Edgecumbe left Horace Walpole trustee for his bequest to a Mrs. Davy, whose name appears to have been very freely on the lips of everyone at White's.

None the less, he indulged his taste for old ladies freely, and at Strawberry Hill he had every chance to gratify it. He loved their company and a few of his sentences will tell what he valued in it. He is describing Lady Cardigan, daughter of the Duke of Montagu, and granddaughter of the great Duke of Marlborough: " Whom I grow every day more in love with; you may imagine, not her person, which is far from improved lately; but, as George Montagu says, *in all my practice* I never met a better understanding, nor more really estimable qualities: such a dignity in her way of thinking; so little idea of anything mean or ridiculous, and such proper contempt for both! "

Lady Cardigan never became one of his intimates. The chief of these was certainly Lady Hervey—the Molly Lepel who was an ornament to George II's court at Richmond when he was Prince of Wales. Indeed she was hardly to be ranked among old ladies, when Walpole settled at Strawberry Hill in 1747: her years ran with the century and she was only sixty-eight when she died. Yet, being seventeen years older than he, she definitely belonged to an earlier generation, and was one of his chief links with Pope, who to Horace Walpole and his friends held the same position that Tennyson did to people born in the latter half of Queen Victoria's reign, as the accepted standard of excellence in poetry, whose work every educated man knew more or less by heart. There was no man of letters in Pope's day—which ended just after Walpole entered Parliament—who had not a good word for this charming woman; and to the end of her life it was recognized (so Lady Louisa Stuart, fifty years her junior, testifies) that " never was there so perfect a model of the finely polished highly bred woman of fashion." She had more than a little touch of the Frenchwoman in her ; her father, General Lepel, was Lord of Sark, still a French-speaking island ; and Horace Walpole liked her none the less for that. But what he singled out to praise when he wrote his lamenting praise after her death was " her friendliness, good breeding and amiable temper "—as well as her patience under long suffering.

Hardly less close was his alliance with another of Pope's allies, Mrs. Howard, Countess of Suffolk, George II's recognized mistress, who when discarded by the King settled herself down at Marble Hill, between Richmond and Twickenham. Walpole wrote of her :

" I have been very unfortunate in the death of my Lady Suffolk who was the only sensible friend I had at Strawberry. Though she was seventy-nine, her senses were in the highest perfection, and her memory wonderful, as it was as accurate on recent events as on the most distant. Her hearing had been impaired above forty years, and was the only defect that prevented her conversation from not being as agreeable as possible. She had seen, known, and remembered so much, that I was very seldom not eager to hear. She was a sincere and unalterable friend, very calm, judicious, and zealous. Her integrity and goodness had secured the continuation of respect, and no fallen favourite had ever experienced neglect less. . . .

Lord Chetwynd and myself were the only persons at all acquainted with her affairs, and they were far from being even easy to her. It is due to her memory to say, that I never saw more strict honour and justice. She bore *knowingly* the imputation of being covetous, at a time that the strictest economy could by no means prevent her exceeding her income considerably. The anguish of the last years of her life, though

concealed, flowed from the apprehension of not satisfying
her few wishes, which were, not to be in debt, and to make
a provision for Miss Hotham."

There was another intimate of Walpole's Strawberry Hill
circle, who however was certainly not a great lady nor, at
least when she first took rank among his friends, old. This
was Mrs. Clive, who delighted London with her comic acting
for a matter of forty years. In 1730 when Walpole was an
Etonian of thirteen she had already made her name in a ballad
opera, " The Devil to Pay " : he mentions it in one of his
first letters from Paris, to illustrate the kind of entertainment that he found popular there. In 1742, just after his
return to London, he praises her mimicry ; and soon after
he acquired Strawberry Hill, we find Mrs. Clive, with her
brother Mr. Raftor (an actor of small parts), settled in as his
tenants at the small house on an outlying part of his grounds,
to which he gave the name Little Strawberry Hill—though
as often as not, he preferred a punning title, Cliveden. Some
people have concluded that she was, as the phrase goes,
under his protection. If so, he took a mistress of mature
years for she cannot have been much—if at all—under forty
when he settled her within so very easy reach ; and readers
of his correspondence will find much more frequent mention
of her in the later years, when the splendour of her jolly
face recalled images of an autumn sunset. Even in 1754
when she had been only a matter of five years at Little Strawberry, he is ungallant enough to quote a saying of Lady
Townshend that Strawberry Hill would be a very pleasant
place " if Mrs. Clive's face did not rise upon it and make
it so hot."

There was perhaps a good deal of insight in another
recorded observation of the same Lady Townshend, in a field
that she had made peculiarly her own. One of Walpole's
neighbours kept a beautiful tiger which Horace greatly
admired. " Lady Townshend says it is the only thing I ever

wanted to kiss." She thought him deficient in natural propensities, and I confess to grave doubt whether he at any time wanted to kiss Kitty Clive. Perhaps his attachment wore the better for that. Young or old, what he valued in her was her gaiety, and the best lines that he ever wrote are in an imaginary epitaph to be set up at Little Strawberry:

> " Ye smiles and jests, here hover round,
> This is mirth's consecrated ground."

That was written after he had composed the Epilogue to be spoken by her when she bid farewell to the stage—in 1769—but long before her buxom presence had the least thought of disappearing. At " Cliveden " there was always supper for him when he wanted company—and cards; she was even more a devotee of loo than he; and there was her garden which he could adorn with his " superfluities "—the overplus from Strawberry Hill.

She was the friend of his friends, too: when George III was crowned, she went with Walpole's party, Lady Hervey, Lady Hertford, Mr. Chute and others, to see the show from a house in Palace Yard, which belonged to his deputy, Mr. Bedford (who performed such duties as were necessary for the work of his office). In 1760 he notes with some disparagement a party specially made up that George III's brother, Prince Edward, then much taken with the lord of Strawberry, might enjoy his company.

" The evening was pleasant; but I had a much more agreeable supper last night at Mrs. Clive's, with Miss West, my niece Cholmondeley, and Murphy, the writing actor, who is very good company, and two or three more. Mrs. Cholmondeley is very lively; you know how entertaining the Clive is, and Miss West is an absolute original."

A year later he writes, complaining, to George Montagu who had been staying at Strawberry and had left abruptly:

" Mrs. Clive is still more disappointed; she had proposed

to play at quadrille with you from dinner till supper, and to sing old Purcell to you from supper to breakfast next morning." In short she was part of his regular company and a most entertaining part : he and his friends laughed at her and with her ; and when he did not go to sit with Lady Suffolk of an evening, he walked in the meadows with Mrs. Clive.

Her brother Raftor was, it seems, a bad actor but a good story-teller, and obsequious to the benefactor. " I should be a cormorant for praise, if I could swallow it whole as Mr. Raftor gives it me."

He was not the only actor who distributed this sweet-meat : Horace Walpole had his share of it from the greatest, for David Garrick owned a house facing the river between Strawberry and Twickenham, and there held great state. Here is a letter to Bentley of August, 1755 :

" I dined to-day at Garrick's : there were the Duke of Grafton, Lord and Lady Rochford, Lady Holdernesse, the crooked Mostyn, and Dabreu, the Spanish Ministry ; two regents " (the King being then in Hanover), " of which one is lord chamberlain, the other groom of the stole ; and the wife of a secretary of state. This is being *sur un assez bon ton* for a player ! Don't you want to ask me how I like him ? Do want, and I will tell you. I like her exceedingly ; her behaviour is all sense, and all sweetness too. I don't know how, he does not improve so fast upon me : there is a great deal of parts, and vivacity, and variety, but there is a great deal too of mimicry and burlesque. I am very ungrateful, for he flatters me abundantly ; but unluckily I know it. I was accustomed to it enough when my father was first minister ; on his fall I lost it all at once : and since that I have lived with Mr. Chute, who is all vehemence ; with Mr. Fox, who is all disputation ; with Sir Charles Williams, who has no time from flattering himself ; with Gray, who does not hate to find fault with me ; with Mr. Conway, who is all sincerity ; and with you and Mr. Rigby, who have always laughed at me in a good-natured way. I don't know how, but I think I like all this as well."

The references to Garrick are countless, as was natural : it is worth while to quote the first of them, written to Mann on May 26, 1742, when Horace Walpole was enjoying his first London season.

" All the run is now after Garrick, a wine-merchant, who is turned player, at Goodman's fields. He plays all parts, and is a very good mimic. His acting I have seen, and may say to you, who will not tell it again here, I see nothing wonderful in it, but it is heresy to say so : the Duke of Argyll says, he is superior to Betterton."

The note of disparagement here runs through the whole : though when Garrick set up his Temple to Shakespeare in his garden at Twickenham, Walpole was ready with a dedicatory inscription, expanding the Latin Horace's " Quod spiro et placeo, si placeo, tuum est."

> " That I spirit have and nature,
> That sense breathes through every feature,
> That I please—if please I do—
> Shakespeare, all I owe to you."

But he thought meanly of Garrick's intelligence, and had far more to say of the cheapness of his writing than of his acting's excellence.

Nor was it only Garrick to whom he assumed this attitude of grudging recognition. Young or old, he was the same. His disparagement of Peg Woffington in 1742 has been quoted. In 1782—when he was sixty-five—he saw Mrs. Siddons, then a new star.

" She pleased me beyond my expectation, but not up to the admiration of the *ton*, two or three of whom were in the same box with me ; particularly Mr. Boothby, who, as if to disclaim the stoic apathy of Mr. Meadows in ' Cecilia,' was all bravissimo. Mr. Crawfurd, too, asked me if I did not

think her the best actress I ever saw ? I said, ' By no means ;
we old folks were apt to be prejudiced in favour of our first
impressions.' She is a good figure, handsome enough,
though neither nose nor chin according to the Greek standard,
beyond which both advance a good deal. Her hair is either
red, or she has no objection to its being thought so, and had
used red powder. Her voice is clear and good ; but I
thought she did not vary its modulations enough, nor ever
approach enough to the familiar—but this may come when
more habituated to the awe of the audience of the capital.
Her action is proper, but with little variety ; when without
motion, her arms are not genteel. Thus you see, Madam,
all my objections are very trifling ; but what I really wanted,
but did not find, was originality, which announces genius,
and without both which I am never intrinsically pleased. All
Mrs. Siddons did, good sense or good instruction might give.
I dare to say, that were I one-and-twenty, I should have
thought her marvellous ; but alas ; I remember Mrs. Porter
and the Dumesnil—and remember every accent of the former
in the same part. Yet this is not entirely prejudice ; don't
I equally recollect the whole progress of Lord Chatham and
Charles Townshend, and does it hinder my thinking Mr.
Fox a prodigy."

Now if there is any trust to be placed in the voice of their
contemporaries, by which alone the genius of actors can
be assessed, all these judgments are not only poor, but
ignominiously inadequate. The truth may as well be spoken
at once : Horace Walpole was a bad critic, and the worst
kind of bad critic ; one who tends to magnify himself by
being supercilious. Where we can judge him securely is in
his reactions to the literature of his own time, and here he is
persistently and abominably wrong. Though a great reader
he had no real love of what is best in literature. He did value
Shakespeare, but the only aspect of Shakespeare's genius of
which he shows real appreciation is represented by Falstaff.

He calls *Midsummer Night's Dream* "forty times more nonsensical than the worst translation of any Italian opera-books." For contemporary work, Pope was his standard; and though he felt Gray's greatness to the full, it is difficult to be sure that this was not chiefly because Gray was in a sense his own discovery. All the rest of what was greatest in the literature of his age, he either ridiculed or tolerated. Fielding pleased him; but he condescended to Fielding much as he condescended to Garrick; Sterne he chose to despise. He attacked with some justice Johnson's pompous vocabulary, but it never occurred to him that Goldsmith, in full opposition to this fashion for verbosity, was writing an English purer, suppler, simpler and more alive than Addison had ever achieved. As to the writers themselves, he is at his very worst in every word he says about them. Though he was free of the ridiculous prejudice which made men of that century affect to think it beneath a gentleman's dignity to earn money by writing—a prejudice by which Gray allowed himself to be governed—still he affected a contempt for the race of authors. As a writer of books, he was an amateur, not a professional; and first and last he is more at ease with the work of amateurs. The praise which he lavished on a fifth-rate poet like Mason makes us very doubtful whether his appreciation of Gray was heartfelt; he was at all events vastly more at home with Mason or with Bentley than ever with the sombre man of genius. When he praised them, and was praised by them, there was no uneasy sense of inequality. I cannot acquit him of a deep-seated jealousy towards those who were doing what he would have given the world to do.

In his youth (so he tells us in his age) he desired fame greatly; and he was too active not to seek it. His only public bid for fame was in the field of literature, and no man was ever more fully possessed by the itch for writing. He masked his ambition under a show of carelessness; but he was too intelligent to deceive himself as to the value of his work; moreover, during the period in which ambition was a spur, he had Gray's opinion to refer to, and Gray never took Walpole's books as more than interesting literary exercises. I do not think that either of them ever guessed that the letter-writer would attain survival hardly less secure than the poet's; certainly Gray did not. But certainly Walpole realized before middle age that none of his publications had any serious importance. It requires some generosity for an ambitious man to recognize that his contemporaries are achieving that which is beyond the reach of his own powers; and Walpole lacked that generosity. Moreover, generosity apart, he had not the sure instinct which welcomes durable quality at first sight, and is indeed perhaps too prone to find it. The best creative intelligences often recognize in the work of their own time something that has already in some other shape profoundly impressed their own minds, and over-rate the expression of a sympathetic thought. But there was nothing creative in Horace Walpole. He was a chronicler: he needed facts to relate: he valued books, not for the thoughts or the imaginings that they stored up, but for the food they gave to his curiosity. Only Gibbon among the great writers of his time meets full acknowledgment from him, and what he recognized in Gibbon was the power of acquiring knowledge and of grouping it so that it should be accessible.

It all comes down to this, that Walpole had no love for poetry in any of its forms—except indeed for *vers de société*, which are far less truly poetry than a work like *Tristram Shandy* or *The Vicar of Wakefield*. Had he possessed that love, or been possessed by it, he would never have spoken of the men who were makers as he permitted himself to do. He had indeed a taste for wit; but even this was by no means a sure one, for he disparaged the *Figaro* of Beaumarchais. Nobody would blame him for this lack of critical acumen, were it not that he did undoubtedly give himself airs as a judge of literature ; and pretentiousness often leads to ill-breeding. He abounds in perfect examples of the *jugement saugrenu.*

It is a pleasure to get away from this least likeable side of him and get on the ground where he is entirely delightful, likeable, writing about what he really liked. One of these likings was for the English countryside, as he understood it, and the best of that lay, to his thinking, between Kew and Hampton Court, along the great river which was the centre of his landscape. Coming back from a visit to the Duke of Bedford's seat at Woburn, he described the place as " rather what I admire than like." " I fear," he adds, " that is what I am a little apt to do at the finest places in the world where there is not a navigable river."

Whatever real feeling for beauty there lay in him was best inspired by the Thames and by his own demesne. Year after year, he went out on visits or pilgrimages to the most famous mansions and parks in England, but always he came back with delight to his own chosen corner which he beautified after his own fashion.

" My present and sole occupation is planting," he wrote to Conway, in August, 1748. August is an odd month to plant in; but the same letter admitted that though he could talk very learnedly with the nurserymen, a lettuce run to seed " overturned all his botany " ; and that the " deliberation now and then with which trees grow was extremely inconvenient to his natural impatience." But the taste grew, and grew quicker than the timber.

" I have made a vast plantation ! Lord Leicester told me the other day that he heard I would not buy some old china, because I was laying out all my money in trees : ' Yes,' said I, ' my lord, I used to love blue trees, but now I like green ones.' "

Verdure—that is the word that recurs a hundred times

in his letters and always with a sense of delight. It was also, as many complainings indicate, the one thing he could count on in an English summer. " An English landscape ought always to be framed and glazed," was one of his favourite sayings—it looked best through a window : and your safest summer was a good fire of Newcastle coals. Nevertheless, June often found Strawberry as he wrote of it to George Montagu, " in the height of its greenth, blueth, gloomth, honeysuckle and seringa-hood " ; and he never if he could help it missed lilac-time and the nightingales. Haymaking too was a festival; but this virtuoso farmer was inclined to let his hay lie too long because a party of ladies were invited down to see it cocked or carried.

At first, the smallness of Strawberry was its distinction : it was a lodge in the wilderness, or anyhow in Arcadia : but before the place had been two summers in his possession a new design had shaped itself.

" I am going to build a little Gothic castle at Strawberry Hill," he wrote to Mann, who protested, for the next letter ends : " I shall speak much more gently to you, my dear child, though you don't like Gothic architecture. The Grecian is only proper for magnificent and public buildings. Columns and all their beautiful ornaments look ridiculous when crowded into a closet or a cheesecake-house. The variety is little, and admits no charming irregularities. I am almost as fond of the Sharawaggi, or Chinese want of symmetry, in buildings, as in grounds or gardens. I am sure, whenever you come to England, you will be pleased with the liberty of taste into which we are struck, and of which you can have no idea ! "

In these years, Horace Walpole, not yet thirty-five, young and active, ran all over England hunting after " Gothic " and exulting in the spread of new ideas. " Capability " Brown was in his heyday and had been let loose on Warwick Castle. ' One sees what this prevalence of taste does,"

From a picture by Marlow

NORTH FRONT OF STRAWBERRY HILL

he told George Montagu, "little Brooke, who would have chuckled to be born in an age of clipt hedges and cockle-shell avenues, has submitted to let his garden and park be natural."

He was indeed a tireless and most influential propagandist. Not even Gray's slow nature escaped a touch of the enthusiasm; for one finds the poet writing to Wharton in September, 1854, "I delight to hear your talk of giving your house some Gothic ornaments already." There was, how-ever, a measure in Gray's zeal. "If you project anything, I hope it will be entirely indoors; and don't let me (when I come gaping into Coleman Street) be directed to the Gentle-man's at the Ten Pinnacles or with the Church-Porch at his door."

Nevertheless, he accepted these vagaries at Twickenham:

"I am glad you enter into the Spirit of Strawberry-Castle. It has a purity and propriety of Gothicism in it (with very few exceptions) that I have not seen elsewhere. The eating-room and library were not completed, when I was there, and I want to know what effect they have."

"Purity and propriety" sound a little odd to us when we look at Strawberry: Gray had more partiality to his friend's hobby than one would have expected of him. Had Walpole not been a friend, Gray's pen might have been em-ployed as it was on the devisings of "little Brooke" at Warwick—

"He has sash'd the great Appartment, that's to be sure (I can't help these things) and being since told, that square sash-windows were not Gothic, he has put certain whim-whams within side the glass, which appearing through are to look like fretwork. Then he has scooped out a little Burtough in the massy walls of the place for his little self and his children, which is hung with Paper and printed Linnen, and carved chimney-pieces, in the exact manner of Berkley-square, or Argyle-buildings."

However, we are under no obligation to take Strawberry Hill seriously, nor, for that matter, its creator. After all, those who knew him and liked him best were always disposed —we have seen his own word for it—" to laugh at him a little." They knew him to have a good heart as well as a quick and busy brain, matched with a pen whose volubility (to use Gray's own word) was never tedious; and they entered gladly into the gay humour with which he went about his multifarious occupations. Here is a sketch of them, written to the friend who perhaps gave him fullest sympathy —George Montagu.

"You bid me give some account of myself; I can in a very few words : I am quite alone; in the morning I view a new pond I am making for gold fish, and stick in a few shrubs or trees, wherever I can find a space, which is very rare : in the evening I scribble a little; all this mixed with reading; that is, I can't read much, but I pick up a good deal of reading. The only thing I have done that can compose a paragraph, and which I think you are Whig enough to forgive me, is, that on each side of my bed I have hung MAGNA CHARTA, and the Warrant for King Charles's execution, on which I have written Major Charta; as I believe, without the latter, the former by this time would be of very little importance."

How complete the man's art is : perhaps completer than he knew, for he puts in with a touch of emphasis just those affectations of aristocratic Republicanism which were so constant a feature of his superficial make-up. It is very youthful for a courtly gentleman entered on his fortieth year —this was written in October, 1756—to be giving himself the airs of an ex-post-facto regicide. But that was thoroughly in the spirit of the part that he was always inclined for playing. I have no doubt in the world that George Montagu knew quite well that if Charles I or any other monarch had come up before this Rhadamanthus for judgment, the instinctive humanitarian would have pushed aside the theoretical executioner. Neither Montagu nor any of " Horry's " friends would have been in the least degree surprised at the way which this republican shrank from regicide when the French Revolution presented him with an example of it.

CHAPTER VII
THE GREAT DAYS OF MR. PITT

THE glorious period—as it looked to him afterwards—in Horace Walpole's life, began when he was forty. But it did not last out the decade. Things had changed with England, and things had changed with him before he reached his half-century in 1767.

Middle-age is an ambiguous expression; but even so long-lived a man as Horace Walpole was half-way through his span when he turned forty. Yet down to the end of George II's reign I confess that the gentleman of forty and upwards seems very much the same as he was in the early thirties—only perhaps a little more so. He had lost none of the spirits which were—as he himself came to see later on—his most attractive quality. He had lost none of the friends that grew up with him : it is only when a first gap comes in that gay group that we meet a change in his tone, a new and sombre note.

But at forty he still kept that keenness of response to any stimulus which is the surest sign of youth. He had a most mercurial temperament and the quicksilver jumped up and down with surprising rapidity, whether it was politics or private life that affected his temperature.

Let us begin with the private gentleman, virtuosc and antiquary. In August, 1758, he was on one of his yearly tours of visitation to places in the country—which he always put off till Strawberry had passed its prime, till lilacs and nightingales had long ceased, till the hay was made, till verdure had lost its freshness, and for that matter till the strawberry season was over.

This time he had gone to Ragley, the seat of his cousin, Lord Hertford, Harry Conway's brother; and he recounted his progress to the sympathetic ear of George Montagu. A great deal had been done to the place—

"Browne" [Capability, of course] "had improved both the ground and the water, though not quite to perfection. This is the case of the house; where there are no striking faults, but it wants a few Chute or Bentley touches. I have recommended some dignifying of the saloon with Seymours and Fitzroys, Henry the Eighths, and Charles the Seconds. They will correspond well to the proudest situation imaginable. I have already dragged some ancestors out of the dust there, written their names on their portraits; besides which, I have found and brought up to have repaired an incomparable picture of Van Helmont by Sir Peter Lely."

Then he goes on to recount one of the feats by which he earned real credit. In a lumber-room he had discovered and recovered "the state papers, private letters, etc. etc., of the two Lords Conway, Secretaries of State. They seem to have laid up every scrap of paper they ever had, from the middle of Queen Elizabeth's reign to the middle of Charles the Second's." There had been whole rooms full, but during the absence of a previous lord all of them were "by the ignorance of a steward consigned to the oven and to the uses of the house." The remainder, save for one mouldering box, when thrown loose, were "spread on the pavement; they supported old marbles, and screens and boxes." On this treasure he flung himself, and so retrieved what in the course of time furnished two valuable volumes—though not till our day. The editing was probably too stiff a job for a dilettante to tackle, and we need not blame him for not doing what has been done excellently by Mr. M. H. Nicolson. But our concern is with the man, rather than with his discovery. There was another visitor at Ragley, Mr. Seward, a learned clergyman—none other than the father of Anna Seward,

the Swan of Lichfield and the scourge of Sir Walter
Scott.

" Strolling about the house, he saw me first sitting on the
pavement of the lumber room with Louis " [his valet], "all over
cobwebs and dirt and mortar ; then found me in his own room
on a ladder writing on a picture ; and half an hour afterwards
lying on the grass in the court with the dogs and the children,
in my slippers and without my hat. He had had some doubt
whether I was the painter or the factotum of the family ; but
you would have died at his surprise when he saw me walk into
dinner and sit by Lady Hertford. Lord Lyttelton was there,
and the conversation turned on literature : finding me not
quite ignorant added to the parson's wonder ; but he could
not contain himself any longer, when after dinner he saw me
go to romps and jumping with the two boys ; he broke out
to my Lady Hertford, and begged to know who and what sort
of a man I really was, for he had never met with anything of
the kind."

Is not that a self-portrait dexterously dashed in ? and is not
there a surprising youthfulness in the zest of it, for a man of
forty-one ?

But the growth of a younger generation was proving to
him and to his neighbours the passage of time ; and from this
period onward we find strong development of the trait which
is proper to an elderly gossip—match-making. He had
indeed tried his hand at it earlier, aiming at a resounding *coup*.
When his brother, the second Lord Orford, died in 1851, the
heir to Houghton was " a wild boy " ; Lady Orford's large
fortune reverted to her own use ; the debts were very heavy ;
and Horace trembled with good reason for what might happen
to Houghton and its treasures, which he valued first for their
own sake, and even more for the sake of Sir Robert who
gathered them. Mr. Chute, the constant counsellor, was at
hand with a suggestion. His friend, the rich young Whithed,
had died suddenly, and so ended the projected marriage

between him and a vast heiress, Miss Nicoll, whose fortune was a hundred and fifty thousand pounds, and who was a minor and an orphan in the hands of untrustworthy guardians —one of whom indeed was later sent to the Fleet for dilapidating the trust funds. Chute, who, as Whithed's friend, had come to know Miss Nicoll, talked to her about the charms of the young Earl (he was it seems very attractive) and got her persuaded to run away to marry him. Nothing could have been more satisfactory to everybody, except to the projected bridegroom, who refused point-blank and left his uncle with a life-long regret that grew yearly more poignant as he saw doom closing in upon the Rubenses, the Guidos and the rest until ultimately they were consigned—of all people—to the Empress Catherine of Russia, whom Horace Walpole abominated beyond all other notorious females.

However, that failure was long past, and in 1758 we find him busy with the fortunes of his nieces, the natural daughters of Sir Edward Walpole, Sir Robert's second son. Whatever ill-will there had been between Sir Edward and his younger brother while Sir Robert lived, evaporated in the course of years; his house at Isleworth was convenient to Twickenham, and the nieces were young women of extraordinary beauty and on the best of terms with their fashionable uncle. In September, 1758, he writes to Mann about the wedding of the eldest, Laura, who was marrying Mr. Keppel, a brother of Lord Albemarle, Canon of Windsor, and (naturally) predestined to be a bishop. It may seem strange to us that a prominent ecclesiastic should wed a lady so irregularly come into the world, but the Keppels themselves were among the motley crew of Charles II's descendants, and the eighteenth century was not squeamish. Sir Robert Walpole while he lived arranged to settle one of his illegitimate daughters by marrying her to a certain Dr. Keene, who in return was to receive a living. The living was bestowed, but Dr. Keene saw and disliked the lady (her appearance is said to have been some excuse for his conduct) and shuffled out, giving her a year's income of the incumbency as compensation. Keene subsequently became a bishop in the days when it did not matter that he had quarrelled with the Walpoles : but the world at large thought badly of him for his shabbiness and apparently would not in the least have been shocked by the marriage. Certainly the history of Horace Walpole's second niece, Maria, leads us to believe that illegitimacy was in these days no serious disqualification, at the worst a slight handicap on personal advantages. She was, in her uncle's opinion, " beauty itself." " Her face, bloom, eyes, hair, teeth, and person are all perfect. You may imagine how charming she is, when her only fault, if one must find one, is, that her face is rather too round. She has a great deal of wit and vivacity, with perfect modesty." In April, 1759, in his budget to Mann he interrupted the recital of military victories (for victories had begun to pour in) with other triumphs.

" I have made a great conquest myself, and in less than a month since the first thought started. I hurry to tell you, lest you should go and consult the map of Middlesex, to see whether I have any dispute about boundaries with the neighbouring Prince of Isleworth, or am likely to have fitted out a secret expedition upon Hounslow Heath—in short, I have married, that is, am marrying, my niece Maria, my brother's second daughter, to Lord Waldegrave. What say you ? A month ago I was told he liked her—does he ? I jumbled them together, and he has already proposed. For character and credit, he is the first match in England—for beauty, I think she is. She has not a fault in her face and person, and the detail is charming. A warm complexion tending to brown, fine eyes, brown hair, fine teeth, and infinite wit and vivacity. . . . My brother has luckily been tractable and left the whole management to me. My family don't lose any rank or advantage, when they let me dispose of them—a Knight of the Garter for my Niece ; £150,000 for my Lord

Orford if he would have taken her; these are not trifling establishments."

I have omitted a couple of sentences in which this austere Republican exults that two of his nieces had married into the house of Stuart, for if Mr. Keppel came from Charles II, Lord Waldegrave was from James II. However, Maria was destined to form even closer connections with royalty and in a less unlucky line.

Another phase of his devotion to family interest showed itself in 1757 when the elder Horatio, Sir Robert's brother, whom the younger Horace had always heartily detested, died within six months of receiving a peerage. His son (" Pigwiggin " of the correspondence), succeeding him, made a vacancy in the borough of King's Lynn—which Sir Robert Walpole had long represented. "The corporation still reverence my father's memory so much that they will not have distant relations while he has sons living " : and so, though reluctantly, the younger surviving son felt called upon to relinquish his seat for Castle Rising (to which he had transferred himself from Callington) and stand for a borough which had a very considerable body of electors to contend with ; though in point of fact nobody seems to have thought it worth while to challenge a Walpole in that Norfolk stronghold.

This transfer, although it involved no contest, had the curious result of leaving Horace Walpole without a seat in Parliament on one of the very few occasions when he really wanted to effect something there.

Matters were going as badly as possible in the newly begun Seven Years War, and public resentment had turned upon the ill-fated Admiral Byng, who was being tried by court-martial for misconduct in face of the enemy. Sentence of death had been passed when the vacancy for Lynn occurred ; but there was doubt if the sentence was final. Horace Walpole, who had resigned his seat, haunting the lobbies of the House of

Commons, heard that two members of the Court, Captain Keppel and Admiral Norris, " desired a bill to absolve them from their oath of secrecy that they might unfold something very material towards saving the prisoner's life." This was on Friday, the execution was fixed for Monday, and the week-end institution was as well established then as now. (" We have a sort of Jewish superstition and would not come to town on a Saturday or a Sunday though it were to defend the Holy of Holies," Walpole wrote to Mann about this date.) There was not a minute to lose ; the House was on the point of rising ; Keppel, though a Member of the House, " said he had never spoke in public and could not," but would allow anybody to speak in his name. Horace Walpole seized a passing member, Sir Francis Dashwood, pushed him across the bar, and Dashwood from the floor of the House, claimed leave to speak. Technically the sitting stood adjourned, but leave was given for the pleading. " The House was wondrously softened " ; it was settled that the Bill should be brought in ; the King gave Byng a fortnight's respite and the House actually sat on Saturday to pass the Bill, which on the Monday was sent up to the Lords. Here, however, the evidence from members of the court-martial was held un-satisfactory, the doubting condemners shuffled, the Bill was " unanimously rejected and with great marks of contempt for the House of Commons." So ended Horace Walpole's part in " a most complicated affair," in which, he told Mann, " I have been a most unfortunate actor, having to my infinite grief, which I shall feel till the man is at peace, been instru-mental in protracting his misery a fortnight, by what I meant as the kindest thing I could do. I never knew poor Byng enough to bow to ; but the great doubtfulness of his crime and the extraordinariness of his sentence, the persecution of his enemies, who sacrifice him for their own guilt and the rage of a blinded nation, have called forth all my pity for him."

In his *Memoirs* Walpole says that Pitt (who was in office though not yet in power) pleaded with the King for mercy but could not get it. The whole episode is characteristic of that unhappy fumbling time. By August of that year Admiral Boscawen who (according to Walpole) was made into a hero to blacken Byng was disgraced. Horace Walpole wrote, " What a melancholy picture is this of an old monarch at Kensington who has lived to see such inglorious and fatal days."

Yet within less than a twelvemonth he was throwing up his cap over successes on the French coast, in Germany, and in West Africa. It is true, he threw it rather higher then than the facts warranted, and was unduly depressed and unduly critical of Pitt when the truth came out—becoming very facetious about " Don William Quixote." But he never allowed the desire for consistency to become an obsession, and on Christmas Day of 1758 he wrote to Mann a chaffing summary, which ends up—" Besides, it may grow decent for Mr. Pitt to visit his gout, which this year he has been forced to send to the Bath without him. I laugh, but seriously we are in a critical situation; and it is as true, that if Mr. Pitt had not exerted the spirit and activity that he has, we should ere now have been past a critical situation." From that onwards there is not much to be found about Pitt save notes of admiration, to which there was only one limiting clause. Pitt did not seem to think highly of Conway's merits as a soldier. Horace Walpole was constantly divided between a desire to see his adored cousin safe at home, and a more creditable desire to see that a brave man got full chance to distinguish himself.

Conway did get his chance, and though he never covered himself with glory, he earned credit, as always; and above all, he did not get hurt. Here is the postscript to a letter to Conway's wife, Lady Ailesbury. He was thanking her for a piece of china, when on the heels of it came a note from her to tell of the victory of Kirckdenkirck over the French—and of Conway's safety.

"Oh! my dear Madam, how I thank you, how I congratulate you, how I feel for you, how I have felt for you and for myself! But I bought it by two terrible hours to-day— I heard of the battle two hours before I could learn a word of Mr. Conway—I sent all round the world, and went half round it myself. I have cried and laughed, trembled and danced, as you bid me. If you had sent me as much old china as King Augustus gave two regiments for, I should not be half so much obliged to you as for your note. How could you think of me, when you had so much reason to think of nothing but yourself?—And then they say virtue is not rewarded in this world. I will preach at Paul's Cross, and quote you and Mr. Conway; no two persons were ever so good and so happy. In short, I am serious in the height of all my joy. God is very good to you, my dear Madam; I thank him for you; I thank him for myself: it is very unalloyed pleasure we taste at this moment! Good night! My heart is so expanded, I could write to the last scrap of my paper; but I won't."

If ever a letter rang true, that does. Horace Walpole is not so much to my liking when he writes to women as to men; there is always a touch of grimace. But here every trace of affectation goes by the board and words come tumbling out from an overflowing heart.

So long as Conway was employed, and was not damaged, there was nothing to check the enthusiasm with which this looker-on threw up his hat for Mr. Pitt.

"And so you don't think we are obliged to Mr. Pitt?" he wrote to Mann. "Yes, I am sure you do. Who would have believed five years ago that France would send to Whitehall to beg Peace? And why should they not have believed it? Why, because nobody foresaw that the Duke of Newcastle and Lord Hardwicke would not be as absolute as ever. Had they continued in power, the Duke of Newcastle would now be treating at Paris to be *Intendant* of Sussex, and Sir Joseph Yorke would be made a Prince of the empire for signing the cession of Hanover."

That was in April, 1761. In June he was telling the same far-off correspondent—"You would not know your own country again. You left it a private little island, living upon its means. You would find it the capital of the world; and, to talk with the arrogance of a Roman, St. James' Street crowded with Nabobs and American chiefs, and Mr. Pitt attended in his Sabine farm by Eastern Monarchs and Borealian electors, waiting, till the gout has gone out of his foot, for an audience."

When matters came, in 1761, to the great Minister's resignation, Walpole's mercury fell to zero: he foresaw " nothing but confusion . . . if Spain bullied when Mr. Pitt was minister, I don't believe she will tremble more at his successors. . . . It required all his daring to retrieve our affairs. Who will dare for him, nay, and against him ? "

But then came letter hotfoot on letter—

" Am I not an old fool ? at my years to be a dupe to virtue and patriotism ; I, who have seen all the virtue of England sold six times over! Here have I fallen in love with my father's enemies, and because they served my country, believed they were the most virtuous men upon earth. I adored Mr. Pitt, as if I had just come from school and reading Livy's lies of Brutus and Camillus, and Fabius ; and romance knows whom. Alack ! alack ! Mr. Pitt loves an estate as well as my Lord Bath ! The Conqueror of Canada, of Afric, of India, would, if he had been in the latter, have brought my Lady Esher as many diamonds as General Clive took."

In short, Mr. Pitt had accepted a pension of £3,000 a year for three lives and a barony for his wife, Lady Hester. George Montagu, Lady Ailesbury and Harry Conway (who was abroad) all received Horace Walpole's outpourings.

We who read them now cannot help saying to ourselves that Horace at four-and-forty was still what he owns in one of his letters to having been—" an absurd young man." Here he was with three or four thousand pounds per annum of sine-cures, for which he had never done a hand's turn, and none the less was righteously indignant with a Minister for not behaving as the ancient Romans are believed to have behaved—in the ages before Rome knew what riches meant. Who was he to set up his judgment of what became a great man's honour against the great man's own instinct? It is all laughable enough, inconsequent beyond words; and yet in a way one likes him for it—and is grateful for the insight. Nothing could possibly make us understand better how England thought and felt about Pitt. Gray, that cold sluggish nature, was for this once in the same cry with his mercurial friend; for Gray also had been caught by the wave of hero-worship which had spread over Britain; and he was not in the least more reasonable than Walpole when Mr. Pitt failed to play the heroic part exactly after their conception of it.

The fact is that Horace Walpole, a worldling of five and forty, was passionately desirous to contemplate examples of disinterested behaviour. He was indeed modestly convinced that his own life gave an example of it; having a very competent provision, he did not clamour for more: still, he was aware that this virtue was not conspicuous, and he longed to see those whom he admired and whom he loved earn crowns of glory. He had evidently given to Mr. Pitt an admiration which was like a schoolboy's or schoolgirl's; that enthusiasm suddenly got a disagreeable knock. But at least one perfect example remained, in Conway. " Oh, my dear Harry, I beg you on my knees, keep your virtue: do let me think there is still one man upon earth who despises money."

Here again Mr. Thackeray or Miss Rebecca Sharp might have discovered that it is not difficult to despise money on four thousand a year, which would have been about Conway's income at this time. But Horace Walpole, whatever airs he gave himself of being a worldling, had not a touch of cynicism in his composition. A cynic would have rubbed his hands over Pitt's pension, instead of being indignant; and even though the indignation was absurd to the point of being impertinent, still it was heartfelt.

There was no inconsistency in his longings after peace, which began to appear at the moment of Pitt's resignation. But they were soon dashed. He wrote to Conway—" This is the most unhappy day I have known of years; Bussy " [the French ambassador] " goes away! Mankind is again given up to the sword. Peace and you are far from England."

Aspirations after tranquillity fill the letters in 1762.

" March 23rd. Well! I wish we had conquered the world, and had done! I think we were full as happy when we were a peaceful quiet set of tradesfolk, as now that we are heirs apparent to the Romans, and overrunning East and West Indies."

" May 20th. I am a bad Englishman, because I think the advantages of commerce are dearly bought for some by the lives of many more. This wise age counts its merchants, and reckons its armies ciphers. But why do I talk of this age?—every age has some ostentatious system to excuse the havoc it commits. Conquest, honour, chivalry, religion, balance of power, commerce, no matter what, mankind must bleed, and take a term for a reason. 'Tis shocking! Good night! "

The influence of Sir Robert was more lasting than that of Mr. Pitt on this philosopher.

Mr. Pitt had of course been replaced by Lord Bute; the transition from George II to George III had taken place earlier. Walpole was attracted as most of his contemporaries were by the young King's frankness and decency. He even went the length of writing a poem in George III's honour, which he sent to Lady Bute—doubtless for transmission;

but it was transcribed in a clerk's hand, and was never acknowledged by its author—nor printed anywhere till more than fifty years after Walpole's death. We may dispense ourselves from reading it. But his letters about the change-over are admirable. The spectacle of struggles for party honour and place which always fed his vein of mockery was profuse in entertainment, and the royal wedding gave full occasion for his gift of description. I need not quote what Thackeray has used so well in his lectures on the Four Georges: but here is a sentence which brings Strawberry Hill close to us, as it was in the days just before the coronation—

" Would you know who won the sweepstakes at Hunting-don ? what parties are at Woburn ? what officers upon guard in Betty's fruit-shop ? whether the peeresses are to wear long or short tresses at the Coronation ? how many jewels Lady Harrington borrows of actresses ? All this is your light summer wear for conversation ; and if my memory were as much stuffed with it as my ears, I might have sent you volumes last week. My nieces, Lady Waldegrave and Mrs. Keppel, were here five days, and discussed the claim or disappoint-ment of every miss in the Kingdom for Maid of Honour. Unfortunately this new generation is not at all my affair. I cannot attend to what concerns them. Not that their trifles are less important than those of one's own time, but my mould has taken all its impressions, and can receive no more. I must grow old upon the stock I have. I, that was so impatient at all their chat, the moment they were gone, flew to my Lady Suffolk, and heard her talk with great satisfaction of the late Queen's coronation-petticoat. The preceding age always appears respectable to us (I mean as one advances in years), one's own age interesting, the coming age neither one nor t'other."

One cause of this gloom was a first gap in his circle. Dick Edgecumbe (who had recently succeeded his father as Lord Edgecumbe) died " a martyr to gaming."

"With every quality to make himself agreeable, he did nothing but make himself miserable. I feel the loss much, though long expected ; and it is the more sensible here, where I saw most of him. My towers rise, my galleries and cloisters extend—for what ? For me to leave, or to inhabit by myself, when I have survived my friends."

So he wrote to Mann, passing on to the mention of that other loss—Mann's brother. "Gal served me to talk of you —now I can only talk to you of him. But I will not—I love to communicate my satisfactions—my melancholy I generally shut up in my own breast."

It was well under control in these years, as a rule ; later in life, he could not so easily keep it locked up. But to speak the truth, from 1757 to 1762—when peace was signed— Horace Walpole had little time for melancholy : his pen was too busy. In May, 1757, while Pitt was trying to shake off the Duke of Newcastle, there appeared a letter from Xo-Ho, a Chinese philosopher at London, to his friend Lien Chi at Pekin which gave an account of the ministerial disputes under a thin veil. This squib ran through five editions in a fortnight. Later, when this period was over, he was prepared to think " nothing more ridiculous in my life than my having ever loved their squabbles, and that at an age when I loved better things too." But in 1757 he loved them dearly, and was enchanted when Mrs. Clive cried out " Lord, you will be sent to the Tower." " Well," said I coolly, " my father was there before me." This account of the episode to George Montagu (who also had thought Xo-Ho a bold performance) has in perfection Horace's jaunty affectation of bold Republicanism.

However, to pass to the " better things " which he loved— meaning, presumably, literature and art—just at this very same time he undertook a new phase of service to them both : in short, he commenced printer. In July, 1757, the *Officina Arbuteana* opened in form. His first idea was to bring out works which would not otherwise be made available, and he had prepared an edition of Hentznerus, with a version by Bentley and a preface by himself, for the first production : but a brilliant chance offered. Gray came to London bringing his two Odes—*The Welsh Bard* and *The Progress of Poesy*—to be published. " I snatched them out of Dodsley's hands and they are to be the first fruits of my press."

Gray, who was not good at entering into the spirit of his friend's adventures, confided his reluctance to Mason.

" Mr. Walpole, having taken it into his head to set up a press of his own at Twickenham, was so earnest to handsel it with this new pamphlet that it was impossible to find a pretence for refusing such a trifle. You will dislike this as much as I do, but there is no help."

It is a pleasure to pass from the damp chilly atmosphere of this presence to Walpole's enthusiasm. He wrote to Chute—

" I tell you no news, for I know none, think of none. Elzevir, Aldus, and Stephens are the freshest personages in my memory. Unless I was appointed printer of the Gazette, I think nothing could at present make me read an article in it."

Apparently people at first suspected some dark political design at the back of this installation. " They don't know how I should abhor to profane Strawberry Hill with politics."

Of course the press was in the first instance a new toy established in a cottage which made part of the demesne.

" My abbey is a perfect college or academy. I keep a painter " [this was Muntz, a Swiss whom Bentley had discovered and who proved to be no great acquisition] " and a printer— not to mention Mr. Bentley who is an academy in himself."

The printer, first of his line, was one Robinson, an Irishman, who very soon left a letter lying about which was no doubt meant to catch the eye. It described his employer and and his employment—" the Hon. Horatio Walpole, son to the late great Sir Robert Walpole, who is very studious and an admirer of all the liberal arts and sciences ; amongst the rest he admires printing. . . . All men of genius resort to his house, court his company and admire his understanding—which with his own and their writings I believe I shall be pretty well employed. . . . The situation is close to the Thames, so is Richmond Gardens (if you were ever in them) in miniature surrounded by bowers, groves, cascades and ponds and on a rising ground not very common in this part of the country—the building elegant, and the furniture of a peculiar taste, magnificent and superb."

Alas, poor Robinson ! he was " a foolish Irishman who took himself for a genius " and grew angry when Walpole thought him " extremely the former and not in the least of the latter." So he found no abiding city in what he called " fair Twickenham's luxurious shades, Richmond's near neighbour where great George the King resides."

The printer at Strawberry Hill had to be handy with a kind of legerdemain, for when fair and distinguished ladies came to visit the establishment there would always be a neat complimentary quatrain duly set to be printed off ; but sometimes also it would be arranged that the printer should set to order some specified piece of verse ; when the setting was done, Walpole would engage the attention of his guests for a few moments and then would call on Robinson—or the printer of the moment; the levers would work, and there would be disclosed what " The Press " had to say—something quite different, unexpected and most flattering to the visitor.

But it was much more than a toy : it was an occupation—one of many : " My mind is of no gloomy turn and I have a thousand ways of amusing myself," he wrote. Yet he was threatened with the loss of these. He had overstrained his eyes with reading and writing at night, and was at this time seriously concerned lest they should wear out and leave him " fit only to consort with dowagers." The press, with all its supervision, made a variety. He was quite prepared to find work for it himself; but there was also always before him the thought of doing real service by making books accessible which would not otherwise be published. He was too much a collector in grain not to know from the first that works printed under such conditions would always be sought after by collectors; yet it was a serious instrument. It pleased him to give the world (with Bentley's help) an edition of Lucan—whom he thought a better poet than Virgil: to publish the Life of Lord Herbert of Cherbury, "a most singular work" of which he was permitted to print 200 copies —only half being for himself. This was indeed a service to literature: and it enabled him to make a rare and acceptable present to Gray's friend, Thomas Warton, the editor of Spenser. Indeed from 1757 onwards the correspondence is full of letters concerning the dispatch of such offerings to the men of learning with whom he was increasingly in touch.

For early in 1758 there issued from Walpole's own press his first important book, the *Catalogue of Royal and Noble Authors*—in an edition of three hundred copies. It was an odd idea to collect details about all the crowned or coroneted heads that had ever produced literary compositions, but at least it led the compiler into out-of-the-way pastures: for instance we owe to this research the edition of Herbert of Cherbury; and genuine scholars wrote to him with suggestion and criticism as well as compliment. One of them, the Reverend Henry Zouch, pressed upon him that he should undertake a life of Sir Robert. The answer was briefly "that I think too highly of him and too meanly of myself to presume I am equal to the task." But there was added another reason that has interest.

"I have too much impartiality in my nature to care, if I could, to give the world a history, collected solely from the person himself of whom I should write. With the utmost veneration for his truth, I can easily conceive, that a man who had lived a life of party, and who had undergone such persecution from party, should have had greater bias than he himself could be sensible of."

That passage indicates one of the qualities by which Walpole has value for us. He had a strong feeling for history, and without the scientific training of a historian, he had a practical sense of the nature of historical testimony. Even for the ordinary man, membership of Parliament confers a considerable privilege. He is very unlikely to make history; but he has the chance to learn the conditions under which, in a parliamentary system of government, history is made. He should have intelligence enough to perceive how differently a series of important transactions may be stated, even with a full desire to give the real facts; above all, how inevitable it is that misleading and even completely untrue interpretations may be issued; and how rapidly a political mythology grows up. Consequently Horace Walpole was never content to accept the conventional, official, and generally accredited estimate of character or record of events. Herein probably lay the secret of the real popularity which attended his productions.

Of course he was a little absurd about it. "My book is marvellously in fashion, to my great astonishment," he tells George Montagu. "I did not expect so much truth and such notions of liberty would have made their fortune in this our day." He was inordinately impressed by what he calls (in a letter to Robertson) the "licentious frankness" of his own way of thinking in history. However, the historian of Scotland took him very seriously and allowed the dilettante to advise him. It is worth noting that Walpole suggests to Robertson "two subjects which I sometimes had a mind to treat myself." One was the *History of Learning*: the other, "what I may in one light call the most remarkable period of the world, by containing a succession of five good princes: I need not say they were Nerva, Trajan, Adrian, and the two Antonines."

This throws a light on what his ambitions had been, when he was young and ambitious. But now, in the forties, even in the early forties, he knew himself to be unequal to any such undertaking. He knew that he had no right to the title of " learned " which Robertson and others threw at him ; if perhaps he ostentatiously underpraised himself when he told Robertson " Nothing can be more superficial than my knowledge, or more trifling than my reading," he was well aware that he had not the real stuff of erudition in him—and, moreover, that he was physically barred from making good the deficiencies of " a very dissipated life, in all the hurry of the world of pleasure." His sight was threatened, and " I own I prefer my eyes to anything I could ever read, much more than to anything I could write."

So much he said to the learned, able and unknown Scotch clergyman. To Montagu he told a good deal more of the truth—mixed up with some affectation. In October, 1758, he was all for a complete stoppage of writing. " I have writ enough—and by what I have writ the world thinks I am not a fool, which was just what I wished them to think." He had lived in horror of that oracular saying which Mr. Bentley translated, " The sons of heroes are loobies." Further, his " little stock of reputation " began to be troublesome, " it has dipped me in erudite correspondences " ; he was afraid of being called learned till somebody abused him for not being what he was called.

" In short, I propose to have nothing more to do with the world, but divert myself in it as an obscure passenger—pleasure, virtú, politics, and literature, I have tried them all, and have had enough of them. Content and tranquillity, with now and then a little of three of them, that I may not grow morose, shall satisfy the rest of a life that is to have much idleness, and I hope a little goodness ; for politics—a long adieu ! . . . at least these are my present reflections—if I should change them to-morrow, remember I am not only a human creature, but that I am I, that is, one of the weakest of human creatures, and so sensible of my fickleness that I am sometimes inclined to keep a diary of my mind, as people do of the weather. To-day you see it is temperate, to-morrow it may again blow politics and be stormy; for while I have so much quicksilver left, I fear my passionometer will be susceptible of sudden changes."

He was right about changes. As happens when a man has many interests and an itching pen, book led to book. By January, 1759 (three months after he had declared off to George Montagu), one of his learned correspondents, Dr. Zouch, was informed that Walpole had bought of the engraver Virtue's widow, " forty volumes of his MS. collection relating to English painters, sculptors, gravers, and architects," and proposed " to digest and complete this work." That was to be after he had completed the Conway papers— which he did not complete. In both cases Walpole had saved for us valuable material; in the latter case though not in the former, he carried out his design, and by his talent for being readable made out of it what he thought possible, " a very amusing work," of which the first two volumes came out in 1760. " It has warmed Gray's coldness so much " (he told George Montagu) " that he is violent about it; in truth there is an infinite quantity of new and curious things about it."

Gray was right as usual. *Anecdotes of Painting* is the one that wears best of all Walpole's shelf-ful. It was rapidly written; the first volume, begun in January, was finished in August; the second was completed between September 5 and October 23. This is quick work, even for a compilation, but there was reason for it. " My tower erects its battlements bravely; my Anecdotes of Painting thrive exceedingly; thanks to the gout that has pinned me to my chair: think of Ariel the Spirit in a slit shoe."

For the almost inescapable doom of that age had come upon him, though he had done all he could to avoid it. He was never a strong man, yet on the whole ailed little; his constitution was, he said, like " grass that escapes the scythe by being low." He was spare of habit, rather tall—Cunningham indeed, from whom I should be slow to differ, says he was short : but really, though we have no record of his height, we may suppose that he knew it, and there are scores of allusions to his own leanness and lankiness. He was temperate to a degree that drew Gray—no toper—to remonstrate ; a little wine and water was his drink at meals and his food was most sparing. He did not take exercise, but he was much on his feet, and moved quickly ; Pulteney said that he " ran like a peewit," which is a most descriptive phrase for the slightly mincing high-stepping gait which was characteristic of him. There seemed to be no loophole for gout to creep in by ; nevertheless it caught him, when he was three and forty. He had even had a visitation of it six years earlier but nobody would believe him.

" Now they may have proof," he told Montagu, " my legs are as big as your cousin Guildford's.

If either my father or my mother had had it, I should not dislike it so much. I am herald enough to approve it if descended genealogically ; but it is an absolute upstart in me, and what is more provoking, I had trusted to my great abstinence for keeping me from it : but thus it is, if I had any gentleman-like virtue, as patriotism or loyalty, I might have got something by them ; I had nothing but that beggarly virtue temperance, and she had not interest enough to keep me from a fit of the gout. Another plague is, that everybody that ever knew anybody that had it, is so good as to come with advice, and direct me how to manage it ; that is, how to contrive to have it for a great many years."

He had a matter of thirty-six years to spend in its company and a whole library of directions for its treatment could be collected from his pages. However, it did not greatly hamper him while George II was king.

That was not for long after August, 1760, when gout first set in. Things then began to happen so fast that so zealous a chronicler had no time to be gouty. The first was an unexpected burst of court sunshine.

On October 14 of a morning:

" As I was very tranquilly writing my ' Anecdotes of Painting,' I heard the bell at the gate ring and called out as usual, ' not at home.' But the footman saw red liveries at the door, thought it would be treason to tell a lie and came running up : ' Sir, the Prince of Wales is at the door, and says he is come on purpose to make you a visit.' There was I, in the utmost confusion, undressed, in my slippers, and with my hair about my ears ; there was no help, *insanum vatem aspiciet*—and down I went to receive him. Him was the Duke of York. Behold my breeding of the old Court ; at the foot of the stairs I kneeled down, and kissed his hand. I beg your Uncle Algernon Sidney's pardon, but I could not let the second Prince of the blood kiss my hand first. He was, as he always is, extremely good-humoured; and I, as I am not always, respectful."

This passage, since it first appeared in print, has led to unflattering comments on its writer. Lady Louisa Stuart in her old age saw some of them and made a spirited defence of one " whom (with the good leave of a swarm of magazine-critics that never saw his face) no one who knew him in his lifetime would ever have accused of servility. . . . When he knelt in form to kiss the Duke of York's hand at his own door, he probably had a politic view quite unsuspected by the aforesaid critics : that of warding off too close an intimacy, and preventing the illustrious young gentleman from skipping in and out of his house at pleasure. To keep at a profoundly respectful distance from our superiors is the true way, as he perfectly knew, of keeping them at a convenient distance from ourselves."

We have also his own explanation of a proceeding in which he had at least the merit of consistency, for a generation later another Duke of York, nephew to this visitant, made an impromptu visit to Strawberry, and Walpole asked leave at the door to kiss his hand. He recorded this to his friend Lady Ossory (sometime Duchess of Grafton), and she, it would seem, found fault : for no doubt fashions were changing. But Horace Walpole prided himself on being *de la vieille cour*. " As I am very secure of never being suspected to pay court for interest," he told her, " and certainly never seek royal personages, I always pique myself, when thrown in their way, upon showing that I know I am nobody, and know the distance between them and me ; this I take to be common sense and do not repent of my behaviour." It was, in short, the traditional behaviour of an English aristocrat in the eighteenth-century Whig world. " Kings and princes were no rarities to him," as Lady Louisa says elsewhere in the passage from which I have quoted, and neither in 1761, nor 1788, had he taken the pains to be presented to these young royalities.

In 1761 that caused inconvenience ; he had not been to court for ten years, and consequently had no standing to return the compliment ; and yet " Could I let the Duke of York visit me and never go to thank him ? "

Preparations were made, everybody was most honorific, and then, just as this long-standing absentee was to make good his neglect, what should King George himself do but die very suddenly on the morning of October 23 ? On the evening of the 28th, Horace Walpole ended his account to George Montagu :

" Would it be news that all is hopes and fears, and that great lords look as if they dreaded wanting bread ? would this be news ? believe me, it all grows stale soon. I had not seen such a sight these three-and-thirty years : I came eagerly to town ; I laughed for three days : I am tired already."

It is not to my purpose to quote from the account of the coronation—though once again, after a long interval, it is possible to compare Walpole's description of a scene with Gray's ; for the poet saw the coronation, no doubt by his friend's good offices. It would be pleasant also to print the story of an evening at Holland House where " Jane Shore " was played by children, Charles Fox, aged eleven, having the leading part, but the children were assisted by Lady Sarah Lennox and her inseparable friend Lady Susan Fox-Strang-ways who played the women—being mature ladies of sixteen. However, it is necessary to concentrate on passages that tell us about Walpole himself ; and since the new reign meant a new Parliament, he was obliged to go to Houghton " to make an appearance of civility to Lynn, whose favour I never asked nor care if I have it or not." But this ungracious mood was soon shaken off, when he found himself among scenes that meant so much to him. Once again, it was to Montagu that he let his thought flow without reserve—and this time at least with real emotion—

" Here I am at Houghton ! and alone ! in this spot where (except two hours last month) I have not been in sixteen years ! Think, what a crowd of reflections ! No ; Gray, and forty churchyards, could not furnish so many ; nay, I know one must feel them with greater indifference than I possess, to have patience to put them into verse. Here I am, probably for the last time in my life, though not for the last time : every clock that strikes tells me that I am an hour nearer to yonder church—that church into which I have not yet had courage to enter, where lies that mother on whom I doated, and who doated on me ! There are the two rival mistresses of Houghton, neither of whom ever wished to enjoy it ! There too lies he who founded its greatness, to contribute to whose fall Europe was embroiled; there he sleeps in quiet and dignity, while his friend and his foe, rather his false ally and real enemy, Newcastle and Bath, are exhausting the dregs of their pitiful lives in squabbles and pamphlets."

Set against that the end of the letter, and there is a contrast which the writer did not fail to mark—

"It is plain I never knew for how many trades I was formed, when at this time of day I can begin electioneering, and succeed in my new vocation. Think of me, the subject of a mob, who was scarce ever before in a mob, addressing them in the town-hall, riding at the head of two thousand people through such a town as Lynn, dining with above two hundred of them, amid bumpers, huzzas, songs, and tobacco, and finishing with country dancing at a ball and sixpenny whisk! I have borne it all cheerfully; nay, have sat hours in conversation, the thing upon earth that I hate; have been to hear misses play on the harpischord, and to see an alderman's copies of Rubens and Carlo Marat. Yet to do the folks justice, they are sensible, and reasonable, and civilized; their very language is polished since I lived among them. I attribute this to their more frequent intercourse with the world and the capital, by the help of good roads and post-chaises, which, if they have abridged the King's dominions, have at least tamed his subjects. Well, how comfortable it will be to-morrow, to see my parroquet, to play at loo, and not be obliged to talk seriously! The Heraclitus of the beginning of this letter will be overjoyed on finishing it to sign himself your old friend,

DEMOCRITUS."

It is right to mention that a couple of years before this, Mrs. Leneve, the kinswoman who had kept house for Sir Robert, was ending her days in Horace Walpole's house in Arlington Street—where a home had been continuously made

HORACE WALPOLE 4th EARL OF ORFORD

for her. She was seventy-three and had been a constant invalid since she was fifty; it was in August and it was the " most gorgeous of all summers "; yet though Horace Walpole pined for Strawberry, he stayed in London by her bedside till she got her release.

There is evidence of his humaneness too in his notice of Walton's *Compleat Angler*, which had been edited by Hawkins, " a very worthy gentleman in my neighbourhood but who, I could wish, did not think angling so innocent an amusement. One of the bravest and best men I ever knew, Sir Charles Wager, I have often heard declare he never killed a fly willingly. It is a comfortable reflection to me, that all the victories of last year have been gained since the suppression of the Bear Garden and prize-fighting; as it is plain, and nothing else would have made it so, that our valour did not singly and solely depend upon these two Universities." Also, in the summer of 1760, when there was a panic about hydrophobia, he wrote:

" In London there is a more cruel campaign than that waged by the Russians : the streets are a very picture of the murder of the innocents—one drives over nothing but poor dead dogs ! The dear, good-natured, honest, sensible creatures ! Christ ! how can anybody hurt them. Nobody could but those Cherokees the English, who desire no better than to be halloo'd to blood :—one day Admiral Byng, the next Lord George Sackville, and to-day the poor dogs ! "

These traits need to be stressed : they take off from the hard glitter of much of his commentary; they even make us forgive his high and mighty reference to " young Mr. Burke's ' authorism,' or his description of " Tristram Shandy " as " a very insipid and tedious performance." Horace Walpole could be actually stupid, and with all his self-scrutiny he probably never guessed this. But he did know that the smart turns of phrase for which people valued him were not the best thing in his nature. There is a letter to Lady Hervey written when he was forty-three; he had offended her and she had scolded him. He says:

"My words failed me—a misfortune not too common to me, who am apt to say too much, not too little. Perhaps it is that very quality which your ladyship calls wit, and I call tinsel, for which I dread being praised. I wish to recommend myself to you by more essential merits—and if I can only make you laugh, it will be very apt to make me as much concerned as I was yesterday. For people to whose approbation I am indifferent, I don't care whether they commend or condemn me for my wit; in the former case they will not make me admire myself for it, in the latter they can't make me think but what I have thought already. But for the few whose friendship I wish, I would fain have them see, that under all the idleness of my spirits there are some very serious qualities, such as warmth, gratitude, and sincerity, which ill returns may render useless or may make me lock up in my breast, but which will remain there while I have a being."

That rings honest: more sincere than his phrase to Montagu at the close of 1761—"Every day teaches me how much I was mistaken in my own past, and I am in no danger now but of thinking I am grown too wise."

Yet that also had its own sincerity: he was quite clear that he was not going to be a great man or a poet. He contented himself with lesser satisfactions and at that moment did his best to endure with philosophy the defection of his printer, Mr. Robinson's successor—the fourth within four years.

CHAPTER VIII

THE TURN OF LIFE

FOR varying reasons a marked change at some given point is to be observed in the lives of many men. Some sudden turn of fortune, for better or worse, may alter the material conditions drastically. To this Horace Walpole was never exposed, and moreover against this he protected himself. He was always amply provided for, and had nothing to fear from fortune—except indeed for the moment when it threatened to bring back the Stuarts. He spent his large income as it came in, lavishly enough: " I drive to the last penny," he wrote to Bentley, when that versatile gentleman suggested to him various speculations. But he never overspent, and all his outlay on Strawberry was made gradually, and always out of income; he prolonged his costly amusements; the work went on little by little. He was the wise man of Swift's saying who should " have money in his head but never in his heart," for more than once he showed prompt willingness to make a very large money sacrifice to friendship, and though he was not taken at his word, there is no doubt that the offers were made in all seriousness.

Further than this, although he had ambitions, he never let them lead him into staking his happiness or ease of mind on their success; they slipped away from him, as imperceptibly as youth does: or rather, they transformed themselves gradually into eagerness for another man's advancement. And here, no doubt, was the limitation to his prudence, which made itself all the more sharply felt because it was disclosed when he was at his full development. The trouble lay deep, for he was that complex and vulnerable creature, a sentimentalist. Even when he acted with all the impetuosity of his nature to bring his cousin Conway into great office; even when he had the additional spur of partisanship in seeking the downfall of other politicians whom he detested; even so, the achievement of this double end brought only a bitter disappointment because it was not accompanied by the further satisfaction of a desire which he had never avowed to anyone—perhaps never explicitly to himself. For he was never at any time quite honest with himself; no sentimentalist can be; self-deceit is the badge of their numerous tribe; and what proportion of men are exempt from it can only be ascertained when psychological statistics are reduced to an accurate science. But the fact is that a sentimental shock of disappointment was sufficient to change the currents of Horace Walpole's nature at least for a period, and to send him seeking for consolations, which he found in a quarter that added very much to the significance of his life and the range of his experience.

The course of the story begins with politics. When Mr. Pitt established his ascendancy in a war so popular and so glorious that parties ceased to exist, Horace Walpole did not think the moral results admirable. "I have a maxim, that the extinction of party is the origin of faction," he wrote to George Montagu, a few weeks after George III succeeded to the throne; and when the new parliament came to be elected, he told Mann: "Corruption now stands upon its own legs—no money is issued from the Treasury; there are no parties, no pretence of grievances and yet venality is grosser than ever."

In this scene of jostling intrigue between persons, not principles, Horace Walpole was well fitted for a part. Pitt went out, Lord Bute came into power; the war went on, and conquests still did not stop; but the Court wanted peace, and Walpole was too much Sir Robert's pupil not to be instinctively a partisan of peace. Fox was called in to win over the

House of Commons and the peace was secured, yet on terms
which Walpole, as Pitt's admirer, thought less flattering than
England's prowess had deserved—and so he would not vote
for it; but as a pacifist he could not vote for protracting
bloodshed. This committed him to nothing; and Conway
whom Fox kept abroad, charged with the duty of bringing
home the British troops from Flanders, was thereby prevented from action in Parliament. Thus neither of the
cousins was involved in hostility to the Court; and Horace
could write—" Well, I shall go into my old corner under the
window and laugh; I had rather sit by my fire; but if there
are to be bull-feasts, one would go and see them, when one has
a convenient box for nothing and is very indifferent about the
cavalier combatants."

However, it became less easy to sit on the back benches
and laugh at ease; the Court assumed a right to inflict
penalties for opposition; and when Bute resigned, power
passed into the less moderate hands of George Grenville.
Then issues were raised which stirred whatever was least
unreal in Horace Walpole's political principles. For the
famous No. 45 of the *North Briton*, Wilkes was arrested on a
general warrant and was triumphantly liberated on appeal to
the Court of Common Pleas who decided against the legality
of the warrant. Before long, Parliament had to give its own
decision " whether the privilege of Parliament preserved the
members from being taken up for writing and publishing
libels." On this Walpole in his *Memoirs* expresses a plain
opinion. " Freedom in speech in Parliament is not so
valuable as freedom of writing." A member of Parliament
who was discovered to have written anonymously what the
Government resented was formerly protected by his privilege.
This privilege the House itself was now asked to surrender, and
it did not delay to do so. Conway with Walpole voted in the
minority. The result was a message to Conway that, if men
in the King's Service were found acting against him, " the

King could not trust his Army in such hands." After this threat, as was to be expected from Conway's character, when the question came up again in another of its phases, he spoke and voted in the division that brought Government to the edge of defeat. Shortly after, Walpole was, in his own words, " stunned with notice of Mr. Conway's being turned out of the King's bedchamber and dismissed from the command of his regiment of dragoons."

Conway made no complaint. " His friends," Horace Walpole says fiercely, " are rejoiced at not being called upon." They were many and high placed. His wife was Lady Ailesbury, daughter to the Duke of Argyll, and the Campbell clan was powerful ; Lady Ailesbury's daughter by her first marriage was now Duchess of Richmond and the Duke of Richmond loved Conway and loved Walpole. Lord Hertford, Conway's brother, was the Ambassador in Paris. Yet none of these potentates stirred a hand, though Richmond agreed to speak if the matter were raised in Parliament. But Horace Walpole took up the fight ; he offered his cousin six thousand pounds—all he had in the funds—then and there ; he altered his will, leaving Conway almost his whole fortune unless the regiment were restored. The Duke of Devonshire, too, who had been removed from his office of Lord Chamberlain and struck off the Privy Council for opposing the Peace, showed his sympathy nobly by offering Conway through Walpole a thousand a year till his regiment should be restored. All these offers were refused, but they were not lightly taken. Conway wrote to his brother, Hertford—" Horace Walpole has, on this occasion, shown the warmth of friendship that you know him capable of, so strongly that I want words to express it." Still that did not advance matters to any practical purpose. Their only hope was to get their enemies out and their friends in.

It is fair to suppose that Horace Walpole, who is here his own chronicler, does not underrate the subtlety with which, when the Opposition showed no power to active union, he fomented dissensions among the various elements of the Government. But we may believe that he worked hard; and events seconded him handsomely. The King's illness in 1765 led to proposals of a Regency Bill, and so led to bitter ill-will between George III and his ministers, of whom, as early as May, he decided to rid himself. In July he succeeded. When the new Government was formed under Rockingham, Conway was one of the Secretaries of State and leader of the House of Commons. The whirligig of time had indeed brought in its revenges, and Horace Walpole could pride himself on the success of his desires. Added to this, he pressed Conway to secure that his brother Hertford should be sent as Lord Lieutenant to Ireland, thus making room for his stepson-in-law, the Duke of Richmond, as ambassador to France.

This was triumph for the partisan. Conway was in a position whence he might easily rise to be Prime Minister; the Grenvilles and Bedfords, who had threatened Walpole and who had shocked him by their support of prerogative, were beaten and disgraced. Yet with triumph came the stab.

There were two grievances. First, while the Rockingham group were in opposition Horace Walpole had been active and considered among them : yet when victory, turning to their side, gave them back the task of distributing preferment, it was galling to learn (at second-hand, for an attack of gout had laid him up) that his name " had not been so much as mentioned." He had never held office; but that was no disqualification; it was a Ministry of inexperienced men; and in that day even more than in Melbourne's, opinion held that " any English gentleman was qualified for any post which he had influence enough to secure." There is no denying that if Horace Walpole had been a seeker either for the distinction of office or its profit, he had a grievance. But he is far from suggesting this. " That I would take no place was well known ; I had frequently declined it," he says in his *Memoirs*—written for publication when all concerned should be dead. None the less, " Was a compliment at least not due to me ? " he asks. And from whom had he a right to expect this sentimental satisfaction ? Not from the Duke of Cumberland to whom he " had never paid court " ; nor from the Duke of Newcastle whom he " had constantly ridiculed " ; nor from Lord Rockingham or the Cavendishes whom he " had treated with a very moderate share of regard.

" Though some notice is due to all men who are respected in a party, they were excusable in proposing nothing for me, when they found nothing demanded for me by my own intimate friend and relation.

But what could excuse this neglect in Mr. Conway ? For him I had sacrificed everything ; for him I had been injured, oppressed, calumniated. The foundation of his own fortune, and almost every step of his fortune, he owed solely to me."

What was more, Conway knew the minor object that his cousin desired for good solid reasons. The collectorship of Customs had been given to Sir Edward Walpole for his life, on the understanding that the bulk of the profits—averaging £1,400 a year—went to Horace. At an earlier period, while the Duke of Newcastle held power, Fox, then in alliance with the Duke, had secured an offer to substitute the younger brother's name. But Horace Walpole had at once, very honourably, objected that this made Sir Edward's interest in his own place dependent on the life of another man who, though many years younger, was by far the more delicate. He suggested then that the grant might be made for the two lives—which would secure both brothers. Newcastle did not see his way to this and the matter dropped ; but Horace Walpole always had it at the back of his mind—and not only at the back of his mind.

" My wish of making this independence perfectly easy, I

had hinted to Mr. Conway during our opposition. He received it with silence. It was not in my nature to repeat such a hint."

This, and not the purely sentimental grievance, was the real sting. One of the two friends had gone to the last limit in his desire to render practical service to the other; that other, when the chance came to repay, let it slip, without appearing to notice what he was doing.

" Whatever was due to me, much or little, he totally forgot it; and so far from once endeavouring to secure my independence, in his whole life after he never once mentioned it. I had too much spirit to remind him of it, though he has since frequently vaunted to me his own independence. Such failure of friendship, or, to call it by its truer name, such insensibility, could not but shock a heart at once so tender and so proud as mine."

The hurt was deepened because Conway showed eagerness to push Hertford into the Irish Vice-royalty, and to help the various Campbells to objects of their desire—though these men had not lifted a voice to protest against his undeserved disgrace. Horace Walpole adds the unkind comment:

" He thought it noble, he thought it would be fame, to pardon the neglect he had met with; and that the world would applaud his generous return of their ungenerous and interested behaviour. No glory would have accrued from his serving me, as it would have been natural and no more than was expected. His heart was so cold that it wanted all the beams of popular applause to kindle it into action."

That is, probably, less than fair to Conway; but it would be much less than fair to Horace Walpole not to give his further comment. After the advent of his friends to power— after the distribution of loaves and fishes—he announced his determination to retire from politics for a while and make holiday in Paris. Conway, he says, was not only vexed by his determination to leave London and its politics for a considerable period; he was puzzled by it, because it had never entered into his mind that Walpole seriously wanted these gratifications.

Much later in the correspondence there is note of a dinner party when three or four party leaders, all presumed to be at daggers drawn, were invited in the hope of a reconciliation. Conway had observed nothing of anybody's demeanour. If his attention had not been specially drawn to it, he would never have noticed that the choice of guests was surprising. It was easy for such a man to be deaf and blind to all that might pass in the soul of an eager sentimentalist.

"But it is justice to him," the sentimentalist writes, "to say, that I think he was incapable of ingratitude. His soul was good, virtuous, sincere; but his temper was chill, his mind absent; and he was so accustomed to my suggesting to him whatever I thought it was right for him to do, that he had no notion of my concealing a thought from him; and as I had too much delicacy to mention even my own security, I am persuaded it never came into his conception. His temper hurt me, but I forgave his virtue, of which I am confident, and know it was superior to my own. We have continued to this day on an easy and confidential footing; but conscious that I would not again devote myself for him, I have taken strict care never to give him decisive advice, when it might lead him to a precipice."

In other words, up to this time, 1765—and Horace Walpole was now no less than forty-eight—his instinct of hero-worship had led him to desire nothing better than to go tiger-hunting with Conway. Now a cold frost had nipped that enthusiasm and the chill of it pierced down to the very marrow of his being. The world was altered for him; life had less charm, and one is conscious of this as one sees the years go by him. He really suffered; although his disappointment was only in a matter when he could well afford to be a loser, it hurt that his friend should have made no effort to serve him when service was honourably possible. And though no doubt a finer nature might have seen that Conway paid his friend the nobler tribute by assuming him indifferent to personal considerations—indeed, by taking all his protestations as literally exact—yet a less generous and constant nature could not have continued both friendship and admiration to the one by whom it had been so deeply offended. For although from this date onward the letters to Conway lack something of the bubble and the sparkle, the happy excitement, that came only when Horace Walpole was writing to those whom he loved best, yet the preoccupation with Conway's fortunes, and the desire for his advancement, never vary. And when Conway showed, as he did show, proof of a disinterestedness in money matters which would be remarkable in any period, and was a prodigy in that age, Walpole " could not bring himself to dissuade " his friend from refusing five thousand a year, even though it might ruin him. His admiration stood the crucial test.

Also, although he confided his resentment to paper, sedulous care was taken that these *Memoirs* should not see the light till all concerned in them were beyond hearing praise or blame ; and Conway himself was kept unsuspicious in 1765 by the most honourable expedient. The aggrieved asked a favour of his friend, the aggriever ; it was that he should secure the Order of the Bath for Sir Horace Mann, which accordingly was granted : Conway being thus convinced that he had done for his cousin the one possible good service.

And now all was clear for the road to Paris. Horace Walpole was late in succumbing to what English papers called " the French disease." Going to Paris had become a rage since the war ended ; and in Paris there was a rage for the English. Garrick had a marvellous reception in 1763. For Walpole, the chief attraction was the presence of Lord Hertford at the Embassy. His estimate of modern France

was very low. " Even in the trifles of which they boast
themselves, they are gone backwards a century." Their
Anglomanie took ridiculous forms. At a vast dinner given
to the Duchess of Bedford, the hostess called out in the
middle of the second course, " Oh lord, they have forgot !
Yet I bespoke them, and I am sure they are ready ; you
English love hot rolls—bring the rolls ! " Then arrived a
huge dish of hot rolls and a sauceboat of melted butter.

Still Walpole constantly returned to the project of what he
told Montagu was " probably the last time he should travel
to finish his education." One of the special attractions was
Madame de Pompadour. " I hope I may live till I see her ;
she is one of the greatest curiosities of the age and I am a
pretty universal virtuoso." But with that one exception he
had—so at least he told Montagu—" much more curiosity for
their habitations than their company."

" They have scarce a man or woman of note that one
wants to see ; and for their authors, their style has grown so
dull in imitation of us that I should certainly not cross the
sea in search of ennui that I can have in such perfection at
home. . . . I go to see French plays and buy French china,
not to know their ministers, to look at their government or
think of the interests of nations—in short, unlike most
people that are growing old, I am convinced that nothing
is charming but what appeared important in one's youth,
which afterwards passes for follies."

That was the mood in which he set out on a disagreeable
journey, to a goal of no very potent attraction. " The change
of scene is my chief inducement, and to get out of politics,"
he told George Montagu ; and for once he was speaking the
literal truth.

In short, when Horace Walpole went to France in September, 1765, he had no realization that he was going to make a
whole group of new connections which would alter the colour
of his life and very greatly extend the kind of celebrity that

THE GALLERY AT STRAWBERRY HILL

he enjoyed. He simply wanted change—partly for health's sake, as throughout this summer he was crippled by the gout, but much more as an escape from scenes made odious to him by a great disappointment. For the first time in his life he had been concerned in a long and strenuous political effort; the result had been to settle in his mind a determination to get clean out of politics. And so, considered this way, as marking the close of his active political life, September, 1765, is a somewhat gloomy epoch. Yet it marks also the opening of a new and surprising range of interests, which must be sketched in another chapter.

But before considering that, let us guard against the impression that politics at any time engrossed Horace Walpole's whole attention. Even while he was trying to get the better of the Bedford and the Grenville factions, he was as busy as ever with Strawberry, and in June, 1763, Chute and he were setting out on a visit to Oxfordshire; they proposed to pass on the way by Bletchley, and stop at " the parsonage of the venerable Cole, the antiquarian of Cambridge "—a friend of Gray, contemporary of both Gray and Walpole at Eton and Cambridge. Walpole's published writings had led to a revival of this early acquaintance, which did not flag, as shall be seen. After that, they would sleep with George Montagu.

" The journey you must accept as a great sacrifice either to you or to my promise, for I quit the Gallery almost in the critical minute of consummation. Gilders, carvers, upholsterers, and picture-cleaners are labouring at their several forges, and I do not love to trust a hammer or a brush without my own supervisal.

Well, but I begin to be ashamed of my magnificence; Strawberry is growing sumptuous in its latter day. In truth, my collection was too great already to be lodged humbly; it has extended my walls, and pomp followed. It was a neat, small house; it now will be a comfortable one, and, except one fine apartment, does not deviate from its simplicity."

Strawberry was always an occupation; so were the researches on which he corresponded with Cole and other learned persons—matter to help out his *Anecdotes of Painting*. But in addition to them, there was a completely new literary adventure; one most astonishing to befall a gentleman approaching fifty. He tells the story himself on March 9, 1765—to Cole, how *The Castle of Otranto* came to be written.

"Shall I ever confess to you, what was the origin of this romance! I waked one morning, in the beginning of last June, from a dream, of which, all I could recover was, that I had thought myself in an ancient castle (a very natural dream for a head filled like mine with Gothic story), and that on the uppermost banister of a great staircase I saw a gigantic hand in armour. In the evening I sat down, and began to write, without knowing in the least what I intended to say or relate. The work grew on my hands, and I grew fond of it—add, that I was glad to think of anything, rather than politics. In short, I was so engrossed with my tale, which I completed in less than two months, that one evening, I wrote from the time I had drunk my tea, about six o'clock, till half an hour after one in the morning, when my hand and fingers were so weary, that I could not hold the pen to finish the sentence, but left Matilda and Isabella talking, in the middle of a paragraph."

It is no wonder that he wrote to Lady Hervey that he would certainly begin to be really eight-and-forty when he got to four-score: this is like the way a gentleman of eight-and-twenty would behave. Walter Scott in his youthful days went wild over German goblinries and made his version of the *Erl König* in a single night; he provided his apartment with a skull and crossbones to furnish such an atmosphere as Walpole had created (more expensively) by outlay of lath and plaster at Strawberry.

At the first contact of his invention with outer air, Walpole lurked unperceived : the first edition was published under a borrowed name in January, 1765—" But it succeeded so well I do not any longer entirely keep the secret," he says to Cole. Indeed it went through five editions quickly ; and if it is fame to be widely known by hearsay, very few novels are more famous. Every student of literature has been taught to repeat these echoing syllables (Walpole had an ear for names). What is more, among those who have tried actually to read it, probably few found any difficulty in doing so. He had the great gift of readability at all times, and such a heat of fervour as he described to Cole always communicates itself, if the one who experiences it can write at all.

Besides, of all his literary progeny this was the favourite child ; he avowed as much to Madame du Deffand in 1767 when a translation in French appeared. " Let the critics have their say : I shall not be vexed : it was not written for this age which wants nothing but cold reason. I own to you, and you will think me madder than ever, that of all my works it is the only one in which I pleased myself : I let my imagination run : my visions and my passions kindled me. I wrote it in defiance of rules, critics, and philosophies : and it seems to me all the better for that. I am even convinced that in some later time when taste resumes the throne from which philosophy has pushed it, that my poor Castle will find admirers ; it has them even to-day coming on ; I have just published the third edition."

He goes on to tell her that he had wished to make it pass for a work of some antiquity and that " nearly everybody has been taken in."

Was he right ? Did *The Castle of Otranto* find admirers when taste resumed its proper station ? We can see it to-day as a kind of signpost, a counterpart in print to Strawberry Hill, indicating that taste was on the turn in 1765 and that a Gothic revival was on the way. Certainly, no one will praise Strawberry as a piece of architecture. It is, however, possible that the creator of Strawberry had some remote hand in bringing it to pass that when the Houses of Parliament came to be rebuilt, they were rebuilt, not following such ideals as had guided the unknown architects who planned, for instance, Dublin's old Parliament House, but on lines that assuredly Horace Walpole would devoutly have approved. It is possible also that his romance was not only a symptom of the coming romantic revival, but a force in it—carried on through *The Mysteries of Udolpho*. Yet it is really pushing the claims for this fantasy much too far to say, as Miss Dorothy Stuart does, that Horace Walpole by his authorship of *The Castle of Otranto* was the progenitor of Walter Scott, Dumas père and such like offspring. He had indeed the will to do something of what they effected. " If I have amused you by retracing with any fidelity the manners of ancient days, I am content," he tells Cole. Again he writes to M. du Beaumont: " It was not so much my intention to recall the exploded marvels of ancient romance as to blend the wonderful of old stories with the natural of modern novels."

The " natural " seemed to him exhausted : " Richardson had, to me at least, made that kind of writing insupportable." In so far as he was looking for scenes where the setting would have an antiquarian interest, where the personages would wear coats of mail, or piked head-dresses, and yet would speak with a natural liveliness, it may be said that he was trying after what Scott was to do with universal applause in *Ivanhoe* or *Quentin Durward*. One may concede even that Scott in his first work of great popularity, the *Lay of the Last Minstrel*, thought it would be attractive to weave into his theme a good deal of supernatural machinery : but it should be remarked also that this was in poetry, where precedents existed in abundance, and that even in his poetry Scott at once perceived the creaking of this machine. In prose, there is not the shadow of a trace that Sir Walter was conscious of the least debt to this pioneer of romance; from the moment when he essayed the novel his feet were planted on solid earth; the scenes which he sought to revive were strange indeed to his readers, but intimately familiar to himself, partly by hearsay from those who took part in the events, but more largely from his own fully nourished observation. The debt which he felt, and which he magnificently acknowledged, was to Miss Edgeworth's studies of the Irish peasantry; and anything more unlike *The Castle of Otranto* than *Castle Rackrent* it would be hard to imagine.

Even Professor Doughty, who has edited *Otranto* with an admirable biographic preface, does not make any high claim for this work of an author whom he knows and loves. He realizes as well as the rest of us that the conception of a monstrous helmet with waving plumes which at suitable moments materializes and strikes terror cannot be taken seriously as a work of art. The book is a literary curiosity, the freakish outcome of certain tendencies in Horace Walpole whose value cannot be better recognized than in a sentence which George Montagu wrote to him when describing a visit to Combe Abbey where Lord Craven had been " routing out a thousand curious ancestors that have been all nailed up in boxes in a long gallery ever since the Queen of Bohemia's time, and many of her things which she pawned." These, he adds, are now ranged about the house " thanks to you who have taught the world to treat their kin and their goods and chattels with respect and to think they are as good furniture as Mr. Reynolds and all our daubers make us pay so dear for."

In short, Horace Walpole, who lived so passionately in the present, nevertheless taught the world to take an interest in the past; and if *The Castle of Otranto* had no other merit, there was education in it which prevented such barbarism in England as was seen in the cultured France of Walpole's day and even under the restored monarchy, when priceless tapestries of the fourteenth century were flung out as "Gothic" lumber.

CHAPTER IX

WALPOLE IN PARIS

WHEN a gentleman of mature years but sentimental disposition feels that he has been badly treated by his closest friend and resolves to lock the wound in his bosom, masked—above all, from the one who has offended—under a show of indifference, one result is all but certain; he will seek, or will find some confidant.

With most men the confidant would be a woman: but Horace Walpole was not like most men. He was indeed what is called—or used to be called—a great ladies' man, constant at tea tables; yet so far as we can judge from the immense volume of correspondence left us, his real taste was for the society of men. He worshipped Harry Conway; and he wrote to George Montagu with a charm and ease that I do not find in any of his letters to women.

One may say even that he made a cult of friendship, and played to his own inner theatre the part of the perfect friend, aiding and encouraging the perfect hero. There was real strong feeling in him, and a real craving to give and to receive affection; but these were mixed with a touch of theatricality. His offers of half his fortune were genuine; but they were also gestures before his own mirror: and as sometimes happens, at a given moment the insincere element corrupted his sincerity. Conway who certainly was not a hero, though certainly a brave and honourable gentleman, failed at a given moment to play his part in accord with Walpole's conception; he lacked sensitiveness, he lacked intuition; he did not say, as he might have said, "All my life I have been receiving benefits from you; cannot I now have the joy of making some return ? " He did not press upon Walpole that which Walpole had always declared his intention of refusing; he did not even request Lord Rockingham to go to the King and insist that the reversion of Edward Walpole's place (which had already been given away) should be none the less secured to Horace. So there followed not merely disappointment, but a new pose. Henceforward it was Horace Walpole's affectation to deny the possibility of friendship, at least for himself; to be on guard once and for all against giving his heart away.

This was easily managed, so far as concerned friendship with men. George Montagu, about whom he had more than a touch of idealizing sentiment, always remained a little elusive. Walpole's only complaint of him was that he could go on loving his friends without feeling a need to see them. After various attempts to settle him in the neighbourhood of Twickenham had been repulsed, he took his " rosy hue, grey locks and comely belly " down to Oxfordshire, and in the end drifted completely away into a mist of silence.—Sir Horace Mann was always available, at the other end of a communication channel : and Walpole did not hide from this old friend the fact of his disgruntlement. But the alliance with Mann had become by this time set, abstract, and bodiless. " I wish you and I had any common acquaintance left that we might chat of something else than Kings and Queens," Walpole writes to him as early as 1762—only twenty-one years after their last meeting; and this sentiment with variations of phrase recurs often in the succeeding twenty-one years over which their correspondence was prolonged.

Other men at varying periods engrossed Walpole's interest and attention; but none of them came into the category in which he placed George Montagu, " one of the very, very few for whom I really care a straw."

But it was not so about women. The two love stories of Horace Walpole's life began well on in the latter half of it.

His relations with the sex were always odd. The type that he conformed to—in so far as he conformed to any type— was not a marrying one. Of the Strawberry Hill group that Reynolds painted, not one married—neither Selwyn, Williams, Edgecumbe, nor Walpole himself; but two of the other three were fully provided with feminine relations. George Selwyn's Mie Mie at least might have been his daughter by the Countess Fagniani: Edgecumbe left a fund for a certain Mrs. Day, of which he made Walpole the trustee: and Gilly Williams was no doubt a patron of Mrs. Naylor's establishment, to which all these gentlemen allude as often as to Almack's or Arthur's. How much Horace Walpole availed himself of its resources there is no means of deciding. But of the ladies in the world that he frequented, whose age approximated to his own, only two had special claims on his devotion. He speaks of " my two Sovereigns, the Duchess of Grafton and Lady Mary Coke." The Duchess had in his opinion the finest figure of her time though she was not the greatest beauty; he thought her a pattern of good breeding and good company; and when she left Grafton and married Lord Ossory, for whom also Walpole had unusual liking, the friendship increased, and she was one of those to whom he wrote oftenest in his later years. But in all this there is no hint of anything beyond a perfectly well-bred and non-committal liking.

Lady Mary Coke was not a character with whom anybody could form so simple, ordinary and sensible a relation. She was a daughter of the great Duke of Argyll, sister of Lady Stafford and of Lady Bute—both of them friends of Walpole. Lady Ailesbury, Conway's wife (daughter of the fourth Duke), was her cousin. The whole history of this fantastic personage has been recounted by her niece, Lady Louisa Stuart. Not the least fantastic part was her marriage to Lord Leicester's mad and dissolute son, who paid out the scorns heaped upon him during courtship by a ceremonious farewell to his bride at the

bridal chamber's door—whence he withdrew to Mrs. Naylor's
or the like and returned drunk in the morning, yet master
of himself sufficiently to hope that she had slept well and
undisturbed. However, it was only after Lord Coke's death
had relieved her from this embarrassing relation that Lady
Mary, a young and handsome widow, began to see much of
Horace Walpole. She saw a great deal : they shared a box
at the opera : in 1759, Prince Edward, Duke of York,
younger brother to the Prince of Wales, asked Walpole when
he was going to marry Lady Mary Coke. " When I get a
regiment," was the answer—for Mr. Pitt was then making
soldiers of all the world—and either Lady Mary believed, or
Horace Walpole affected to believe that she believed, that her
beaux yeux gave Mr. Pitt his most potent inspiration. She
was quite capable of believing it : and Horace Walpole, who
adored persiflage, heaped it on her. " I will take my death,"
he wrote, " that Lady Mary was one of the first admirers of
Mr. Pitt and all the world knows that his eloquence gave the
spirit to our armies. But unluckily my deposition can only
be given in person " ; and he goes on to deplore the lack of
such a poet as shall be heard for ever. " Though a historian
should with as many asseverations as Bishop Burnet inform
mankind that the lustre of the British arms under George II
was singly and entirely owing to the charms of Lady Mary
Coke, it would not be believed : the slightest hint of it in a
stanza by Gray would carry conviction to the end of time."

Walpole was prudent : he knew that his attentions were
safe, since Lady Mary believed herself to be the object of
passion in no less than a royal heart : and when Prince
Edward, the silly, chattering Duke of York, died in 1761, she
was more than inconsolable : she flew at anyone who rashly
in her presence mentioned his name—or even spoke of
Windsor : for such associations, it should be known, were a
brutal assault on her sensibility. To escape them, she went
abroad, and set her cap at Frederick the Great : he evaded

her attentions : then she moved to Austria, and according to her own reading of the facts incurred the deep and lasting hostility of the Empress Queen, who was fearful lest her son should be captured. Nothing inconvenient thereafter happened to Lady Mary for any simple cause : if she slipped on a piece of orange peel in the street, an emissary from Maria Theresa had put it there to destroy her.

In short, she was an absurd personage whom Horace Walpole loved to laugh at, but she was also handsome and in a way good company—and good humoured : when gout laid him low, she was one of those he counted on for visits. But Lady Mary was a habit, a standing joke, and never by the wildest possibility a confidant.

His real taste in women's society was for the old. "Horry has gone a progress into Northamptonshire to Lady Betty Germaine's," Gilly Williams wrote to Selwyn in July, 1763. "Is it not surprising how he moves from old Suffolk on the Thames to another old goody on the Tyne, and does not see the ridicule which he would so strongly paint in any other character." But Lady Betty, the "divine old mistress" of the great house at Drayton, had been Swift's ally; Lady Suffolk, George the Second's mistress, was a mine of old-world stories; and his *Anecdotes of Painting* were dedicated to Lady Hervey "who has conversed familiarly with the most agreeable persons dead and living of the most polished ages and the most polished nations." These intimates could all feed his thirst for the kind of knowledge that is not in written histories; but he loved also laughing with them and making them laugh. Here is a picture of him in 1763, after the Peace, when the rush to Paris had begun and the Bedfords had gone over officially, taking George Selwyn "to add gravity to the embassy."

"I dined last week at Lady Blandford's, with her, the old Denbigh, the old Litchfield, and Methusaleh knows who. I had stuck some sweet peas in my hair, was playing at quadrille, and singing to my *sorcières*. The Duchess of Argyle and Mrs. Young came in ; you may guess how they stared ; at last the Duchess asked what was the meaning of those flowers ? ' Lord, Madam,' said I, ' don't you know it is the fashion ? The Duke of Bedford is come over with his hair full.' Poor Mrs. Young took this in sober sadness, and has reported that the Duke of Bedford wears flowers."

What pleased him most in Paris when he had settled in there was that old people could still be charming, and nobody thought it odd. "Though the fountain of youth is not here, the fountain of age is, which comes to pretty much the same thing," he wrote to Lady Hervey, the greatest lover of France among all his English friends. "One is never old here or never thought so. One makes verses as if one were seventeen—and has no fear of being laughed at."

The gayest of all the gay people, the wittiest of the witty, the best maker of these verses of light mockery or airy compliment, was a lady of sixty-eight who had been blind since she was fifty, yet whose salon was one of the most reputed in that age.

It is well to put together the dates of this extraordinary pair of allies. Madame du Deffand was born in 1697, while Louis XIV and William III were still fiercely at war. In 1717, the year when Horace Walpole was born, she was a young woman married to a dull man, and flung herself into the society over which the Regent presided : for a fortnight she was even the Regent's mistress. After ten years' experience of libertinage, she settled down, in 1730—when Horace Walpole was an Eton boy—to live with her brother, a Canon, in the Rue de Beaune, and maintained a steady liaison with President Henault, a distinguished lawyer and man of letters, who was her senior by some ten or twelve years. When she received her friends in the Rue de Beaune, or (after her husband's death) in the rooms once occupied by Madame de

Montespan in St. Joseph's convent, Henault was always of the company.

Indeed from the time when she settled into this apartment, the President and she appear to have seen each other only as old friends between whom inveterate habit was the strongest bond. She was fifty when she moved in to the apartment that she rendered so famous; and though when she was forming her salon, her sight had not failed, this tragedy was not far off. It left her terribly alone : and the idea came then that she should go down to live with her kindred in the country. There she found installed at Champrond Julie de l'Espinasse, the illegitimate daughter of Madame d'Albon, whose legitimate daughter was married to Madame du Deffand's brother, Gaspard de Vichy, master of Champrond. Madame du Deffand may or may not have known then, but she knew later, and Julie knew later, that Gaspard de Vichy had been the lover of Madame d'Albon, and by her the father of Julie, before he became the husband of her other daughter.

It is not surprising that the family were trying to push Julie into a convent. Madame du Deffand saw another way and took the girl to Paris to share her household and help in her entertainments. That was in 1754. By 1764 Julie de l'Espinasse was a serious rival to the mistress of the salon, and had above all secured the devotion of d'Alembert, one of the chief notabilities among its habitual guests. Matters came to a breach, and Madame du Deffand, a passionate woman, had little welcome for those who frequented the rival salon which Julie had set up.

Her anger, her disappointment, were still rankling and unappeased when Horace Walpole—he also with his load of grievances—came to Paris in the middle of September, 1765, alighting at the door of Lady Hertford, wife of his cousin, who had just ceased to be ambassador. The Richmonds, who were to succeed the Hertfords, had not yet arrived.

From the background of Paris, Madame du Deffand does

not at once emerge on the picture which Walpole's correspondence builds up. We can trace the growth of her ascendant in the hundred pages or so of Cunningham's edition that cover the six months of his story in Paris. Indeed we can follow the whole of his reactions to this new and stimulating scene. Lady Hervey got the first account of them, and it is chiefly concerned with the narrowness of the streets, the trees clipped like sweeping brooms—and the dirt. None the less, he found himself wonderfully disposed to like the country. "Indeed, I wish I could wash it." All Lady Hervey's friends, all Lady Hertford's friends, gave him welcome. David Hume, the philosopher, who had been Hertford's secretary and who now was chargé d'affaires, proved a valuable standby; for Hume was prodigiously the fashion, being an Englishman, a philosopher and a free-thinker. Walpole was a good deal shocked by the tone of conversation.

"Freethinking is for one's self, surely not for society; besides, one has settled one's way of thinking, or knows it cannot be settled, and for others I do not see why there is not as much bigotry in attempting conversions from any religion as to it. I dined to-day with a dozen *savants*, and though all the servants were waiting, the conversation was much more unrestrained, even on the Old Testament, than I would suffer at my own table in England, if a single footman were present."

He was presented at Court, and found there as elsewhere "a mixture of parade and poverty"; people selling all sorts of wares in the colonnades, on the staircases and in the very anti-chamber of the royal family: two fellows sweeping the floor of the Dauphin's sumptuous bedchamber and dancing about in sabots to rub the floor even while company waited there to see him emerge.

The Dauphin was dying; that was the daily news of the day; or rather it came next to the "*bête du Giraudan*," a monstrous wolf which had just been slain after legendary depredations and was to be viewed in the palace. Indeed, even to-day books are still being written about this portent; it easily outlasted the poor Dauphin in public interest.

Madame du Deffand's name appears first in October: "an old blind debauchée of wit, at whose table the President Henault, very near deaf and much nearer superannuated," was the principal person. There is no suggestion that Horace was attracted by her or by her company; but six weeks later he quotes a verse riddle of hers to Lady Hervey and says, "I sup there very often." And to George Selwyn he writes this acknowledgment for what appears to have been the fateful introduction:

"I was in your debt before, for making over Madame du Deffand to me, who is delicious; that is, as often as I can get her fifty years back; but she is as eager about what happens every day as I am about the last century. I sup there twice a week, and bear all her dull company for the sake of the Regent. I might go to her much oftener, but my curiosity to see everybody and every thing is insatiable."

In short, from the first he was inclined to treat her as a living document—especially concerning a period celebrated for its improprieties—while she on her part was finding him just the company that suited her. Her mind, like his, had a great dislike of all enthusiasm; she liked facts, not theories; she hated metaphysics and loved the dry light of the intellect—sometimes for the fine things it showed her, but more often for the pleasure of laughter. He kept her laughing; she said he had *le fou moquer*, that he went into convulsions of mockery. But also she wanted his affection, and by the New Year it was clear that she had at least his partisanship. A very long letter to Gray describing Paris and its people makes complaint of Frenchmen's dullness.

"They have taken up gravity, thinking it was philosophy and English, and so have acquired nothing in the room of their natural levity and cheerfulness. The women do not seem of the same country; if they are less gay than they were, they are more informed. Enough to make them very conversible. I know six or seven with very superior understandings."

Then follows a list of them with this central passage:

"Madame du Deffand was for a short time mistress of the Regent, is now very old and stone-blind, but retains all her vivacity, wit, memory, judgment, passions, and agreeableness. She goes to Operas, Plays, suppers, and Versailles; gives suppers twice a week; has everything new read to her; makes new songs and epigrams, ay, admirably, and remembers every one that has been made these fourscore years. She corresponds with Voltaire, dictates charming letters to him, contradicts him, is no bigot to him or anybody, and laughs both at the clergy and the philosophers. In a dispute, into which she easily falls, she is very warm, and yet scarce ever in the wrong: her judgment on every subject is as just as possible; on every point of conduct, as wrong as possible for she is all love and hatred, passionate for her friends to enthusiasm, still anxious to be loved, I don't mean by lovers, and a vehement enemy, but openly. As she can have no amusement but conversation, the least solitude and ennui are insupportable to her, and put her into the power of several worthless people, who eat her suppers when they can get nobody's of higher rank; wink to one another and laugh at her; hate her because she has forty times more parts—and venture to hate her because she is not rich."

That is written with detachment to one remote from the scene: but it gives the key to all that followed: She still wants to be loved, "I don't mean by lovers." A blind woman at sixty-eight with this craving is singularly vulnerable: and Horace Walpole was soon involved, for the first time perhaps, in a relation charged with emotion.

One of the men who always frequented Madame du Deffand's salon was James Crawford, a Scotch member of Parliament, much younger than Walpole but a fellow-

Etonian : Eton had given him the nickname by which he is
known all through the Memoirs of that period—" Fish Crawford." There had been chaff as to whether he or Walpole
were the ruling favourite : but he had disappeared to England
and made no sign, till in March a letter came which Walpole
hailed with joy, " not so much for my sake as for Madame
du Deffand's, because it wipes off the reproaches she has
undergone on your account."

" They have at once twitted her with her partiality for you
and your indifference. . . . Your good old woman wept
like a child, with her poor no eyes as I read your letter to her.
I did not wonder ; it is kind, friendly, delicate and just—so
just that it vexes me to be forced so continually to combat the
goodness of her heart, and destroy her fond visions of friendship. ' Ah ! but,' said she at last, ' he does not talk of returning.' ! I told her, if anything could bring you back, or me
either, it would be desire of seeing her. I think so of you, and
I am sure so of myself. . . . You will forgive these details
about a person you love, and have so much reason to love ;
nor am I ashamed of interesting myself exceedingly about her.
To say nothing of her extraordinary parts, she is certainly the
most generous friendly being upon earth—but neither these
qualities nor her unfortunate situation touch her unworthy
acquaintance. Do you know that she was quite angry about
the money you left for her servants ? Wiart would by no
means touch it, and when I tried all I could to obtain her
permission for their taking it, I prevailed so little, that she gave
Wiart five louis for refusing it."

Every word in that rings true ; there is genuine affection
and genuine concern. But observe what follows. Crawford
had made protestations of friendship to Walpole, who
promptly mounts the pulpit :

" I must preach to you as I do to your friend " (meaning
Madame du Deffand). " Consider how little time you have
known me . . . consider my heart is not like yours, young,

good, warm, sincere, and impatient to bestow itself. Mine is worn with the baseness, treachery, and mercenariness I have met with. It is suspicious, doubtful and cooled. I consider everything round me but in the light of amusement, because if I looked at it seriously, I should detest it. . . . I converse with Madames de Mirepoix, Boufflers, and Luxembourg, that I may not love Madame du Deffand too much—and yet they do but make me love her more. But don't love me, pray don't love me. Old folks are but old women, who love their last lovers as much as they did their first. I should still be liable to believe you, and I am not at all of Madame du Deffand's opinion, that one might as well be dead as not love somebody. I think one had better be dead than love anybody."

All this is play-acting : the sham cynicism that is the obverse to sham sentimentalism. Here was a creature full of generous impulses, and affectionate instincts, who could not let himself be himself because he was afraid of his own image in the glass : about to destroy all the charm of what might have been a beautiful relationship, and to neutralize the worth of his own very remarkable fidelity and devotion, for the paltriest apprehension.

This failure had yet to come : but the factors which caused it were present from the first. For the moment however, it is to be noted that Walpole came away from England, hurt in his heart by disappointment in friendship. He found in Paris a new friendship whose quality he never questioned, heaped upon him by a nature of whose distinction, to do him justice, he was fully aware. He never doubted, in his own mind, that the old blind woman's choice of him did him high honour ; and when he said to Crawford that if he came back to Paris, it would be for her only, he spoke sincerely—even if there was a touch of exaggeration.

Yet Paris had been more than commonly kind to this witty foreigner, and he amused himself to the top of his bent, when the gout would let him. For gout came on him and he was laid up in the apartment he had taken on the left bank of the Seine, in the Rue du Colombier which prolongs the Rue Jacob. We have a description of his day there from Cole the antiquary who—to Walpole's great joy—came out that autumn and got quarters near to his friend. On the day in question, October 17, 1765, Cole went to dine at three with Mr. Walpole (he had a standing invitation). After dinner came in the young Duke of Beaufort with his governor, Mr. Lyte, and Lord William Gordon. The two young men and their bear-leader having withdrawn, in came an elderly French lady of about sixty years of age, to drink tea with Mr. Walpole. This was Madame Geoffrin who immediately flung herself carelessly " into an Elbow Chair, almost half reclined, with a leg thrown on the knee of the other," and indeed Mr. Cole did not like the look of her. But she stayed and talked for two or three hours. Next Mr. Wilkes was announced. But though Wilkes was then in Paris, this proved to be Lord Ossory, a young man with whom Walpole was greatly taken. After these calls, there would be a sally forth into the world, Walpole would " fix at nine for the evening," sup, drink coffee and sit up till half-past two ; " if I meet Madame de Mirepoix, drink tea and stay later." For, as he told Lady Mary Coke, in the letter from which these words are quoted, " having no terrors of gravity before my eyes, I amuse myself as foolishly as I please all day long."

Mornings were spent in bed, unless he went out in his carriage with Cole to see churches or convents, or to buy china, at prices that even now sound stiff. The dinner at three was apt to be " a no-dinner " ; he ate like a sparrow. But there was no doubt of his social success. " It would sound vain to tell you the honours and distinctions I receive, and how much I am in the fashion ; yet when they come from the handsomest women in France, and the most respectable in point of character, can one help being a little proud ? " he wrote to Conway.

All this had been heightened by a *jeu d'esprit*. Rousseau was then at the zenith of his fame and of his foppery, and when there was talk of his personality at Madame Geoffrin's house, Walpole said some things that diverted the company. He said in effect that Frederick the Great, so noted an admirer of the French genius, ought to offer Rousseau an asylum, adding, " If you really want misfortunes, I am a king and can provide them, as many as you please ; but I can stop persecuting you when you cease to pride yourself on being persecuted." That was the pith of the idea which was put in a letter, signed " Frederick " and duly published. Paris was enchanted, Rousseau was furious, and there were reverberations of the affair in England where Rousseau was then staying.

Walpole wrote to Mann from Calais on his way back :

" How I like France upon the whole ? So well that I shall certainly return hither. I have received most uncommon civilities and real marks of friendship and shall ever preserve great gratitude for them."

After all, it was not only Madame du Deffand : *Me voici à la mode* counted for something. He had forgotten for a while that horror of the discomforts of travelling which made him write to Conway from Paris, " if I once get to London again, I shall be scarce tempted to lie in an inn more." Yet I think there can be no doubt that when he wrote to Mann from Calais, his heart was full of enthusiastic purpose to fulfil the expectations which he had left behind him.

For it is plain from Madame du Deffand's letters to him (of which we have three large volumes) that this sentimentalist turned cynic had forgotten his own chosen attitude. The parting with his friend had been charged with emotion on both sides ; and from the first halting-place at Chantilly, he had written to her as a lover might have done to his mistress, with assurances of his speedy return. And though after a few score leagues more were past, he resumed his old admonitions against demonstrative affection, still his mind was full of her.

From a picture by M. Carmontel formerly at Strawberry Hill

DUCHESSE DE CHOISEUL, AND MADAME
LA MARQUISE DE DEFFAND

For while he waited for the tide at Calais, he addressed to Lady George Lennox, who with her husband had made part of the Richmond household, a letter full of his characteristic elaborate ingenuity—and evidently written for the sake of the last word in it. "Thank Lord George and yourself for all your goodness to me, and now and then spare a moment to my dear old woman." The lady acted on his wish, and in September another letter of witty compliment went to her with this for its burden: "Tho' I have a mind to scold you, I cannot help thanking you, because the less you like the French, the more sensible I am of the goodness you have had for my old woman." And in England his friends evidently heard a great deal about this adoration. Another elderly countess settled down near Twickenham. "If she is only lame, what with the deaf one and the blind one, I shall see nothing of you," said Mrs. Clive.

We have it on Walpole's authority that the likeness of her in the picture reproduced opposite to page 208 is very good. It hung at Strawberry Hill. He was by no means pleased with the presentment of Madame de Choiseul (who is shown offering a doll to the old lady: it was a joke between them that Madame du Deffand was young enough to be the young Duchess's granddaughter and Madame de Choiseul was always "*la grand'maman*.")

As for Horace Walpole himself, Eccardt's portrait shows him as he may have been at this time. It is very hard to reconcile it with the other likeness given opposite page 60; and Hone has certainly suggested admirably the young gentleman who masqueraded joyously at Venice and was a "dancing senator" in London. But the mouth is full and sensuous to a degree that one can hardly reconcile with all we know of the man's abstemiousness; and Eccardt shows it tightly primmed up. The artists agree on one point, the character of his eyes. All that Madame du Deffand ever knew of his appearance was that her friends told her that he had *les plus beaux yeux du monde.* Hone perhaps fits with that. Eccardt's view of him lends itself to illustrate the wonderful pen portrait which a score of commentators have quoted, beginning with Sir Walter Scott in his preface to a reprint of *The Castle of Otranto.* It shall be given here once more.

The writer was Miss Laetitia Hawkins, daughter of Walpole's neighbour at Twickenham, the Sir John Hawkins who figures largely in Johnsonian literature. But those who turn to her " Anecdotes," hoping to find more of this quality, risk disappointment. Walpole's " highly gentlemanly " personality was the perfect subject for her pen.

" His figure, as has been told, and every one knows, was not merely tall, but more properly *long* and slender to excess ; his complexion and particularly his hands, of a most unhealthy paleness. I speak of him before the year 1772. His eyes were remarkably bright and penetrating, very dark and lively :—his voice was not strong, but his tones were extremely pleasant, and if I may so say, highly gentlemanly. I do not remember his common gait ; he always entered a room in that style of affected delicacy, which fashion had then made almost natural ; *chapeau bras* between his hands as if he wished to compress it, or under his arm—knees bent, and feet on tip-toe, as if afraid of a wet floor.

His dress in visiting was most usually, in summer when I most saw him, a lavender suit, the waistcoat embroidered with a little silver or of white silk worked in the tambour, partridge silk stockings, and gold buckles, ruffles and frill, generally lace. I remember, when a child, thinking him very much under-dressed, if at any time except in mourning, he wore hemmed cambric. In summer no powder, but his wig combed straight, and showing his very smooth ·le forehead, and queued behind :—in winter, powder."

CHAPTER X

MADAME DU DEFFAND

PARIS had thrown something of a spell on this Englishman to whom it gave so warm a welcome; and the
bright air suited his constitution. He had left it in March,
1766, and before the next spring came he told Mann that
he was meditating another visit "not for pleasure, but a
little for health, and still more for my charming, blind old
woman, Madame du Deffand." She on her part had hoped
for him in November, and was counting on him for February.
But Walpole was still in parliament, and still making it the
main business of his life to serve Conway, whose position
in the midst of all the current intrigues for place was complicated by his own vacillation. Conway indeed wanted to
be out of political life, and entrusted with a military post, for
which he had more talent. But his cousin, more ambitious
for him than he for himself, staved off various tendencies to
resignation, and (at least by his own account in the *Memoirs*)
served the King by retaining to the Court these valued
services. It was indeed so plain to him that George III
knew of this debt that he once more considered that an
easy opportunity offered itself to Conway of gratifying his
supporter's chief wish. There was the more occasion because
Sir Edward Walpole was seriously ill, and Horace was
threatened with that considerable loss of income which came
later. But once more Conway took no step, and once more
Horace Walpole committed to paper the resentment that he
hid from his friend.

By July matters were to some degree settled. Parliament adjourned, and Horace Walpole was free to pay in

1767 the visit that had been so long and so impatiently desired.

Indeed, when we come to read in Madame du Deffand's letters the reiteration of that longing, it is impossible not to feel (as, for example, Mr. Lytton Strachey does) that Walpole was a paltry creature not to have gone to her much earlier and returned much oftener. It is well, therefore, to recall how things looked to Walpole's contemporary George Montagu, who realized what travelling meant in that age.

Walpole had written to him from Calais, just arrived after a crossing of nine hours—of which he makes no complaint; but for George Montagu the sea had awful terrors. What Walpole dreaded more particularly was the inn—especially the French inn; and to reach Paris he must lie at least four nights in inns, French or English, and spend at least four days driving over bumpy roads in a postchaise. George Montagu thought this no small matter. "Why then the Lord above Reward your love to an old woman poor and blind," he wrote. "Your letter is a proof you are well and in good spirits to take such a trip *de gaieté de cœur*. I would give half the money I have been scraping together to be able to please myself at a moment's warning and run to Paris as easily as to Hampton Court. You have enlightened me all over by seeing you so light."

Indeed, the journey to Constantinople nowadays would be far less formidable to a chronic invalid, such as Walpole had become. Mr. Lytton Strachey, and the rest of us, before we find fault with this " Knight errant " (as he called himself to Montagu), and write him down laggard in the quest for his " old fairy," ought really to consider whether if, say at Fez, there was a lady of seventy who loved us, we should be oftener on the road to pay homage than was this elderly martyr to gout.

Still, I defy anyone who reads the correspondence not to become the lady's partisan; her vitality, her sincerity, and her passion are so astonishing, her spirit so high. For she is none of the meek ; she hits back, she slaps his face when his lecturing becomes insufferable ; but in the end nothing offends against good sense, and real affection. She humbles herself, this proud fierce woman, yet she keeps her essential dignity. Instinct drives her to rebel, to push matters to a final quarrel ; but her clear trenchant intellect soon brings her to a sense of the realities. She is giving more than he gives, in one sense ; yet in another she knows that she gets more than she has the power of giving. She even exaggerates the inequality : " Fate has decided that I should be able to contribute nothing to my tutor's happiness and that he should be the trouble, the occupation, and the delight of my last years."

That word " tutor " is at the root of the mischief. Walpole always liked to behave as if he were in a comedy, to play the fool a little, to put sweet peas in his hair, one way or other, with his *sorcières* : and the game that had been established during his long evenings with Madame du Deffand was that he should be the wise elder and she the tender pupil. It was not entirely of his devising ; her perpetual youth was a byword and the tiny exquisite Duchesse de Choiseul always insisted on being *grand'maman* to the old blind maker of songs and epigrams. Horace Walpole, entering into the spirit of this, assumed the rôle of tutor to Madame de Choiseul's " granddaughter," and she—since she had fallen in love with him, there is no other word for it—gladly adopted his humour, and they were " *mon tuteur* " and " *ma petite* " to each other. Since in a society that professed devotion to metaphysics and philosophy, they agreed in common detestation of these abstract subjects, what was there for him to instruct his pupil in but the lessons of experience ? He told her, for his mind was full of it, that he had suffered greatly through friendship ; it is plain enough from many passages that she at least knew of his grievance against Conway ("*votre cousin*"). If he had gone to her experience for counsel, he could not have done better than unpack his bosom of this poison. But unluckily that was not in the part. He was there to teach, not to be taught, and he was bitten with a deadly temptation. Stevenson has written in *Weir of Hermiston* about the schoolmaster latent in all men, who raises his head when there is a plain issue to be complicated. Kirsty in the story is in her lover's hands to do with as he will; his love of power finds a gratification in trying to protect her against herself; he must be wiser than all the promptings of nature. This other story is like a caricature of that; but in essence one finds, I think, a man subject to the same intoxication. So far as the multifarious volumes of correspondence can inform us, no woman had ever before put herself unreservedly in Horace Walpole's hands, giving him the power to make daylight and dark for her. Now, in this fantastic way, a woman who was still admired and courted, still a power, who had gone through her period of *galanterie*, and her later period of a settled liaison, but now was done these many years with all tie of the senses, still had the impulse to give her affection so unreservedly that her happiness was in the hands of him to whom she gave it. Power makes tyrants; that was one of the commonplaces to which Horace Walpole was specially addicted. But he never guessed that it made a tyrant of him—benevolent no doubt, and affectionate, but tyrannical and capricious; for he did not even play the game according to the rules he had laid down.

One is hampered here by the variation in shades of meaning: "*aimer*" has more meanings than "to love"; there had evidently been much discussion of this, and the word was ruled out as dangerous. So at least it would appear from the first of all these letters—more than eight hundred, spread out over fourteen years.

"Vous avez raison d'aimer Mme. de Choiseul (*aimer*,

pardonnez moi ce mot, nous sommes convenus de sa significa-
tion), elle pense de vous comme moi—elle en parle comme
j'en parlerais si vous ne me l'aviez défendu."

But then comes rebellion : woman goes direct to her
end. · " I can follow neither your advice nor your example :
I might add, nor my experience. Come what may, I shall
be *votre amie* in spite of you and in spite of common sense."

Who was to blame her ? The pedant had written her
a line to reach her on the morning of his departure which
had " increased in me—this forbidden word." More than
that, from the first halt at Chantilly, he had sent her back a
letter which we have not got, but which appears to have
been almost a declaration. But there was time to reflect in
the postchaise, and from the next stage came what was
designed for an antidote ; a warning against " indiscretions "
and " romantic effusions." When this reached her, swift as
lightning—for the process of breaking in had only begun—
comes the slap. " Si vous etiez Français, je ne balancerais
pas à vous croire un grand fat ; vous êtes Anglais, vous
n'êtes donc qu'un grand fou. 'Romantic effusion' indeed!
I, the declared enemy of whatever has the least touch
of such things, I, who have always made war on them, who
have made enemies for myself of all who fall into such
absurdity, am I to be accused of it to-day ?"

Still, she put up with it. Fierce creature though she was,
she had learnt in twelve years the dreadful meekness of the
blind. She could not afford to risk this tie that was the
trouble and the pleasure of a life without resource except
the spoken or the written word. In her strange existence
there was only one mechanical contrivance against the scourge
of ennui. Hours and hours she would be busy pulling to
shreds old fragments of silk, and separating out the threads,
so that they could be woven up again into new pieces which
she gave her friends. All the rest of her life, when she had
not company, went in listening to books read to her, and

dictating letters—or now and then making up little songs. Sleep was hard to come by and it came mostly after the nights were over. She saw no one, she went nowhere, till four in the afternoon; then she came alive, received guests, gave them supper at nine o'clock or so, and stayed up talking as late as anyone could be found to sit with her. Then came the dark hours, great part of which she would spend in writing, sometimes with a machine devised to guide her hand, but oftener dictating to her devoted secretary, Wiart—whose existence must have been almost as strange as hers.

It was worth more to her than anything imaginable to have a friend on whom she could bestow these vacant hours : to whom she could pour out her talk on paper, since he was not there to hear. All she asked was leave to talk freely, to let her fondness for him find vent in words. But this was harshly denied her. Letters—he was willing to have as many letters as she could send; but they must keep within the prescribed bounds; they must be gossip and commentary, all she had learned, all she had observed—but nothing of what she felt. Feeling brought in inevitably the forbidden words; and he was haunted by the knowledge that letters were opened in the post, that letters to a man close in confidence of ministers would certainly not escape notice (indeed we know that several of his to her were copied in the French government's *cabinet noir*; the official copies have been unearthed). They would go to the King and his circle : they would be talked of; and he would be laughed at for maintaining a love correspondence with a lady of seventy. Again and again he scolds her as if she were a schoolgirl because she risked bringing ridicule upon him. She must watch her tongue as well as her pen; she must not talk of him. And again and again she submits to defend herself, to assure him that his name has not crossed her lips, not even when she had natural occasion to talk of him.

He makes no scruple of admitting his obsession. She

need not think, he says, that she put it into him. " Long
before our acquaintance began, this dread of ridicule had
taken root in my heart and you must remember how I was
possessed by it and how often I spoke of it. Ever since I
ceased to be young, I have had a horrible fear of becoming
a ridiculous old man." It never weighs with him, though as
time goes on she points it out sharply, that these letters of
his with their sermons upon discretion, assuming them to
be read in the post, are the surest means to make a laughing
stock of her; and she has enemies enough.—One loses all
patience with the man. If he had been content to say, " let
us suppress these pet names, *mon tuteur* and *ma petite* " —
(for these did give a handle to mockery), he would have
written sensibly : but when she is moved, when she is writing in all seriousness, her phrase, *mon bon, mon très bon
ami*, is touching and is beautiful. As for what she has to
say, for what she wants to say, there is never matter for
mockery, not even to the coarsest mind. We know what
she valued in him ; she liked his mind, his wit, but above
all she thought him honest, genuine, kind and sincere beyond
other men she had known. What she loved in him was,
in short, not the thin-skinned sentimentalist, so easily tortured
by dread of what other folks might think, but the friend
who for fifteen years would keep up week by week this
correspondence with an old blind woman, and five times
would push aside his valetudinarianism and his padded ease
to undertake a long disagreeable journey for her sake.

If we are to be fair, we have to keep on remembering
the whole story, this long tract of time from his forty-eighth
year to his sixty-third ; we must say to ourselves that few
men in that day, or in any day, would have been capable
of so long sustained a devotion. But we cannot shut our
eyes to his stupidity. A few weeks after he came back from
that first visit in 1765–6, he found on his table in Arlington
Street a tiny box with a medallion portrait of his adored

Madame de Sevigné. Enclosed with it was a letter signed by the lady herself, to her adorer—dated " from the Elysian Fields " where there were no dates, for no time changes. Here is a translation—

" I know your mad passion for me ; your worship of my letters, your recent pilgrimages to the places I lived in ; I have been aware of the homage you paid me ; it has touched me so deeply that I have asked and obtained permission from my Sovereign to come and stay with you always. . . . I was allowed to choose the age at which I should wish to appear to you ; I choose five and twenty that you might be better pleased. Have no fear of alteration ; the Shades have this singular privilege that though light they are unchangeable. I chose my shape as small as possible so that I need never be separated from you. By sea, by land, in town, in country, I desire to be your companion everywhere ; but what I demand is that you should bring me without delay to France and let me see my own country and Paris town, and that you should choose the Faubourg St. Germain to live in : my best friends lived there, yours live there now ; you shall make me acquainted with them ; I should be glad to see if they are worthy of you, and worthy to be the rivals of
RABUTIN DE SEVIGNÉ."

Naturally the happy man was delighted with his offering, showed it to all his friends, French and English—and confided to them his conviction that it came from Madame de Choiseul, the tiny, enchanting wife of Louis XVI's chief Minister. He consulted everybody as to what he should do, and some advised him to write the Duchess his acknowledgments at once. Never for an instant did he guess who the author was : he wrote to his old friend, she answered him in riddles— secretly piqued, as she admitted later, that her hand should not have been recognized at once. Meanwhile, however, seeing that he was on a wrong scent, she sent him word through " le petit Crauford " that she was the guilty one.

Thereupon, instead of abusing himself for stupidity, he flies
out into rages over the absurd figure that she would have
made him cut, had he indeed written to Madame de Choiseul.
Letter follows letter, she scolding him for his absurdities, he
still raging against her indiscretion ; and in the end, although
while he believed Madame de Choiseul to have been the
author, she heard praise heaped on the wit and the charm
of the dear ghost's letter, the true and only begetter
and devisor of this charming mystification gets not a word
of thanks, not a trace of tenderness, in response to her
ingenious way of saying that France wants him back.

In short, he does his best to kill all springs of gaiety
in her, he checks the natural flow of her mind ; and then
when her letters begin to be full of lamentations, he writes
her from Strawberry Hill a letter which is only excusable
because it is written in a language for whose inflections he
has not the complete feeling that a man has for his native
tongue :

" Vraiment si l'amitié a tous les ennuis de l'amour sans
en avoir les plaisirs, je ne vois rien qui invite à en tâter. . . .
Si vous voulez que notre commerce dure, montez-le sur un
ton moins tragique."

She may well talk in reply of " l'insolentissime correction
que vous me faites." It is not conceivable that Horace
Walpole would have permitted himself language of such
brutality if using his own tongue, for he always exaggerated
deference when he wrote to a lady. Yet, in this case, he was
writing to a woman who put herself unreservedly in his
hands ; he has almost a marital freedom ; and he uses it to
inflict his lordly anger.

So it goes on ; and except for a few brusque movements,
there is no limit to her patience, nor to its clear-sightedness :

" If I had any self-love, you would have crushed it long
ago ; but it is a feeling that I never let myself listen to when
you are in question ; your outspokenness has never hurt me,

I have never felt humiliated. Your fears about ridicule are a panic, but there is no cure for fear : I have never met a weakness like yours : I know that at my age one is protected against the possibility of scandal : if one loves, there is no reason to hide it : *amitié* will never be a ridiculous sentiment when it does not lead to folly ; but let us avoid the name since you have such excellent reasons for banning it : let us be *amis sans amitié* : it is a new system, but after all no more incomprehensible than the Trinity."

She knows him for " a mixture of kindness, of harshness, of reasonableness, and of caprice . . . a man made of stone or of snow, in short, an Englishman, who would be all this on theory if it were not his birthright." She uses phrases about her old ally, President Henault, which perhaps are meant to carry further.

" His head is as full of trifles as his heart is empty of affection ; he wants a perpetual magic-lantern, which will keep all sorts of objects moving before his eyes, and all of them equally indifferent to him. They say (it is your theory) that he is lucky to care for nothing. Ah ! I am far from thinking that way."

Yet this is only one side of the picture. He has spoken to her of his gratitude. She answers—

" You owe me nothing : I followed my inclination : I thought you different from anything I had seen, you answered to the conception I had formed of what an honourable man should be (*d'un parfaitement honnête homme*). . . ."

The tie was not only of friendship : it was of taste : " a feeling " (she says) " that youth knows less of than any other age ; not in the least a seduction of the senses, but a bond, a suitability—something hard to define : deepseated."

It had to do with his race.

" I would choose an Englishman for my intimacy, but for ordinary intercourse, for society, give me Frenchmen. One likes to see one's friend as he is, but it is better to see the rest of the world as they wish to appear. Englishmen do not live by rule : they let their genius develop on its own lines ; their minds would be what they are, if no one had had a mind before them. We are not like that ; we have our books ; manuals on the art of speaking, of writing, of judging, and so on. We are the children of art : anyone perfectly natural among us would be fit to show at a fair ; a phenomenon—but it will never occur."

None the less, praise him or blame him, we cannot ignore what he was worth to her. She says :

" I take care of my health for your sake, for without you I should have no concern to live : everything shocks me, annoys me, and bores me. I had a friend for thirty years " (this was a M. Formart) ; "I lost him ; I loved two women most passionately ; one is dead—the other lives and has betrayed me. You have made up for these three losses, but you are a foreigner, any day you may be an enemy : and then, the ocean, your business, and most of all, your health, inevitably keep us apart. Still, I am thankful to have known you ; to live without loving someone is to die daily, and, as La Fontaine says, better suffer than die is the motto of all mankind."

That was written in March, 1767, a year after he had first left her ; he had raised her hopes of seeing him in February and then coolly dashed them. Yet here is her considered judgment : it was worth the pain.

Affection apart, he was a bewilderment to her : now he was writing about his project of a new book " Historic Doubts of Richard III," undertaken to consider whether after all this monarch had so many ugly stains on his hands.

" How did you come to form such a queer project, and how can you possibly look for amusement in it ? Oh ! your head is indescribable " (*ineffable*—it was one of her pet words). " All that I understand is that, thanks to all your hobbies, you must be sure of never being bored, and that gives you the greatest advantage that there is in the world."

She comes back to this again in another letter. "Your head is a shipload of resources against boredom ; each has its little compartment, you skip from one to another, and are equally happy with them all. I would rather have this gift than be heir in general to the Pulteney millions."

So the litany goes on : divided between pleasure and vexation, the cry for his coming always repeated, yet always checked by fear for his health and fear of importunity. And when at last his return was settled for August, she was full of terror lest a new meeting should bring him disappointment.

All passed off radiantly on that visit ; her letters are happy after his departure and give little suggestions of his drawling French " *Non, po-int du tout ; au contr-aire*," and his way of shaking hands, one finger out, and then the " *petite secousse.*" But soon the scoldings and the remonstrances begin : she complains that his letters, though they come as regularly as pay-day, look like the settlement of a debt of gratitude ; they are impersonal and might as well be addressed to any one else. Worst of all, when things go wrong, he calls her " Madame "—" It is like the whip for children," she says, " you are too harsh a schoolmaster."

Still he filled her life—he, and the delightful little Duchess who played at being grand'maman. " You two have the exclusive privilege of putting up with my melancholy," she writes. But it is the grand'maman who always gives her spirit to carry on, not the *tuteur* : " Ware the post—a sheet of paper can upset all my cardhouse of happiness."

The extraordinary thing is that when he did set out again to see her, in August, 1769, things were better than ever between them : her spirits were so high that he told her she " would go mad with age,"—and his description of her to George Montagu, written in this year, is the best known of all. " She r akes songs, sings them, remembers all that were ever made; and having lived from the most agreeable to the most reasoning age, has all that was amiable in the last, and all that is sensible in this, without the vanity of the former or the pedant impertinences of the latter."

The only trouble was that she lived too strenuously. If they were back by one o'clock in the morning from a supper in the country, she would propose a drive in the Boulevard because it was too early to go to bed. Everything that could be organized to amuse him was organized. Yet he tells Montagu that he felt ashamed to be dragging his withered person through a round of diversions that he had quitted at home; he sighed to be in his quiet castle and cottage. "But it costs me many a pang, when I reflect that I shall probably never have resolution enough to take another journey to see this best and sincerest of friends, who loves me as much as my mother did."

That rings true. And when that visit came to a parting, once more he wrote a letter from a halt on the road, that seemed to her even more affectionate than the earlier note from Chantilly.

"I am content with you beyond words, but am ill-pleased with myself; I cause you a thousand troubles and fatigues, I abuse your kindness; I am not worth it; I feel all this more than I can say," was her acknowledgment.

He was by this time almost as well known in Paris as in London; and during that stay he had been able to glut his curiosity about the promoted courtesan, of whose rise Madame du Deffand's letter had been full. She was well placed to know, for the du Barri's chief object was to displace Choiseul, whose wife was Madame du Deffand's closest intimate. Walpole was the less concerned for this, because he thought Choiseul ambitious and eager to get revenge on England for Pitt's victories. He loved Madame du Deffand, he liked many Frenchwomen but few Frenchmen, and he had no feeling for France as France. "Paris revived in me that national passion, the love of my country's glory," he writes to Mann. " I must put it out : it is a wicked passion, and breathes war. It is self-love and vanity at bottom, and insolence easily rekindles it. Well! I will go home, love my neighbour, and pray for peace."

Three months later another letter fills this out.

" I have received an odd indirect overture myself, not from Administration nor Opposition, but from France. M. de Choiseul has a great desire that I should be Ambassador at that Court. As no man upon earth is less a Frenchman, as you know, than I am, I did not at all taste the proposal, nay, not his making it. I sent him word in plain terms that he could not have desired a person that would suit him less ; that whatever private connections or friendships I have in France, however grateful I may be for the kindness I have met with there, yet, the moment I should be Ambassador, he would find me more haughty and inflexible than all the English put together ; and that though I wish for peace between the two countries, I should be much more likely to embroil them than preserve union, for that nothing upon earth could make me depart from the smallest punctilio, in which the honour of my nation should be concerned. I do not think he will desire me to be sent thither."

The overture had come, of course, through Madame du Deffand.

After that journey in 1769, Walpole was relieved of one anxiety ; he carried back the whole packet of his letters. When she restored them, she bade him, if he re-read them, remember that *l'amitié a plus d'un langage* ; and that, to her thinking, a lady of seventy writing to her friend might use the tone *of a mother to her daughter*. That was her way of reminding him that his cherished Madame de Sevigné was not slow to let her love find words.

Yet next year things were worse than ever between them. He had been gravely ill ; his niece, Mrs. Cholmondeley, was in Paris, seeing much of Madame du Deffand; of her, Madame du Deffand made inquiry concerning his health; when he learned this, he accused her promptly of theatrically affecting an indecent anxiety. Then indeed she turned on him.

"Either you have no more affection for me or are ashamed to have it. My age and the misfortunes that go with it give a fine opening for fools and bad-hearted people to laugh at you about our connection. The shadow of ridicule is enough to make you give up the truest friend you have had or can have. Still, if you believe that I am playing a part, there is nothing for it but to leave me. Only, Sir, if you were mistaken, would not you need to reproach yourself all your life with having put the crowning stroke to the sorrows of these last days of mine?"

Once more there was a gradual renewal of confidence; yet at the beginning of 1771 one finds her owning to a "sort of terror when I write."

"It is a great trouble in friendship not to be able to speak out what one thinks, what one feels, in short not to be free to give affection after one's own fashion. You have not lessened my regard nor even my attachment, but you have toned down their keenness and perhaps have taken the sweetness out of them."

There was too always hanging over her the dread of war that must bar all meetings: but the threat passed and that year, in 1771, he came again.

"Nothing, I think, but my dear old woman could draw me so far, and nothing but her shall I see," he wrote to Mann, with sad complaints over leaving Strawberry, which was "in the most perfect beauty, the verdure exquisite, and the shades venerably extended." "I have made a gothic gateway," he added, "to the garden, the piers of which are of artificial stone and very respectable." And the country to which he was going had no admiration for Strawberry.

"When I once asked Madame du Deffand what her

countrymen said of it, she owned they were not struck with it, but looked upon it as natural enough in a country which had not yet arrived at true taste. In short, I believe, they think all the houses they see are Gothic, because they are not like that single pattern that reigns in every hotel in Paris; and which made me say there, that I never knew whether I was in the house that I was in, or in the house I came out of. Two or three rooms in a row, a naked *salle-à-manger*, a white and gold cabinet, with four looking-glasses, a lustre, a scrap of hanging over against the windows, and two rows of chairs, with no variety in the apartments, but from bigger to less, and more or less gilt, and a bed-chamber with a blue or red damask bed; this is that effort of taste to which they think we have not attained—we who have as pure architecture and as classic taste as there was in Adrian's or Pliny's villas."

Yet with all that, though he had no kindness for the people nor the country, the most vital part of his life was in France. Lady Suffolk was dead in 1767, " votre pauvre sourde," as Madame du Deffand wrote pityingly. Lady Hervey followed her at no long interval. Conway—there was always Conway, but it was not the same thing. Madame du Deffand, who knew best, kept urging him to see more and more of Montagu, and Walpole asked no better.

" My t'other dear friend," he wrote to him, " I am sorry to say I see you almost so seldom as I do Madame du Deffand. However it is comfortable to reflect that we have not changed to each other for some five and thirty years." That was in 1769. A year later at the end of a letter describing the philosophy of his life, the last word is : " You see I never let our long-lived friendship drop, though you give it so few opportunities of breathing."

It takes two to keep up such artificial respiration. There are other letters : but the last is on October 16, 1770 : Horace Walpole speaks of " seven long weeks " cripplement with gout at Strawberry : then there is a word or two of chaff;

and with that, George Montagu quietly fades out of the story. There were still the young Lennoxes and Foxes of the second generation ; there was still Horace Mann, faithful at the end of postal communications after thirty years of it ; there was the kind old Cole, general referee on antiquarian matters : there was Conway : there was Chute—but Chute, though always an ally, was less of an affection. He wanted variety and so it was not only for the sake of the dear old woman that he set out for Paris early in July, 1771.

At Amiens the inn was so suffocating that he rose at five and drove straight through, arriving at eight o'clock " tired but rejoiced."

He found little to admire : the du Barri régime was disastrous ; the King's tradesmen were ruined, his servants starving, "and even angels and archangels cannot get their pensions and salaire." There was even nothing new in their shops !

"'I know the faces of every snuff-box and every teacup. Between economy and the want of novelty I have not laid out five guineas—a very memorable anecdote in the history of my life."

Then suddenly in the midst of all this vacuity, came the news of Gray's death. That cut deep.

" 'Tis an hour that makes one forget any subject of complaint, especially towards one with whom I lived in friendship from thirteen years old. As self lies so rooted in self, no doubt the nearness of our ages made the stroke recoil to my own breast : and having so little expected his death, it is plain how little I expect my own. . . . I thought that what I had seen of the world had hardened my heart : but I find that it had formed my language, not extinguished my tenderness. . . . Nay, I am hurt at my own weakness as I perceive that when I love anybody, it is for my life."

So he wrote to Chute, adding, " Of being here I am most heartily tired, and nothing but this dear old woman should keep me here an hour—I am weary of them to death—but that is not new."

He left early in September. In her letters to him, both before his going and on his departure, there is now a studied moderation. What she is not afraid to express is gratitude. "You will have the satisfaction of having given a great mark of affection to the person in the world who loves you best," was the welcome she had for him; but when he goes, she is almost painfully limited to the tone of a journal. Her resentment does not go beyond an ironical assurance. "You will seldom find any interesting facts, but a quantity of proper names, sometimes facts, all the gossip I hear, and never, no never, one thought or a reflection." Even so, after a fortnight she is saying, "I see you are still afraid. Be reassured; your lessons have been salutary. . . . If what I write you bores you, it's a revenge that I joyfully allow myself."

In short, he gave her much and was worth much to her, but far less than he might have been: and he forced her, on his absurd theory, to bring him less vitality than she would gladly have poured into his rather starved existence.

For in this period of life, in his late fifties and the sixties, all of the man seemed to dry up: the wit of his letters grows forced and the new correspondent who now takes a front rank was of a kind to develop whatever in him had least vitality. Mason, that insufferable prig and poetaster, was taking in hand to write Gray's life, and so naturally came to Walpole for assistance.

The tie with Gray had long been purely literary and the pleasure was much gone out of it for Walpole since literary confidences ceased to be mutual. Gray wrote nothing, would write nothing: and though he was always ready to assist Walpole with the resources of his knowledge and power of research, he never greeted his friend's work with enthusiasm. When Walpole urged him to produce more, "If I do not write much, it is because I cannot," he answered. "As you have not this last plea I see no reason why you should not continue as long as it is agreeable to yourself and to all such as have any curiosity or judgment in the subject you choose to treat." That is a chilly encouragement : but Gray was cold of temper and his lack of warmth in friendship was certainly no way disguised from this old intimate. None the less, his withdrawal left a great gap : something changed in the whole landscape. One is probably justified in connecting with it the fact that the *Memoirs* which had been Walpole's main literary preoccupation and the part of his work most approved by Gray, were allowed to drop at the end of the year. In many ways he grew moodier, more whimsical ; and as often happens, he vented his discomfort on the person whom he could be sure of hurting.

As early as April, 1772, Madame du Deffand had spoken of a visit to Chanteloup, where the Duc de Choiseul, banished from Court to please the du Barri, was living on his estates. It would only, she said, be a last resource against ennui. Thereupon he sent a furious letter. " The way you talk about ennui is really a mania : you might be a girl of sixteen forbidden to amuse herself as much as she would like. I beg of you, and I advise you, give up this mad plan." " Very well," she answered, " I won't go to Chanteloup, my health forbids it ; I will talk to you no more of my ennuis, for you give the lie to that verse of Corneille's—' By telling troubles we can often soothe them.' " Yet she looked forward to a lonely summer ; all her intimates were leaving Paris ; and then suddenly on May 20 a letter was posted to him. " Guess from where : From Chanteloup." One of her friends, the Bishop of Arras, had come and, so to speak, whirled her away with him, by Étampes, Orleans and Blois, only staying at these places ; then, it was only an afternoon's drive and her reception was enthusiastic. Weeks passed and she was made much of by these people who loved her and wanted

to keep her till October: but she had always an anxiety—
what her dearest friend would say.

He took the line that would be most painful; he left
her without news of him; and there is a pathetic change
from the delighted bubbling over in her first reports to the
anxious impatience of the last. Soon she was in a fury to
get back to Paris and distressed because her travelling companion was delayed. At the end of June she got back and
there was his letter. "What a letter! Nothing could be
more wounding, colder, ruder." She had thought he
would be pleased to hear that she had stood the journey
and had been well and happy; and all he had to say was
that she had broken her word and made him ridiculous.
There was an exchange of angry letters. Was she to be
called a coquette because she had expressed anxiety about
his health? Were her letters really a persecution? So,
seeing that he clearly wanted a rupture, she broke off—on
July 25. On August 30 she was begging for news of him;
proposing peace and an amnesty. From that time on, his
despotism was established, and from that time on he contrived
to keep her (not without frequent chastisements) to a tone
that conformed to his prescription. She hated writing
"gazettes"; he kept her to that occupation—supple-
mented, it is true, by the expression of her opinions on literature—for instance on the English novel, which she thinks
much more life-like than he does. She is increasingly
unhappy, and yet her attachment never varies. "The truth
is you are a very good man," she tells him, "sometimes
a little harsh and unjust and angry, but it doesn't last; and
one forgives you because of your very great honesty."

There was no question of his paying another visit; she
was careful not to suggest such a thing; and indeed during
the latter part of 1772 he was closely confined by the gout
and in great torture; yet not without alleviations. "Five
young ladies, the finest and youngest, have made it the fashion

to visit me," he writes to Mann; "as old ladies never fail
to go after the young, I have wanted neither sort."

As soon as he got better, a different trouble fell on him;
Lord Orford, his nephew, went mad and the two uncles had
to take charge; but Horace did the work and it was strange
to him, for it involved disposing of a racing stud.

"I intended," he told Mann, "to trifle out the remnant
of my days; and lo! they are invaded by lawyers, stewards,
physicians and jockeys! Yes; this whole week past I have
been negotiating a sale of race-horses at Newmarket, and,
to the honour of my transactions, the sale has turned out
greatly. My Gothic ancestors are forgotten; I am got upon
the turf. I give orders about game, dispark Houghton, have
plans of farming, vend colts, fillies, bullocks, and sheep, and
have not yet confounded terms, nor ordered pointers to be
turned to grass. I read the part of the newspapers I used
to skip, and peruse the lists of sweepstakes: not the articles
of intelligence, nor the relations of the shows at Portsmouth
for the King, or at Oxford for the Viceroy North. I must
leave Europe and its Kings and Queens to you; we do not
talk of such folks at the Inns of Court. I sold *Stoic* for five
hundred guineas: I shall never get five pence by the
Monarchs of the Empire, and therefore we jockeys of the
Temple, and we lawyers of Newmarket, hold them to be
very insignificant individuals."

Moreover, his little dog Rosette, who adored him, was
dying. "I have been out of bed twenty times every night;
I have had no sleep, and sat up with her till three this morning." Madame du Deffand was no stranger to this last
trouble; she pressed for news of Rosette, whose death scene
grew prolonged. It pleased her to hear of something where
feeling was involved. Long after, when she was near her
end, looking back she admitted that in her feeling for him
there had always been "some trace of passion." "But is
there not always when one loves?" she added. "Remember

231

Rosette!" When she used irony, it was always pointed against herself.

There was a new attraction to Paris in September, 1774, for Louis XV died, the du Barri and all her crew vanished and the young king came in surrounded by reformers ready to restore parliament and abolish all the bad old ways. Horace Walpole "mighty pleased with this convulsion," cries, "What a century, which sees the Jesuits annihilated and absolute power abolished!" Nevertheless, when Conway who was travelling on the Continent proposed a rendezvous in Paris, Walpole's courage failed him.

"As the period is arrived when the gout used to come, it is never a moment out of my head. Such a suffering, such a helpless condition as I was in for five months and a half, two years ago, makes me tremble from head to foot. I should die at once if seized in a French inn; or what, if possible, would be worse, at Paris, where I must admit everybody—I, who you know can hardly bear to see even you when I am ill, and who shut up myself here, and would not let Lord and Lady Hertford come near me—I, who have my room washed though in bed, how could I bear French dirt?"

But he sent out with Lady Ailesbury a paper of directions concerning Madame du Deffand, begging that Conway would take "a great deal of notice of this dear old friend." He was especially anxious to find out from her if her pension stood in any danger from the change and how she stood at Court. Next, Conway was to get Walpole's letters to her and bring them back. And lastly, he must remember that she hated *les philosophes*, and if he went to Madame Geoffrin's house, "whither all the pretended *beaux esprits* and *faux savants* go," he must not talk of it to her. But above all, he must not let himself be taken to call on Mademoiselle de l'Espinasse.

Conway came and had a great success. Her enthusiastic

description of him is skilfully used to renew some of her old reproaches; but one thing is plain. Though Walpole had confided to her some of his disappointment, she was convinced that she could not please him better than by praising this hero of his youth. Lady Ailesbury and her daughter, Mrs. Damer, were also in high favour and they all did their best to return the old woman's kindness by urging Walpole to revisit her. Conway indeed, wrote at once in that sense. This was the reply:—

"My intention is certainly to see her again, if I am able; but I am too old to lay plans, especially when it depends on the despot gout to register or cancel them. It is even melancholy to see her, when it will probably be but once more." . . .

Many passages indicate that the Conways kept up the pressure, and she herself of course added her voice. On August 9 he wrote to Conway—

"Well, I am going *tout de bon*, and heartily wish I was returned. It is a horrid exchange, the cleanness and the verdure and tranquillity of Strawberry, for a beastly ship, worse inns, the pavé of the roads bordered with eternal rows of maimed trees, and the racket of an *hôtel garni*! . . . Madame du Deffand, I am sure, may be satisfied with the sacrifice I make to her!"

However, when he got to Paris on the 20th, after being, as he told Lady Ailesbury, seasick to death, poisoned by dirt and vermin, stifled by heat and choked by dust and starved for want of anything he could touch, yet, none the less, he found himself "almost as young as when I came hither first in the last century . . . and thank your Ladyship and Mr. Conway for driving me hither."

Madame du Deffand came to him the moment he arrived, stayed while he dressed—"for, as she said, since I cannot see, there was no harm in my being stark": and he sat with her till half past two in the morning and had a letter from her before his eyes were open again. " In short her soul is immortal, and forces her body to bear it company."

He stayed his usual six weeks and was once more received with open arms, not only by the dear old friend but by maréchales and duchesses who embraced him on both cheeks till he was " smeared with red like his own crest the Saracen." Above all he saw the young queen, " a statue of beauty, when standing or sitting; grace itself when she moves." And of course Madame du Deffand crowded up the time with engagements and parties in town and country, and all these parties were " so many polypuses that would shoot out new ones and there was no chance to get to bed from supper till two or three o'clock.

"If possible, she is more worth visiting than ever," he told Selwyn. " So far am I from being ashamed of coming hither at my age, that I look on myself as wiser than one of the Magi, when I travel to adore this star in the East. The star and I went to the Opera last night, and when we came from Madame de la Valiére's, at one in the morning, it wanted to drive about the town, because it was too early to *set*."

By October 12 it was all over and this was her note written in the morning before he started:

" Adieu, ce mot est bien triste; souvenez-vous que vous laissez ici la personne dont vous êtes le plus aimé, et dont le bonheur et le malheur consistent dans ce que vous pensez pour elle. Donnez-moi de vos nouvelles le plus tôt qu'il sera possible.

Je me porte bien, j'ai un peu dormi, ma nuit n'est pas finie; je serai tres-exacte au régime, et j'aurai soin de moi, puisque vous vous y intéressez."

Once more for a while the glow of assurance given by personal contact, and by the proof of devotion, spreads itself over the letters; though here and there she underlines her attention to his orders, and assures him that after the first rush there will be only one message a week. The result is a string of communications throughout all of which one feels constraint—something held in check. Now and then, fire breaks out.

"You mocked at me so much for the store I set by friendship that you convinced me at last : but you have given me nothing to put in its place : and it may be happiness to take oak leaves for gold. Your summing up of all my good fortunes made me laugh : long life for instance : you will know some day perhaps what to think of that."

Or again—and here irony and passion both stir under the polished surface :

"The list you send me of your occupations makes me feel that you must regret the time you waste in writing to me : your days are full. I should be truly grateful for the moments you give me, all the more because I know the effort writing costs ; for nothing can be truer than that you are the only one for whom that costs me nothing."

The letters get sadder as the note of resignation deepens.

"Do not be vexed, but I cannot help saying that I would give everything in the world to see you once more. Don't be afraid, I won't speak of it again."

That was more than two years after their parting in 1775, and the next letter renews apology for this one lapse. Again she admits his right to be surprised that her spirit does not age. "It has the same cravings as at fifty, at forty even ; for I was by then clear of all appeal to the senses. I had then, and shall have to the end of my life, the craving to love and be loved : but you are the only one who knows this. La grand'maman (Madame de Choiseul) is the same in everything ; everything with her is on principle, by rule or by habit ; nature never breaks through. As for you, you have smothered your self as much as you could, and I really believe that nothing is any longer a necessity to you."

Between people so different, between what she was and

what he affected to be, there can be no free communication:
and she tells him so plainly once:

"The determination not to see me again, and your refusal
to admit this even though you perceive that I guess the truth,
raise a sort of fog in your feelings for me which makes you
misconstrue all I say."

A year later, still in 1779, she thanked him for "the
first letter that has shown me so much friendship for several
years." But then she comments grimly enough on the
reasons for the change. War as well as the sea divided
them now: France had gone to support America. Yet in
the easy way of those times the communications were still
open, by Ostend instead of by Calais, the post was only
a couple of days longer. For that matter, English subjects
could still come to France. But it was a barrier—and
she asked him whether this change, this unwonted tone of
affection, came because he could never see her again.

She knew that he could not; and she was almost re-
conciled to this because now at eighty-three she was afflicted
with deafness as well as blindness. "I should be ashamed
for you to see me in so deplorable a state: one would gladly
rouse sympathy, but not pity." And when he replied with
protestations, she answered:

"I do not doubt of your affection, but I shall see you no
more. I will not say it would be better never to have seen
you, for regrets are better than a mind without feeling, and
that is what I should be if I did not know you."

At the very end there was a period of bitter anxiety, for
no letters came to her: Walpole was crippled again, Selwyn
who used to act as amanuensis failed him; but at last Conway
came to the rescue and took the pen. But she had little
news to send in her gazettes: at eighty-three, she was weaken-
ing: sleep had left her: she had four people reading to her
—three of her servants and a veteran from the Invalides—
but there was nothing new that gave her pleasure. Her life

was so monotonous that she had almost lost, she said, the faculty of thought.

Yet to the very last she was being reprimanded. " Qui bien aime, bien châtie. Ah, que de preuves je reçois de votre amitié ! " That was written on August 3, 1780. There was one more note, and then on August 22 the last of them. She spoke only of her weakness which she took for a warning of her end. " I have no strength left to be frightened at it, and since I am never to see you again, there is nothing I am sorry to leave. . . . Amuse yourself as much as you can, my friend, do not trouble about my state : we were almost lost to each other : we were never to meet again : you will miss me, for we all like to know that we are loved."

The rest was told by her servant Wiart. Like all her household, he was devoted to the Englishman.

She left Horace Walpole her papers, many of which had interest ; a little gold box with the picture of her favourite dog ; and finally Tonton, the dog of her last years. He was incredibly cross and celebrated his arrival at Strawberry Hill by a quarrel with larger dogs, but was soon established in almost as great favour as the deceased Rosette. Walpole tells how he had been dining at Richmond House and had said he was going on to another party ; but the Duke asked : " Own the truth, shall you not call at home first and see Tonton ? " and Walpole admitted it was so.

The long story, then, ends with Tonton. It is easy to believe that Horace Walpole was glad to be able to continue at least some good offices to a creature that his friend had loved. It is less easy to believe that he did, as she foresaw, miss the sensation that somewhere in the world one lived whose life for long years had centred upon the thought of him. " She loves me better than all France," he wrote to Conway in 1774. But it is a question whether the most self-satisfied is content with a relation where so much more is given on one side than on the other. Each habitually spoke of gratitude to the other : but to her it was a delight to be in his debt for courtesy and kind observances. He would have hated to be outdone in these, and in these she left herself willingly his debtor ; knowing, always, that in what really mattered she was incomparably the greater giver. However lacking in comprehension he showed himself at times, he too must have known this. I should not wonder if her death relieved him of an almost intolerable weight of gratitude where he could make no return.

CHAPTER XI

THE LEES OF LIFE

HORACE WALPOLE was fifty-one in 1768 when he gave up his seat in Parliament. He was told that he would regret quitting it, but four years later he wrote to Mann:

" I have done nothing but applaud my resolution. When I compare my situation with my former agitated and turbulent life, I wonder how I had spirits to go through the former, or how I can be charmed with the latter without having lost these spirits."

Yet it is doubtful whether he was a good judge in his own case. He had the power of making occupations for himself, but these gradually left him, and none had importance. Parliament was a duty, and a man with so much activity is the better of a duty. At first the preoccupation of literature and the encouragement of success in it helped to fill his life. His *Historic Doubts on Richard III* sold very largely—1,250 copies at once. Then he plunged into tragedy in his blank verse drama of the " Mysterious Mother," with a theme of involuntary incest. Gray, he says, approved it ; we may leave the matter at that. After Gray's death, as has been seen already, he dropped the writing of his contemporary memoirs : more than that, the impulse to any considerable literary production died away altogether. The necessity for occupying himself with Lord Orford's affairs helped to kill the habit ; when that necessity was ended, he was more and more limited to being a busy idler ; and his value to us as social chronicler is distinctly lessened by his lack of first-hand contact with the parliamentary scene. He was, it is true, a member of White's ; but the House of Commons in those days was, even more than White's, the central club of London men's society.

Indeed as the years went on he was less and less a Londoner, more and more a dweller in what he called the country. Twickenham was his world. Writing to George Montagu, he says that he has withdrawn decently " out of the world into London," and goes on to explain that this is done on principle : " I always intend to place some months between me and the moroseness of retirement. We are not made for solitude. It gives us prejudices ; it indulges us in our own humours and at last we cannot live without them."

In so far as he carried out this theory of life, nature helped him. Strawberry was very well, but the Thames valley has its mists and he got his health, though he hated to admit it, better in London. Still the new way of life reflects itself in his correspondence. There is less of narrative and description —at which he excelled ; and much more philosophy, in which he did not get beyond the neat expression of rather shallow thought. Now and then, when social contacts are concerned, his observation rings true, as when he reproaches George Montagu with settling down in Oxfordshire " under the nose of an infant duke and duchess, that will understand you no more than if you wore a ruff and a coif."

" Your wit and humour will be as much lost upon them, as if you talked the dialect of Chaucer ; for with all the divinity of wit, it grows out of fashion like a fardingale. I am convinced that the young men at White's already laugh at George Selwyn's *bon-mots* only by tradition. I avoid talking before the youth of the age as I would dancing before them ; for if one's tongue don't move in the steps of the day, and thinks to please by its old graces, it is only an object of ridicule, like Mrs. Hobart in her cotillon."

Socially also he becomes a somewhat shocked recorder, writing for instance in February, 1770, of the gaming at Almack's.

" The young men of the age lose five, ten, fifteen thousand pounds in an evening here. Lord Stavordale, not one-and-twenty, lost eleven thousand there last Tuesday, but recovered it by one great hand at hazard : he swore a great oath—'Now, if I had been playing *deep*, I might have won millions.' "

Then follows the inevitable allusion to Charles Fox, who " shines equally there and in the House of Commons, where at twenty-one he is already one of our best speakers," and a Lord of the Admiralty. The rise of this prodigy, scion of two friendly houses (Horace Walpole had been of those who helped to reconcile the Richmonds to their daughter's runaway match), was of unceasing interest to the looker-on. Five years later, in 1775, he records that " Charles Fox has tumbled old Saturn (Chatham) from the throne of oratory, and if he has not all the dazzling lustre, has much more of the solid materials."

But except for this case, where there was so strong a tie, one feels that his comment on men is less and less nourished by personal contact. He feels himself something of a stranger in this world. An instance gave him one in no way pleasing glimpse of the House of Commons of which he had been so long a member. Lord Orford, before his malady completely incapacitated him, had used his patronage to return as member for one of his boroughs, a waiter at White's, from whom he had borrowed money. Horace Walpole had the disagreeable experience of finding himself supposed to have written a speech which the new senator delivered. All the good things in it were George Selwyn's, he told Lady Ossory, from whom the accusation came ; he adds sharply :

" Madness is an excuse for my nephew, and they who make a friend of Macreth without being out of their senses, have, I suppose, very good and very bad reasons for it."

That sentence has a sharp ring in it which recalls Lady Louisa Stuart's observation that certainly nobody ever accused Horace Walpole to his face of servility. Indeed, he was otherwise occupied than with such buffoonery; it is a pleasure also to quote what he wrote to Mason in 1774, after the charge of Lord Orford's affairs had filled his life for an anxious twelvemonth:

"I have found I have sense enough to learn many common things that I never believed myself capable of comprehending. I have found that better sense of acting as I ought, when it was necessary; for till this year I never really had anything to do. I shall be rejoiced to resume that happy idleness: I know not whether it will be my lot."

It was not to be his lot; he never tasted again with the same eagerness his old amusements of books and virtú. A few months later one finds him writing to Conway: "I see nothing, know nothing, do nothing. My castle is finished, I have nothing new to read, I am tired of writing, I have no new or old bit for my printer."

For there was no more to be done to Strawberry. "I have finished this house and place these three years," he told Mann in 1775, "and yet am content with and enjoy it. . . . I choose my house should enjoy itself, which poor houses and gardens seldom do, for people go on mending till they die and the next comer who likes to improve too, begins to mend all that has been done."

One of his constant occupations was the issue of cards to view the place; and Margaret, his housekeeper, did so well out of the traffic that when, during some financial stringency, parliamentary inquiry into the profits of places was set up, Gilly Williams wanted to know why there was no mention of Margaret's place.—One must not grudge Margaret her vails. It was she who took charge of the wounded Tonton when on his arrival older dogs resented his arrogant arrival, and she who cried out, "Poor little thing, he does not understand my language." Tonton was safe with her for, as Walpole wrote, she "loved all creatures so well that she would have been happy in the Ark, and sorry when the Deluge ceased; unless people had come to see Noah's old house, which she would have liked still better than cramming his menagerie."

How should one not like a man who can write so about his housekeeper? Indeed it seems likely that a great array of witness on behalf of Horace Walpole could have been mustered at the judgment seat from among those who once were his domestics. A letter of thanks to Lord Harcourt, who had recommended him a gardener, says that he will take the man recommended, if he can. But there is a hitch. He has had a gardener for five-and-twenty years, who is useless but refuses to leave :

"I have offered him fifteen pounds a year to leave me, and when he pleads that he is old, and that nobody else will take him, I plead that I am old too, and that it is rather hard that I am not to have a few flowers, or a little fruit as long as I live. I shall now try if I can make any compromise with him, for I own I cannot bear to turn him adrift, nor will starve an old servant, though never a good one, to please my nose and mouth."

A great preoccupation of these autumnal years was furnished by the fortunes of his beautiful niece, the widowed Lady Waldegrave. So far back as 1766, she had secretly married the Duke of Gloucester, George III's brother. Horace Walpole knew, though unofficially, what was in the wind and strongly disapproved. Yet so late as 1771 he was without official knowledge, and it was only in June, 1772, that the lady was allowed to inform her father. In the following September the Duke of Gloucester formally notified the King also. But in the previous autumn another brother, the Duke of Cumberland, had suddenly gone off with another widow, Mrs. Horton, after much less circumspect proceedings, and was forbidden the Court. The same prohibition was imposed, though with more tenderness, on the Duke of Gloucester, and those who went to his house were officially excluded from St. James's. Accordingly Horace Walpole, who had so far carefully avoided any recognition of the marriage, asked leave to go and kiss hands, and thereafter thought it his duty to be a constant attendant at this secondary and somewhat disconsidered court. This involved seeing a number of new faces and young people, which he professed to dislike. " To converse with young people is like asking for the beginning of a story of which one is never to hear the end," may be noted among his many *obiter dicta* on such acquaintanceships. But he made an exception for his nieces, whom he owned to loving—even to liking them. Still, he based his interest mainly on " family pride." " For the whole rest of the young world, they are as indifferent to me as puppets or black children," he wrote to Conway when he was sixty. When he was seventy, indeed—but that comes later.

Conway was still the nearest to his affection, and in 1776 Conway had a slight stroke : what was worse, Conway's daughter, Mrs. Damer, found herself ruined. She was married at eighteen to a man who had five thousand a year and the reversion of twenty thousand : within a few years he had run himself in debt to the tune of seventy thousand pounds and ended matters by blowing out his brains in a tavern whither four wenches and a blind fiddler had been summoned to spend the evening with him. Conway had insisted on making over all his capital to furnish a marriage portion for his stepdaughter, and now her very jewels were, by her own desire, sold for the benefit of the creditors. The young widow went back to her father's house and in the end became Horace Walpole's heiress. " I love her as my own child," he wrote to Mann when Mrs. Damer went to Italy for her health and to develop her gifts as a sculptor. She was erudite as well, knew Latin and some Greek, and her companionship was always a pleasure to the old virtuoso.

Chute's death, which came at this time, when Horace Walpole was passing out of the fifties, left a dreadful gap. " He was my counsel in my affairs," so the letter ran which reported this loss to Florence, where the friendship had begun, " was my oracle in taste, the standard to whom I submitted my trifles, and the genius that presided over poor Strawberry. His sense decided me in everything ; his wit and quickness illuminated everything. I saw him oftener than any man ; to him in every difficulty I had recourse, and him I loved to have here, as our friendship was so entire, and we knew one another so entirely, that he alone was never the least constraint to me. We passed many hours together without saying a syllable to each other ; for we were both above ceremony. I left him without excusing myself, read or wrote before him, as if he were not present. Alas ! alas ! and how *self* presides even in our grief. I am lamenting myself, not him—no, I am lamenting my other self. Half is gone ; the other remains solitary."

It is after this that he writes to Conway an excuse for withdrawing a good deal from society. Gout has crippled him, and he does not like to hobble where others walk or run : and he could not persuade himself that he had wit enough to make up for deficiencies.

" I find what small share of parts I had, grown dulled— and when I perceive it myself, I may well believe that others would not be less sharp-sighted. It is very natural ; mine were spirits rather than parts ; and as time has abated the one, it must surely destroy their resemblance to the other."

So he wrote to one of his most likeable friends, the antiquarian Cole, whose " disciple in antiquities " he professed himself. However, Cole's way of life was too unlike that of the man of fashion, which Horace Walpole never ceased to be, for them to come into close contact ; and the later volumes of his correspondence were filled up with effusions to that unlikeable person Mason. To him Horace Walpole poured out the hysterical spleen with which the contemplation of public affairs afflicted him.

It was not unnatural. In 1767, though the splendours of

Chatham's day had passed, he could still write to Horace Mann, when the House of Commons was busy at once on the East India Company and on America : " Is not this very magnificent ? A senate regulating the Eastern and Western worlds at once. The Romans were triflers to us ; and yet our factions and theirs are as like as two peas." But things in America, as we all know, went sadly amiss and in ten years he was telling Lady Ossory : " I am at last not sorry you have no son, and your daughters, I hope, will be married to Americans and not in this dirty despicable island." And again : " In truth I am content that liberty will exist anywhere and amongst Englishmen, even across the Atlantic." For, like most of his friends, he was vehemently against the attempt to enforce the will of Parliament against the instincts of an English-speaking people.

In 1778, when France entered the struggle, other impulses came into play.

" My first object in politics is to demolish the French marine," he told Lady Ossory. " My Whig blood cannot bear to part with a drop of the Empire of the ocean. Like Romans, I would have Rome domineer over the world and be free at home."

He was aware that there was " little equity in this," but " a good citizen of the world, as this world is constituted, would be the most useless animal in creation." He was, in short, at bottom a very representative Englishman.

Once more, too, a private anxiety was added to his concern for the State. Conway was Governor of Jersey, and with the French fleet threatening in the Channel had at once hurried to his post, where the defenders could be only a handful. Under this stimulus all that was sincere in Walpole found expression.

" Such I am, ardent for England and ever shall be," he wrote to Mann at Florence ; " it is all an useless old man can do, to pray for its prosperity. My father is ever before my eyes—not to attempt to imitate him, for I have none of his matchless wisdom, or unsullied virtues, or heroic firmness; but sixty-two years have taught me to gaze on him with ten thousand times the reverence that, I speak it with deep shame, I felt for him at twenty-two, when he stood before me."

Altogether it was a period of much unhappiness : and the "Short Notes of my Life" compiled for the use of his literary executors stop abruptly in 1779, as if he had found no further matter worth recording.

One episode which bulks larger in the correspondence and has its place in literary history belongs in the main to these years—though its origin went farther back.

In March, 1769, Walpole wrote a letter to Mr. Thomas Chatterton at Bristol thanking him for a communication of a copy from specimens of *Rowley's Poems*. It is courteous and even flattering; asks, without the least suggestion of doubt, where Rowley's poems are to be found : "I should not be sorry to print them; or at least a specimen of them if they have never been printed." It inquires after the period of Rowley's life and notes that the manuscript contains a reference to an oil painting. But Walpole's inference is to dispute the tradition that John van Eyck was the inventor of oil painting—not in the least to suggest that allusion to this art raises doubt as to the authenticity of the poems. In short, he was taken in by Chatterton's ingenious forgery.

Another letter from Bristol enclosed more extracts and suggested that Chatterton would like assistance to enter upon a literary career. Walpole wrote back, giving prudent advice against abandoning a definite livelihood. At the same time, he wrote to Bristol for information about his correspondent; and he communicated the specimens of Rowley to Mason and to Gray. They at once pointed out, what Gray of all men living was the most certain to detect—that although the language was archaic, the metrical structure spoke of a comparatively modern date. Walpole was righteously indignant, although he himself had brought out *The Castle of Otranto* anonymously with a hope that it might be taken for a genuine antique. Still, the case was different: Chatterton was indisputably trying to get help on false pretences; and Walpole now replied to his letters by a demand to see the originals—and held on to the specimens submitted, neglecting a request for their return. Meantime he went off to Paris, and on his return found a very angry letter from Chatterton, to which he sat down and wrote a very arrogant reply; but thinking better of it, simply returned the manuscripts without a word. Two years later, he heard, at a literary dinner, from Goldsmith, the tale of Chatterton's suicide, and was naturally moved.

But, as legend grew up about the marvellous boy, Walpole found himself figuring in the mythology as " the fastidious and unfeeling being to whose insensibility we owe the extinction of the greatest poetic luminary, if one may judge by the brightness of its dawn, that ever rose in our or perhaps any other hemisphere." The kind of commentary which expressed itself thus appropriately through the pen of Lichfield's egregious swan, Miss Anna Seward, naturally ruffled Walpole a good deal: he was drawn into a defence of himself, and his handling of the matter is in his least likeable vein; so much so that it elicited a rhymed epistle in praise of it from Mason. He was worried into regarding Chatterton as a very clever young man who had tried to cheat him and had not been clever enough to do that. It would have been pleasanter if we had found him sorry for a chance missed to help struggling genius; but he is too anxious for his own vindication, and we find no trace of any such remorse— nor, for that matter, the least suggestion from either Gray or Mason that so brilliant a young man was worth helping.

It would be idle to trace out a detail of his life during these years. In 1779 he moved from Arlington Street into a house on the east side of Berkeley Square, which pleased him, and well it might: a charming piece of Georgian architecture. One is only surprised that it did not a little disgust him with the eccentricities of Strawberry. It was from Berkeley Square that he observed the beginning of the Gordon riots which are vividly described in several letters. One of these (to Mason) is of interest as indicating his attitude on the Catholic question. He had always, he says, disliked the repeal of the penal laws, and lamented the Duke of Richmond's " toleration of Popery "; but Lord George Gordon went entirely beyond his approval in pointing out the Duke to the mob as a fit mark for their attentions.

Again we have passing impressions of Gibbon, one of the few contemporary great authors whom Walpole cordially praised. None of his praise is so interesting as the story of what happened when Gibbon came to be patted on the back for his second volume and was told that Constantinopolitan history was so disgusting that few would have patience to read it, however well written.

" He coloured; all his round features squeezed themselves into sharp angles; he screwed up his button-mouth, and rapping his snuff-box said, ' It had never been put together before '—so well, he meant to add—but gulped it."

Politics fill many pages. In 1782 Conway was again in office for a moment, in the Ministry which Lord Rockingham's death dissolved at the end of three months. But Walpole felt in his own words that he " had neither youth nor perseverance enough to form any new plans of hopes for my country." So he " took the resolution of abandoning even speculation and observation and now, literally, never so much as asked a political question." It would be easy to demonstrate out of his own mouth that this was far from being the essential truth, to say nothing of the literal. He was more than a little displeased at feeling himself outside the fray at whose beginning the old parliamentarian in him had begun to prick up ears.

But in truth, his only place was on the shelf. His hands were so disfigured by the recurring discharge of chalkstones that he would not accept invitations outside his familiar beat. " I have not enough philosophy to stand stranger servants staring at my broken fingers at dinner. I hide myself like spaniels that creep into a hedge to die. . . . Sleep is my great restoration ; no dormouse beats me. Nay, I do not even look so ill as I have a right to do, though to be sure I might be admitted at the Resurrection without being rejected for a counterfeit corpse."

Yet the vitality in him which gave him spirit to make such neat phrases over his own affliction, was to carry him on for another fifteen years : though their passage was marked by little but deaths and the dropping out of friends. His brother, Sir Edward Walpole, died in 1784, and thereby Horace lost £1,400 a year : but this, as he said, only meant "buying fewer baubles for a year or two " ; besides, " the old child's baby-house is quite full of playthings."

Mason drops out too, as the result of a quarrel ; he had gone over to the Court side, following his patron, Lord Harcourt ; and Walpole was censorious. The correspondence becomes better reading from this date (1784) ; henceforward he is writing mainly to his old intimates.

Long before this he had told Sir Horace Mann that they were the Pylades and Orestes of letter writers—then in the thirty-seventh year of their correspondence. Earlier still, in 1774, an excited postscript tells of the heartfelt pleasure he had felt in seeing Mann's picture. " It brought tears to my eyes : though thirty years have fattened you, made you florid, I traced every feature and saw this whole likeness in the character and countenance—yes, there is all your goodness."

It is difficult to account for the continuance of so warm a stream of affection for so long a period through the post's chilly channels : but no doubt Horace Walpole owed his excellence as a letter writer to a power of projecting his personality across space. He was a good chronicler because he was interested in people, concerned for all the detail of their lives—which indeed became part of his own : and he had a special love for Mann because Mann was specially identified with his youth. It was to Mann that he reviewed his life in 1785 ; the letter had been postponed to report all well after a dangerous fit of gout.

" Pray give me as good an account of yourself. Have you driven yet in your coach to the Cascines or the foot of Fiesoli ? or about the streets to the Duomo and Annunziata, as I used to do in the heat of the day, for the mere pleasure of looking at the buildings, when everybody else was gone into bed ? What a thousand years ago that was ! yet I recollect it as if but yesterday ! I sometimes think I have lived two or three lives. My thirteen months at Florence was a pleasant youth to one of them. Seven months and a half at Paris, with four or five journeys thither since, was a middle age, quite different from five-and-twenty years in Parliament which had preceded—and an age since ! Besides, as I was an infant when my father became Minister, I came into the world at five years old ; knew half the remaining Courts of King William and Queen Anne, or heard them talked of as fresh ; being the youngest and favourite child, was carried to almost the first operas, kissed the hand of George the First, and am now hearing the frolics of his great-great-grandson ;—no, all this cannot have happened in one life ! "

The correspondence lasted yet another year : it brought the opening scenes of Warren Hastings' trial among the things which Walpole described for his far-off friend. Finally, in June, 1786, it ceases ; there is no valedictory. But its end surely may be allowed to mark the close of a chapter in Horace Walpole's life.

CHAPTER XII

INDIAN SUMMER

IF Walpole could have been told, when the news of Mann's death reached him, that Pylades must survive Orestes by a matter of fifteen years, he would assuredly have heard it with genuine dismay. He was indeed, at sixty-nine, not past an age at which many men retain their activity and power of enjoyment with little diminution. But what he had told Conway was true; he was in fact twenty years older than any of his contemporaries. Long before this George Selwyn had written to Carlisle that the sight of him was shocking, so crippled in all his limbs (*perclus de tous ses membres*) was this vivacious person. Movement was impossible except between his two centres of Berkeley Square and Twickenham, with an occasional excursion to Conway's home, Park Place, near Henley.

Moreover, if the revelation had been complete, he must have seen that long before the spectacle of events had ceased to unroll itself before him, the polite world, all the established order that he cherished, would be menaced as never before in modern times, and that in one of the capitals he knew the pageant of existence in which he had taken part would be, not merely menaced, but shattered, and, as it seemed to him, replaced by brutal savagery. Even as it was, his letters show us that while the French Revolution ran its course, his mind, when it had leisure for brooding, chewed a bitter cud, extracting nothing but poisonous nourishment from the gazettes and gossips on which it had always browsed.

He had lost the resource on which Gray congratulated him, and which Madame du Deffand, if she did not admire it, recognized as a perfect remedy against ennui—the power to invent occupations for himself; and when a man has used this gift to the utmost till decrepitude and then finds it leave him, he has never learnt to do without occupations.

There was, of course, society: but even the habits of society were shifting, in the decade that led up to 1789—which, as we shall have to note, was an epoch in the life of Horace Walpole as well as in world history. Nobody goes out of town till July, he complains, and consequently if he wants to see his friends he must stay in London when he would sooner be at Strawberry. At Strawberry or in Berkeley Square he dined at four o'clock, which is still the dinner hour of parish priests in Ireland—the last upholders of eighteenth-century tradition; but already his friends, even his contemporaries, had pushed this function back shamelessly to six. What was more, a rage for movement had set in, and ladies, even elderly ladies, were no longer to be found in their houses after dinner. Lady Bute he mentions as an honourable exception, and he regretted her death the more because she was one of the few on whom he could look in of an evening. Except the Conways and their daughter, Mrs. Damer, and two or three other standbys, nobody called on him after his frugal meal. On the other hand, from half-past one to four his " coffee house was always crowded "; so he tells Lady Ossory, the sometime Duchess of Grafton, regretting that more than once when she had come to see him he had been surrounded by company. But she also, though always willing to write letters and receive them (she was after Mann's death the most regular recipient of his political observations), would not pay evening visits; and in one way or another he spent a deal of time alone— talking to Tonton. For Tonton persisted in living up to the great age of sixteen, though stone deaf and blind, nursed up by constant attention by a master always afraid lest the dog should be the survivor, " as it was scarcely possible he could meet a third person who would study his happiness equally."

Tonton died in Berkeley Square but was carried to Strawberry to be buried " behind the chapel near Rosette." " I shall miss him greatly and must not have another dog," Walpole wrote to Lady Ossory. " I am too old and should only breed it up to be unhappy when I am gone."

However, by the time that was written in February, 1789, he had a better resource than Tonton, or the two marble kittens that Mrs. Damer had sculptured and given him, " and which are so much alive that I talk to them as I did to poor Tonton." For time dealt indulgently with this spoilt child whose mouth had been always furnished with silver spoons ; yet the indulgence had in it a colour of mockery as if providence said to him, " You need not be unhappy if you will learn to be natural. But you must recant in public."

And so providence presented him with an inverted copy of the situation which had arisen when Madame du Deffand fell in love with her Englishman.

Only—for providence does not do things by halves when it deals in irony—all the features of the situation were to be emphasized to the point of caricature. He had marred and maimed the happiness his old friend might have had : he had contributed little—nothing, one may say—to the beauty of an attachment which kept its beauty in spite of him ; and all because he had a panic fear of ridicule. Yet when Madame du Deffand at sixty-eight lavished her *amitié* on an elderly man whom her blind eyes could never see, no living soul in her surroundings was in the least degree likely to put any construction on it but the true one. Twenty years earlier—ten years earlier even—people might have said cruel things about this infatuation for a man twenty years her junior, and might have jeered at his compliance. But at sixty-eight the society in which she moved, the only public for whose opinion she cared, had not a thought of misunderstanding her ; and since she was Madame du Deffand, had no difficulty in understanding her attraction for a clever man. It was probable, however, that Englishmen who could not understand that a woman should exercise fascination in any way but one, might laugh : Crawford admitted to her that he also was afraid of being laughed at for his devotion ; and Horace Walpole let their whole relation be overclouded by his fear of that laughter. He had now to face what before he ran away from, and to face something more than a mere shadow of it. For if a gentleman in his seventies becomes enamoured of a lady in her twenties, people will laugh in a way that cannot be agreeable to the laughed at.

Yet in the last resort Horace Walpole found the necessary courage—even though providence heightened the touch of caricature, by making him appear the senile admirer not of one young woman but of two. The explanation is simple enough, of course. Strong feeling kills everything less real than itself : Madame du Deffand had that feeling for Horace Walpole, but he lacked it for her. In another case he found it.

Here is how it happened. In the circles that he frequented there began, about 1787, to be much talk of the two Miss Berrys, said to be paragons. Horace Walpole saw them for the first time in October of that year and refused to be introduced to them, having heard so much in their praise that he " concluded they would be all pretension." In 1788 they and their father happened to take a house for the season at Twickenham, and one night at the house of his friend Lady Herries, in a very small company, he sat next to Mary (the elder) and " found her an angel both inside and out." By the time he wrote this to Lady Ossory, he did not know which he liked best, Mary or Agnes, except that Mary's face was " formed for a sentimental novel, but ten times fitter for a fifty times better thing, genteel comedy." This delightful family—they and their father, a " little merry man with a round face "—came to Strawberry almost every Sunday evening, as Twickenham did not admit of cards on the seventh day.

For the benefit of these new flames the old wit " recollected his gallantry of former days," and when the Berrys came to see his printing-press, stanzas were ready set with appropriate tribute ; for Mary was a Latin scholar and Agnes drew divinely :

> " To Mary's lips has ancient Rome
>   Her purest language taught,
> And from the modern city-home
>   Agnes its pencil brought.
>
> Rome's ancient Horace sweetly chants
>   Such maids with lyric fire ;
> Albion's old Horace sings nor paints—
>   He only can admire.
>
> Still would his press their fame record,
>   So amiable the pair is !
> But, ah ! how vain to think his word
>   Can add a straw to Berrys ! "

And here is the first stanza of Mary's reply :

> " Had Rome's famed Horace thus addrest
>   His Lydia or his Lyce,
> He had ne'er so oft complain'd their breast
>   To him was cold and icy."

This was only the beginning of a round of versifying. Mr. Richard Cambridge, author of the *Scribleriad,* and general purveyor of news to Twickenham, went on with plays on the word, and Mary Berry writes on November 1 to say that there were half a dozen others, " some of them by people we never saw." In short, this new allegiance was blazoned abroad, and not merely confided to the sympathetic ears of Lady Ossory— who no doubt laughed a good deal when she received within the space of a week two rhapsodies about the charmers, but was, as the correspondence shows, more and more concerned that they should be available for her old friend's solace.

As to ridicule, it is plain from the first that he had it in mind, and equally plain that he took a line of resistance : determining, so to say, to outface it by a vehement protesta-

From a painting by Zoffany

MISS BERRY AND MISS AGNES BERRY

tion of being in love with both young women at once. His way to avoid ridicule was to present an exaggeration of what it might invent. He wrote to them :

" I am afraid of protesting how much I delight in your society, lest I should seem to affect being gallant ; but if two negatives make an affirmative, why may not two ridicules compose one piece of sense ? and therefore, as I am in love with you both, I trust it is a proof of the good sense of your devoted

H. WALPOLE."

He had certainly chosen well. In addition to good looks they were unusually well bred and well educated : and Mary, for whom Horace Walpole formed his real passion, was kind-hearted beyond his deserts. The only trace of a time when she was hurt was one when she was moved by feelings that he of all men was prone to admire ; for she could not bear the idea of mercenary motives ; her family history was all against it.

Her father was bred up by a very rich uncle, with a business in the City. But because he made a love match against the uncle's wish, he sacrificed chances which went to his younger brother. The wife died, leaving Mr. Berry with two daughters to educate on very small means ; however, the younger brother, on succeeding to his uncle's fortune (of £300,000), settled on Mr. Berry an annuity of £1,000 a year, so that there was ample means to take the two girls abroad for a couple of years. They profited by their opportunities and returned " exceedingly sensible, entirely natural and unaffected, and being qualified to talk on any subject, nothing was so easy and agreeable as their conversation." They had, moreover, the admirable quality of being good listeners.

Horace Walpole had long before this attained to what might be called celebrity. Yet being a competent critic, at least of himself, he was not deceived as to his literary merit, and considered that he had done more service to letters through his journeyman printer than by his pen, " having sometimes," he told Lady Ossory, " obtained for the public works of intrinsic value or variety : I shall sit mighty low on the bench of authors ; but Kirgate and I shall not give place to many printers in the Temple of Fame."

He had, however, and he knew it, real celebrity as a personality and a talker ; but old age brought disgust for general society and almost physically disabled him. Besides, it was part of his philosophy that such celebrity was transient and did not pass current with the younger generation. He apologized to Montagu for belonging to " a club of both sexes " being set up at Almack's ! What should he do in so young and fashionable a society ? Still : " Age ought sometimes to polish itself against younger acquaintance," yet " it must be the work of folly if one hopes to contract friendships with them, or desires it. In short, they are a pleasant medicine that one should take care not to grow fond of." That was his creed at fifty-three. Now at seventy-three he found that his disvalued reputation could attract younger women to whom society showed every goodwill ; not only that, but beyond yea or nay they took pleasure in his conversation ; and his old age with its long memory was a new claim to their regard. They listened eagerly to his recollections ; the proof is that within a few weeks of forming their acquaintance he had begun to write for them his Reminiscences of the Courts of George I and George II, which were begun on October 31, 1788, and finished by January 13 of the next year. In short, they had restored to him his zest for life, and his occupations. But in truth, they were his occupation. Whatever he did, he did with them, or for them.

They were of course introduced in form to his relatives, who accepted them with goodwill. Mrs. Damer, an able and cultivated woman who loved her elderly kinsman, made a close friendship with Mary Berry ; there could be no better proof that none of his intimates suspected the new-comers of interested designs. Yet he gave every occasion for misconstruction; by summer-time it was regularly established that he should call them "his two wives." This is how he wrote when they had gone on a visit to Yorkshire in that first summer of their alliance:

"I passed so many evenings of the last fortnight with you, that I almost preferred it to our two honeymoons, and consequently am the more sensible to the deprivation; and how dismal was *Sunday* evening, compared to those of last autumn! If you both felt as I do, we might surpass *any* event in the annals of Dunmow. Oh! what a prodigy it would be if a husband and two wives should present themselves and demand the flitch of bacon, on swearing that not one of the three in a year and a day had wished to be unmarried! For my part, I know that my affection has done nothing but increase; though were there but one of you, I should be ashamed of being so strongly attached at my age; being in love with both, I glory in my passion, and think it a proof of my sense."

During their absence, which lasted some months, he made it his main business to find a house for them near his own; reports of the search fill no small part of the letters, of which eight were posted in forty days, as he points out. There is a good deal of complaint because they do not reply often enough and because they put off their return. "A month later is a century to a husband that is old," he writes. Mrs. Damer and he had settled that he and the Berrys should meet at Park Place at the beginning of September: now they were not coming back till the end of it. "Long evenings without a fire are tiresome and without two wives insupportable."

He filled up the time with bulletins of the news from France, written with a good deal of his old light touch—and quite unlike the sententiousness of his musings to Lady Ossory on the same themes. He had plenty to muse on: London was filling up with refugees with whom he had lived much when in Paris—Madame de Boufflers, and others. Later, Richmond became a perfect colony of them, but in 1789 the flight had only begun.

By the beginning of October the Berrys were settled into the house which he had found for them and he was happy. Writing to Lady Ossory on December 6 he said, " The Berrys are at Teddington and it is on their account that I have stayed here later than I ever did. They go to town next week and so shall I."

His occupation in these months was completing the Catalogue of Strawberry Hill which he had begun years before for Cole : the book was printed long before it was published, but the Berrys received a copy at once, offered " from a heart overflowing with admiration, esteem and friendship."

This day-to-day intercourse lasted till summer of 1790, when the Berrys made a journey to Lymington and there are more letters. But a longer absence was in prospect; their father proposed another continental journey. Horace Walpole made no concealment of his feelings. Writing to Conway while they were at Lymington he says : " The loss of them is irreparable to me and I tremble to think how much more I shall feel it in three months when I am to part with them—for who can tell how long."

He might well tremble. " The society of the young is a pleasant medicine ; one must be careful not to get too fond of it " ; so he had philosophized to George Montagu, in the years when an old woman in Paris was wearying for his presence. Now he felt the pain of separation long in advance. They were both to sit for their pictures before going on their long journey ; yet, " portraits are but melancholy pleasures in long absence. With what different emphasis does one say adieu for a month and for a year. I scarce guess how one can say the latter—alas ! I must learn."

He spent all his energy during that July in pointing out the dangers of a journey through revolutionary France—which might deter them from going. There was still a period of felicity to look forward to, but too brief.

"I feel all the kindness of your determination of coming to Twickenham in August, and shall certainly say no more against it, tho' I am certain that I shall count every day that passes, and when they are passed, they will leave a melancholy impression on Strawberry, that I had rather have affixed to London. The two last summers were infinitely the pleasantest I ever passed here, for I never before had an agreeable neighbourhood. Still, I loved the place, and had no comparisons to draw. Now, the neighbourhood will remain, and will appear ten times worse, with the aggravation of remembering *two months* that may have some transient roses, but, I am sure, lasting thorns."

Not a day of that July went by without his writing, and the affectation of writing to both becomes a thin screen. "Oh, my beloved friend! can I be interested about you and not alarmed? Lyons is all tumult and violence. . . . Are these vain terrors in me? And tho' I did not remonstrate at first, can I love you and be silent now?"

The end came.

"Sunday, October 10, 1790; the day of your departure. In happy days I smiled and called you my dear wives— *now*, I can only think of you as *darling children*, of whom I am bereaved! As such I have loved and do love you; and charming as you both are, I have had no occasion to remind myself that I am past 73. Your hearts, your understandings, your virtues, and the cruel injustice of your fate, have interested me in everything that concerns you; and so far from having occasion to blush for any unbecoming weakness, I am proud of my affection for you, and very proud of your condescending to pass so many hours with a very old man, when everybody admires you, and the most insensible allow that your good sense and information (I speak of both) have formed you to converse with the most intelligent of our sex as well as your own; and neither can tax you with airs of pretension or affectation. Your simplicity and natural ease set off all your other merits—all these graces are lost to me, alas! when I have no time to lose!"

(Madame du Deffand also in her old age had been haunted for many months by the terror of time at her back, hurrying her to an end before she could again have speech with what she loved.)

"If I live to see you again, you will then judge whether I am changed—but a friendship so rational and so pure as mine is, and so equal for both, is not likely to have any of the fickleness of youth, when it has none of its other ingredients. It was a sweet consolation to the short time that I may have left, to fall into such a society—no wonder then that I am unhappy at that consolation being abridged. I pique myself on no philosophy but what a long use and knowledge of the world had given me, the philosophy of indifference to most persons and events. I do pique myself on not being ridiculous at this very late period of my life; but when there is not a grain of passion in my affection for you two, and when you both have the good sense not to be displeased at my telling you so (though I hope you would have despised me for the contrary), I am not ashamed to say that your loss is heavy to me."

Madame du Deffand also had protested with as good right that no grain of passion entered into her feeling, but she was bidden to conceal that feeling, even from her closest friends. He put no such restrictions on himself. Mrs. Damer, who about the same time was going to Lisbon, wrote to Miss Berry that "it was a distress to her that her own departure must deprive him of the satisfaction he may, heaven knows! indulge with me of saying all he thinks."

The whirligig of time might bring in its revenges, but everyone was in a conspiracy to temper the wind to this shorn, bleating, elderly lambkin.

Madame du Deffand cannot have been out of his mind,

for he had enjoined the plan which she enforced upon him of numbering all letters in a series so that each correspondent could know if any went astray. His count went up rapidly, and for months he was tormented by a fear that the missives would not reach their destination. Already, too, when they reached Italy, he was busying himself to dissuade them from another journey through France. Burke's *Reflections* were just out and all the world was agog about them : Horace Walpole heard the passage about Marie Antoinette condemned for its extravagance, and yet he says " it paints her exactly as she appeared to me the first time I saw her when Dauphiness. She shot through the room like an aerial being. . . . I like the ' swords leaping out of their scabbards.' "

All this was in the first months after their departure, and he had a year to wait—for fulfilment. Cliveden, Little Strawberry Hill, was vacant and at his command, for the Clive was dead since 1785. He had prevailed on these new friends to say that on their return they would settle in as his tenants.

Yet before 1790 was out, nature gave him grave cause to doubt whether his desire could be achieved. Gout, going to the stomach, brought him to death's door, and for a further admonition, George Selwyn, his " oldest acquaintance and friend," was despaired of. In that day's addition to his journal-letter (exactly such a letter as Madame du Deffand used to pile up by instalments) he wrote to Mary Berry—" These misfortunes, although they come to us for but a short time, are very sensible to the old ; but him I really loved, not only for infinite wit, but for a thousand good qualities."

His own recovery continued, yet with no return of spirits ; and now indeed the echo of Madame du Deffand becomes tragic.

" I see and thank you for all the kindness of your intention ; but, as it has the contrary effect from what you expect, I am forced, for my own peace, to beseech you not to continue a manœuvre that only tantalizes and wounds me. In your last you put together many friendly words to give me hopes of your return; but can I be so blind as not to see that they are vague words?"

He had counted on their return in autumn: now he was warned not to expect them till the following spring.

"I shall not; nor do I expect *that* next spring. I have little expected this next! My dearest Madam, I allow all my folly and unreasonableness, and give them up and abandon them totally. I have most impertinently and absurdly tried, for my own sake merely, to exact from two young ladies, above forty years younger than myself, a promise of sacrificing their rooted inclinations to my whims and satisfaction. But my eyes are opened, my reason is returned, I condemn myself; and I now make you but one request, which is, that, though I am convinced it would be the most friendly and good-natured meaning possible, I do implore you not to try to help me to delude myself any more."

When they wrote to say that they were changing their plans for his sake to a return in autumn, he protested, he begged them: "Do not unsettle me: I dread a disappointment as I do a relapse of the gout." The end was, of course, apologies: he had repented of his murmurs. "Even my complaining letter, though original and unreasonable, proved that the more I thought myself to be quitting the world, the more my heart was set on my two friends." And his excuses were accepted; not only that, but the time was definitely shortened. One asks oneself if he ever cast a glance over his shoulder into past years and felt remorseful twinges.

Probably not: he was too busy with the present, putting in his year of waiting ("the longest year that ever was, a baker's year, it has thirteen months to the dozen"), much perturbing himself because Miss Mary had fallen down a slope and damaged the loveliest of all noses (happily not a lasting damage); chronicling the gossip, the rage for Sir William

Hamilton's Mrs. Harte and her " attitudes," her plastic poses ; and incidentally sketching the place he loved. There was a boatrace at Richmond and he was with the Duke of Clarence and other fine company :

" The day had been coined on purpose, with my favourite south-east wind. The scene, both up the river and down, was what only Richmond upon earth can exhibit. The crowds on those green velvet meadows and on the shores, the yachts, barges, pleasure and small boats, and the windows and gardens lined with spectators, were so delightful, that when I came home from that vivid show, I thought Strawberry looked as dull and solitary as a hermitage."

He could not have done that better at forty-seven than he did it at seventy-four.

Meanwhile all his friends made inquiries about his " wives " as a matter of course ; and he was proud and flattered. " I am in the utmost perplexity of mind about them ; torn between hopes and fears," he wrote to that good creature Hannah Moore, who figures largely towards the end of his correspondence. Yet the pith and marrow of what he has to say is sent to the wayfarers.

" Could I believe that when my clock had struck seventy-four, that I could pass a year in such agitation ! . . . I will swallow my apprehensions, for I doubt I have tormented you with them. Yet do not wonder, that after a year's absence, my affection, instead of waning, is increased. Can I help feeling the infinite obligation I have to you both, for quitting Italy that you love, to humour Methusalem ? "

He got them back on November 11, 1790, and no doubt within the next day or two radiantly invested them with Cliveden ; there was no secret of his intention to bequeath it as part of his desire to secure their ease when he " should be no more." But other people, naturally, heard of this ; and he was to a new degree in the world's eye, for the death of his nephew had made him Lord Orford, at seventy-five, " the poorest earl in England." The result was seen in newspaper paragraphs and Mary Berry showed her vexation. There is a letter from him:

"You have hurt me excessively! We had passed a most agreeable evening, and then you poisoned all by one cruel word. I see you are too proud to like to be obliged by me, tho' you see that my greatest, and the only pleasure I have left, is to make you and your sister a little happier if I can; and *now*, when it is a little more in my power, you cross me *in trifles even*, that would compensate for the troubles that are fallen on me."

He has the lover's egoism: he asks her to set aside her own feelings and consider only her tenderness for him. But she did not give way at once. We have her answer. Even Cliveden and the "compliment of settling in near you," seemed to her only a misfortune if they were to be represented as seeking his society "with some view beyond its enjoyment." Yet she ended with leniency. "I am relieved by writing and shall sleep the sounder for having thus unburthened my heart." It sounds stilted, but that was how a lady of eight-and-twenty expressed herself even in the last years of the eighteenth century.

His reply begins—"My dearest angel" and he renews the appeal to her feelings. Vexation and fatigue have brought back the flying gout. "I shall want but your uneasiness to finish me. . . . But I talk of myself when I should speak to your mind." He argues—"Is all your felicity to be in the power of a newspaper?" He brings in royalty: the Duchess of Gloucester "when she heard of my intention about Cliveden, came and commended me much for doing some little justice to injured merit." And then he goes back to his appeal. "I am too exhausted to write more. . . . How could you say you wish you had not returned?"

Of course he had his way—with the approval of everybody. They settled in under his wing, and there was no disappointment for this spent old man, now valiant against his own bugbear.

" Since the ridicule can only fall on me, and not on them, I care not a straw for it being said that I am in love with one of them—people shall choose; it is as much with both as either, and I am infinitely too old to regard the *qu'en dit-on*."

At the close of 1793 he was looking back happily on a summer " because you two made it so delightful to me that six weeks of gout could not sour it "; confident that " I shall be as happy with a third summer if I reach it as I have been with the two last."

He did not miss the third of these Indian summers that lit up the wreckage of his prime. He reached a fourth in 1795 and this delightful companionship carried him through a blow that otherwise would have left him desolate indeed : for Conway died, and there was no premonition. On July 7 Horace wrote to the Field-Marshal (as Conway had become) thanking him for his kindness about some soldier who would be released from service if he got a substitute, and then went on to tell of his preparations for an impressive visitation : Queen Charlotte was to come bringing six princesses and the Duchess of York and the Princess of Orange as well. He was to wear a sword when he did the honours of Strawberry to all this assemblage. " Woe is me at seventy-eight with scarce a hand and foot to my back." On July 7 he reported the results.

" The Queen was uncommonly condescending and gracious, and deigned to drink my health when I presented her with the last glass, and to thank me for all my attentions. Indeed my memory *de vieille cour* was but once in default. As I had been assured that her Majesty would be attended by her Chamberlain, yet was not, I had no glove ready when I received her at the step of her coach ; yet she honoured me with her hand to lead her upstairs ; nor did I recollect my omission when I led her down again."

Mrs. Damer, who had been called in to assist, returned to

Park Place able to report "how prosperously he had succeeded " : she found her father " remarkably well and cheer-
ful" at supper on the evening of July 8. He was dead shortly
after dawn the next morning.

We have no letter in which Horace Walpole uttered to
anyone his feelings on this occasion. Among his papers
were a brief biographical note and a long " character of
Marshal Conway " in the form of an epitaph. Perhaps his
silence is the best measure of what he felt.

Yet in the following month he was writing to Mary Berry
just as gaily as ever about trifles ; there is no trace that
Conway's loss had struck deep. In truth all the faculties of
his being were engrossed by his attachment. If he was
lonely, it was not painful : he could talk to everybody about
it. " Richmond is deserted," he told Mr. Lysons, the parson
of Putney, " but if I spoke fairly I should sum up all my
grievances in the absence of the Berrys."

They were at Cheltenham, for a cure ; and things were
happening at Cheltenham of which Lord Orford had not the
least inkling.

In 1784, when the Berrys were at Rome making part of
the English society, they met Conway there on a tour by
himself ; and in his company they visited St. Peter's. With
him was his friend, General O'Hara, a soldier of distinction
who had experienced the misfortune of being captured in the
American war.

Horace Walpole, when he came to know the Berrys, of
course heard of this earlier meeting with Conway and his
friend, and when his " wives " had left him disconsolate
during their second tour of Italy, he writes, in 1791 : " O'Hara
is come to town. You will love him better than ever. . . .
He has been shockingly treated." Seemingly he was disappointed of preferment.

Again in April there is mention of him. " He is so
dispersed and I so seldom dine from home, that I have not

seen him, even at General Conway's. When I do, can you imagine that we shall not talk of you two ? " A little later they met. " I have seen O'Hara, with his face as ruddy and black, and his teeth as white as ever ; and as fond of you too. . . . He has got a better regiment."

In 1792 O'Hara was made Governor of Gibraltar and there is no trace of a meeting between him and the Berrys. In 1793 he was moved from Gibraltar to take command at Toulon, and there had again the misfortune to be captured, and was most uncomfortably a prisoner till 1795, when his exchange was effected, and chance or choice brought him to Cheltenham.

" I am delighted that you have got O'Hara," Horace Walpole writes. " How he must feel his felicity in being at liberty to rove about as much as he likes. Still, I shall not admire his volatility if he quits you soon."

In fact this good-looking soldier did not show the least disposition to quit Miss Berry. On the contrary, they became engaged—though the difference in age was very considerable : she was thirty-two, he fifty-four. It was only natural that when he returned to his post at Gibraltar that autumn he should have wished to take her with him as his wife. But she refused to go so soon—" out of consideration for others."

She had always been the directing member of her home : her father, an easygoing man, and her sister, depended greatly on her. Yet she had agreed to marriage, and there is no reason to suppose that they would have regarded this as a catastrophe. On the other hand, there was no doubt about it ; if she were taken away from him, Horace Walpole's lamp would simply go out.

At all events, she let O'Hara go, and correspondence, in war time, was difficult ; there were " questions unanswered, doubts unsatisfied," complaints and a gradual decay of confidence, till the engagement was broken off. Yet she did not cease to hope that all might be set right. " And so it would had we ever met for twenty-four hours," she noted, when as a woman of seventy, she opened the packet of his letters ; for at seventy she still looked on those six months as the happiest of her existence. But they never met : he died in Gibraltar in 1802. We who know that General O'Hara left a large fortune to be divided between two ladies resident in Gibraltar, by both of whom he had children, may restrain our romantic feelings : but it is recorded that when Miss Berry learnt in some public place the news of his death, she fell down fainting. There is no question of the sacrifice she made. " In submitting to this absence," she wrote when she put aside the immediate marriage, " I *think* I am doing right. I am sure I am consulting the peace and happiness of those about me and *not my own*."

" Those about me " certainly included the old man at Strawberry. It is not certain that he ever knew the sacrifice. The letters show no reference to it. I do not think he knew.

If there is in the last year of his correspondence with her less sign of delight than formerly, that is no matter for surprise : he is chiefly concerned with his own health or hers, which was affected—no doubt by her sentimental troubles, for she was a strong woman and lived to be ninety : and moreover he was too far gone to feel any sort of elation. Writing with his own hand had become almost impossible ; and we can feel the quick brain show numbness at last.

The end was not lenient. In December, 1796, he was moved up to Berkeley Square and the Berrys followed : but in the last weeks that remained, hallucination set in ; he believed himself neglected and abandoned by the only persons whom he desired to see. If they returned to the room after an hour's absence, they could not persuade him but that he had been left alone for weeks. At last he sank into mere exhaustion, and so flickered out on March 2, 1797.

He left Cliveden to the Berrys, and it continued to be their home in summer till the father died and his annuity with him : thereafter the sisters had reason to be grateful for the bequest

to each of them of £4,000.   Mrs. Damer, his general legatee—
she inherited some £80,000—was his executrix, but his will
appointed Mr. Berry as editor of his literary remains—except
his *Memoirs*, which were left, as has been said, sealed up
for twenty years.   The effect of this was that Mary Berry,
though not named, had the task of preparing for publication
the series of quarto volumes of which the first four were
issued in 1798, nominally under Mr. Berry's direction; and
that she was throughout in consultation with Mrs. Damer.

I disbelieve the legend that Horace Walpole, either
before or after his succession to the peerage, asked Mary
Berry to marry him.   If she had wanted the offer, she could
undoubtedly have had it; there is nothing he would not
have given to retain her society.   But unless pressure were
put on him, nothing could be more unlikely than that he
would alter the position he had taken up in the face of the
world.   For one consideration, such a marriage would
threaten the close friendship between Miss Berry and his
niece, which must have greatly heightened his satisfaction.
For another, he was attached by all the habits of a lifetime
to a way of existence which forced no companionship on
him; which enabled him to shut himself up completely if
and when he chose.   Stronger still, there was the fear of
what the world would say.   Up to a point it had been
prepared to refrain from ill-natured mockery: but such a
union would let all the tongues loose.   That, if he ever
had the wish for marriage, would have been a formidable
deterrent; yet perhaps another was even stronger.   All that
was sentimental in him loved to glory in the Berrys' private
disinterestedness, just as it had done in Conway's public
example of the same virtue.   If he made Mary Berry Lady
Orford, he must destroy the picture of her which he loved
to show to all beholders.

And, in fact, he and she, or rather he and his two wives,
come down to us in a group that presents an old man

receiving the devotion of attractive young women who courted him for his company first, and later than that, out of sheer loyal affection. I even think that he made the legacies to them smaller than they would have been, had he not wished to emphasize to the world the quality of their attachment.

Well, that is the story. I feel no need to sit in judgment on the character it discloses. There was a real humanity about him, a warm-heartedness, which expressed itself also in what he himself called his " dogmanity." If he had had a tomb—he would have liked to—in the fashion of the old Dukes of Burgundy, Tory and Patipan, Tonton and Rosette should have been among the mourning figures, with old housekeeper Margaret conducting the procession. Madame du Deffand, and the Berrys with their father duly in attendance, might have filled one end, at the feet. Horace Mann deserved the whole of a side, yet Gray and Conway would go in with him, at the head—while on each of the longer sides between the columns, there should have defiled George Selwyn, Gilly Williams and a host of others representing White's and Almack's ; and in sequence behind these, the whole array of fashion, Lennoxes, Gunnings, and who not else. The other side should be left to the Members of Parliament, Pitts and Foxes of the two generations, the Duke of Newcastle present in proportion to his frequency in the pageant as comic relief ; and royalties and sub-royalties in large retinue. They all live for us largely through Horace Walpole.

It is true that Mr. Oliver, in those volumes on Sir Robert Walpole which make eighteenth-century politics much livelier than our own, goes out of his way to caution us against Horace Walpole as a witness. Careful scrutiny of his facts, still more of his judgments, will always be necessary : but what he renders to us unapproachably is what he rendered unconsciously—the temper of his times.

The value of his work in other ways, writers far better qualified than I have assessed ; and I have not concealed my agreement with his own somewhat disparaging estimate of his books and of their success. His place is by no means among " the mob of gentlemen who wrote with ease " ; yet his success, as he saw himself, was partly due to his position in a society which had a good deal of culture and a good deal of money and, as libraries in eighteenth-century houses testify, still bought books—a habit that gradually waned among such circles in the nineteenth century and perished in the twentieth.

What we owe to his active curiosity and his collector's instinct for picking up and preserving, is best witnessed by the existence of a Walpole Society created to edit those manuscript notes of Virtue's which he saved from disappearance, and from which by a mere casual delving he drew his *Anecdotes of Painting*—in his own judgment his most useful work.

There remains the achievement by which he was perhaps best known in his own day : his creation of Strawberry Hill, the concrete example to which he and his friends could point when they made propaganda for a revival of Gothic. Mr. Tipping, a great authority, admits that Horace Walpole, with his allies, Chute and Bentley, were practically the originators of this movement, though not absolutely first in the field. But Mr. Tipping cannot bring himself to take Strawberry seriously. How should he ? If indeed we should go there and seriously consider the fabric as " exhibiting " (these are Walpole's own words in his Catalogue) " specimens of Gothic architecture as collected from standards in cathedral and chapel tombs and showing how they may be applied to chimney-pieces, ceilings, windows, balustrades, loggias, etc.," we should go away revolted by a display of tawdry gimcracks. What medieval craftsmen had wrought with chisel and mallet out of supporting stone, Walpole's clever artisans copied, pinching it with clever fingers out of papier mâché, and pinning it on to lath and plaster. Inevitably this fundamental incongruity led on to worse. Gray was partly a convert, and describes elaborately as being " in the best taste of anything he has yet done " a bedchamber at Strawberry whose chimney-piece was borrowed from the high altar at Rouen; but Gray had nevertheless instincts in his bones that made him disdainful of such trumpery. One hears the note of it in a letter to Wharton:

" My slumbers were disturbed the other day by an unexpected visit from Mr. W., who dined with me, seemed mighty happy for the time he stay'd, and said he could like to live here: but hurried home in the evening to his new Gallery, which is all Gothicism, and gold, and crimson, and looking-glass. He has purchased at an auction in Suffolk ebony-chairs and old moveables enough to load a waggon."

What is Strawberry after all, when we look at it to-day, but " the old child's baby house "? Its contents, the " baubles " with which he had it crammed, did indeed include real treasures. Miniatures and enamels were its strong point, and he did well to be proud of having gathered together the only large collection of the works of Isaac and Peter Oliver. But is it not characteristic that he names drawings and wax bas-reliefs by Lady Diana Beauclerk almost in the same breath with Raphael's missal?

The contents of Strawberry are scattered, as their collector foresaw and almost intended: one might say he looked forward with eagerness to the sale as a day of judgment when his connoisseurship would stand out triumphantly justified. He left Strawberry to Mrs. Damer for her life, with two thousand a year for its upkeep—providing that, if she wished to abandon it, the place should go to his kinsfolk, the Waldegraves. For Sir Edward Walpole's daughter, Maria Duchess of Gloucester, had three daughters by her first marriage to Lord Waldegrave. The eldest of them married her cousin, a younger Lord Waldegrave. It was the son of this marriage, the sixth Earl Waldegrave, who acquired Strawberry Hill from Mrs. Damer in 1811, after she had held the place fourteen years. In 1842, the next Earl grew tired of this possession and the sale of its contents took place. On the whole Horace Walpole's ghost must have been satisfied with the prices.

Four years later, Lord Waldegrave died, still quite young, and left the empty Gothic castle to his widow, Frances Lady Waldegrave, daughter of the singer Braham, a lady of great charm, who remarried twice. It was only in her second widowhood that she took up her abode at Strawberry and re-equipped it in a revival of its prime—herself working embroideries for some of the rooms, which are, to speak truth, more awful than anything of Bentley's. She added to it, again more or less in the original manner, but altered definitely for the worse: however, when she married Lord Carlingford, one of Gladstone's Liberal colleagues, the house became noted among the pleasant places for a week-end, as Memoirs of the 'seventies and 'eighties testify. But then and thereafter, it was first and foremost a monument of its creator.

The creation has been strangely transformed; like other big houses, it passed after the war from private to public uses; the Vincentian Order acquired it for their work of training Catholic school teachers. Thus by an odd irony of fate the pseudo-monastery has become a real one; and in one of the oddly-shaped chambers wedged in between the house and the round tower, the ecclesiastical ornament now decorates a real oratory where mass is said. Mr. Walpole, as we have seen, did not like popery; one might even say that he did not much care for things that were real. But his friend, Mr. Cole, would have rejoiced, for he was an Anglo-Catholic before the name began; and Walpole's own prejudices might have melted to see how carefully what remained of his invention was treasured, so that when pulling down became necessary, the original design was restored. Not, however, in the original materials ; the battlements, once a frowning array of lath and plaster, that had to be thrice renewed in his lifetime, are of concrete now.

There it is. One cannot help laughing at Strawberry and its creator ; but after all, his friends who knew him best— we have it on his own word—always laughed at him a little. But they liked him none the less ; and I for one cannot help liking him, not indeed for the sake of Strawberry, but for his real love of all that lay about Strawberry in what is still perhaps the most characteristically English of all England's beauty spots, the stretch of silver Thames from Richmond to Hampton Court.

For his letters it would be superfluous to praise him. The last of them all, written to Lady Ossory, deprecates her treating his " idle notes " as works of art to be handed about and shown. " Oh ! my good Madam, pray send me no more such laurels. . . . I shall be quite content with a sprig of rosemary thrown after me when the parson of the parish commits my dust to dust."

A sprig ? No, but a whole thicket of rosemary for remembrance grows, sharp and pungent, out of those " idle notes."

INDEX

INDEX